Media Practice in Iraq

Media Practice in Iraq

Ahmed K. Al-Rawi

Erasmus University Rotterdam, the Netherlands

First published 2012 by
PALGRAVE MACMILLAN

Palgrave Macmillan in the UK is an imprint of Macmillan Publishers Limited, registered in England, company number 785998, of Houndmills, Basingstoke, Hampshire RG21 6XS.

Palgrave Macmillan in the US is a division of St Martin's Press LLC, 175 Fifth Avenue, New York, NY 10010.

Palgrave Macmillan is the global academic imprint of the above companies and has companies and representatives throughout the world.

Palgrave® and Macmillan® are registered trademarks in the United States, the United Kingdom, Europe and other countries. ⁄

ISBN 978–0–230–35452–4

This book is printed on paper suitable for recycling and made from fully managed and sustained forest sources. Logging, pulping and manufacturing processes are expected to conform to the environmental regulations of the country of origin.

A catalogue record for this book is available from the British Library.

A catalog record for this book is available from the Library of Congress.

10   9   8   7   6   5   4   3   2   1
21   20   19   18   17   16   15   14   13   12

Printed and bound in the United States of America

For my late father, the scholar and the man

Contents

Figures

Tables

Acknowledgements

This book is based partly on my PhD thesis, which I wrote during my study from 2008 to 2011 at Leicester University. The contribution of my supervisor, Professor Barrie Gunter, is very evident since he cultivated my knowledge of communication research and encouraged me to look critically at different concepts and views relevant to the Iraqi media. I am truly grateful for his kind patience, timely feedback, and continuous follow-up.

I am also indebted to my wife, Dr Alaa Al-Musalli, who supported me from the beginning in pursuing my second PhD study and writing this book; she also assisted me as a second coder in the pilot study. Without her great love and encouragement, this book would not have been written. Also, my mother, Nawal, was very encouraging and supportive; she was always concerned about my health rather than my research. Indeed, my late father, who got his PhD on the Iraqi media from Keele University in 1983, was one of the inspirations to work on the current book since he wrote several books in Arabic on the history of journalism in Iraq.

Furthermore, I would like to thank Mr Abbas Hamid from Sultan Qaboos University, who helped me to explain some statistical tests that I used during the content-analysis phase of the study. I am also really grateful to the following people who assisted me in filling in the questionnaire used in this study and in different ways during writing this book: Dr Saad Al-Mashhadani from Tikrit University in Salahideen; Dr Ahmed Abdul Majid, editor-in-chief of *Al-Zaman* newspaper in Baghdad; Dr Fadhil Al-Badrani from the Grand Imam University in Baghdad; Dr Sabah Nahi from Al-Arabyia channel; Dr Ammar Tahir; and Mr Na'im 'Abd Muhalhal. I also thank the library staff of Leicester University who assisted me in obtaining some PhD theses through the inter-library loan service. Special thanks go to the peer reviewers, whose feedback was very useful in revising this book, and Kate Boothby and Flora Kenson for their patience in reviewing the book as well as their thorough and detailed feedback.

And finally, thanks to the Palgrave Macmillan editorial team members, especially Felicity Plester and Catherine Mitchell, for their follow-up and support during the publishing process.

Glossary

CMC	Communications and Media Commission (previously NCMC)
IAF	Iraqi Accord Front (Sunni slate)
IHEC	Iraqi High Electoral Commission
IMN	Iraqi Media Network
INA	Iraqi National Alliance (Shiite slate)
INC	Iraqi National Congress (Ahmed Chalabi)
KA	Kurdish Alliance
KDP	Kurdistan Democratic Party (Masud Barazani)
PUK	Patriotic Union of Kurdistan (Jalal Talabani)

Introduction

When I worked for the official Iraqi TV back in 1997, a great deal of attention was given to the media during the Ba'ath rule. A military tank never left its position in front of the TV station's main gate and the small road leading to it was always blocked. Every Iraqi driver knew it was forbidden to approach this road. The kind of security checks that everyone had to undergo to enter the main building were thorough. It looked like a place for the privileged, though its employees got very low salaries that could not sustain them for a whole month, mainly due to the economic sanctions. It was a rather surreal place where rumours spread about Uday Saddam's torture chamber at his Al-Shabab TV station. It was believed that it contained different torture tools to be used against anyone who, intentionally or not, made a mistake. Other confirmed reports were about employees whose job it was to censor 'suspicious' TV material lest anything obscene or political, such as a half-naked woman or an anti-revolutionary message, was shown. For example, a colleague who translated George Orwell's film *1984* was shocked when he knew that the authorities had refused to air the film because Iraq's political system bore some similarities to Orwell's imaginary authoritarian regime, especially in the way that the Iraqi security forces monitored the activities of the people. If any prohibited scenes were aired, the responsible employee would have his hair shaved and be sent to a remote prison as a punishment. In the end, the station's employees were in constant fear, which killed a great deal of their creativity. Added to that was the old and ill-maintained equipment used. One Iraqi technician told me in 1998 that it was a miracle that Iraqi TV was still broadcasting and airing programmes, since most of the equipment – dating from the 1970s – should be sent to the museum of science and technology.

As for print journalism, the situation was even more difficult; some people might overlook a scene on TV which disappears afterwards, but newspapers remain. Sometimes unintentional typos could cause a great deal of controversy and lead to imprisonment. For example, an article published in one of the main newspapers mentioned Ezat Al-Douri, once a vice-president, but one letter from his name was replaced by another making it Al-Doudi, with the connotation of being 'wormy'. Everyone I knew who read the article laughed and expected that its author would face severe imprisonment for such a mistake. I was later informed that no Iraqi official noticed the mistake, so the author was spared punishment. Such cases, no matter how trivial they were, frightened journalists and drove them to become receptors of information instead of producers. After decades of this, many Iraqi journalists became passive and preferred to depend on the Iraqi News Agency for information instead of making news themselves.

After the 2003 US-led invasion of Iraq, media freedom was finally felt for a short period. Due to their previous repressions, many Iraqis hurriedly published their own newspapers and started writing without having a proper background in journalism practice. It was completely chaotic, like going to a bazaar where various noises and odours are felt to come from everywhere. Many newspaper publishers realised soon after they started that they were losing money because their newspapers were not sold properly, so they just quit. Another positive outcome of the invasion was having hundreds of foreign journalists who needed Iraqi partners to work as editors, translators, fixers, or stringers. This generated a decent income for Iraqis working for foreign news outlets and enriched their experience in Western journalism standards.

Yet, the darkest period was to come, when armed groups from Al-Qaeda and its affiliates on the one hand, and Shiite militias on the other, started gunning down journalists who opposed their views or burning newspaper stores for selling certain publications. Many journalists did not stop writing, so they began to use pseudonyms or avoided using their photos in order not to be recognised. When I worked as a spokesperson for the International Committee of the Red Cross in Baghdad, I did my utmost best not to show my face by mainly communicating via the telephone. This was essential because the armed groups with their various agendas would recognise a person easily and eliminate him if they did not like what he said.

The situation is not any better now. The Iraqi government is pressuring journalists with libel suits and allowing threats to be made against them without providing proper protection. In the end, most journalists are confined to self-censorship to avoid any repercussions. It is sad to see how the state of journalism improved for a short period after 2003 but quickly regressed to a gloomy reality, and fear continues to characterise the work of Iraqi journalists.

This book

This book attempts to give to the reader an understanding of the Iraqi media and its development from the 19th century onwards. The main focus of this work, however, is on the current media landscape that is shaped by different internal and external factors. To give the reader a brief overview of the media landscape, it is important to cite the following example. On February 22, 2010, the state-run Iraqia channel, the Shiite Al-Furat TV, the Sunni Baghdad channel, and the Kurdish Al-Hurria TV aired news reports on a savage murder that took place in the neighbourhood of Al-Wahda in southern Baghdad. A family consisting of a father, mother, and their six children were all mercilessly slaughtered (and some were beheaded) by a criminal gang. According to a Wikileaks cable, the father worked on hanging election posters to promote the candidate Entifadh Qanbar, who was part of the infamous Ahmed Chalabi's party that was affiliated with the Shiite Iraqi National Alliance (INA) (Wikileaks 2010d). Hence, the murder was conducted for political reasons by a group of four young men who apparently opposed Chalabi's political group or INA. However, the four TV channels decided to use this crime as part of their election-campaign coverage by covering it from different perspectives.

Iraqia TV emphasised the success of the Iraqi security services that managed to capture the murderers on the same day; thus Maliki's government, which exercises great influence over the channel's management and editorial line, was accredited with this success. The news correspondent stated: 'The fact that the gang was captured few hours after committing the crime proves that the Iraqi security forces are ready to handle the full responsibility of security; in addition, it increases the citizens' confidence in the performance of their security forces.' On the following day, a news report praised the Iraqi security officers who managed to solve the crime riddle. The anchorwoman of Iraqia TV stated that the crime was carried out by the 'hands of blasphemy, darkness, and terrorism', which echoes the usual rhetoric of the Iraqi government that always links criminal crimes with the insurgency in the country that destabilises the whole state.

As for the Shiite Al-Furat TV, it claimed that the motives behind the action of the 'terrorist group were unclear' though 'election promotional publications were found in the house'. The news report showed a brochure printed by INA and a large subtitle was shown four times that read: 'Crimes of the Saddamist Baath'. The channel was directly accusing former Ba'ath members, who are erroneously believed to be mostly Sunni, of being behind the attack in order to disseminate a culture of fear and drive potential voters from electing any candidate suspected of being lenient with the Ba'ath Party, such as Ayad Allawi. The news correspondent wondered at the end of the report about what is better to select: 'those who call for [political] change or others who want to establish security', which refers to INA's electoral programme.

On the other hand, Baghdad TV, which is affiliated with the Sunni Iraqi Islamic Party (IIP), presented this event very briefly (27 seconds; talking head) without any accompanying film; the channel downplayed the importance of this crime since it took place in a predominately Shiite neighbourhood, and it devoted most of its newscast coverage to promoting IIP.

Finally, the Kurdish channel Al-Hurria TV showed more attention to this crime than Baghdad TV by showing a voice-over and a newsreader. The channel called it 'Terrorist crimes' and praised the Iraqi security forces that managed to arrest the gang within '24 hours' from the time the crime was committed. As the channel is supported by President Jalal Talabani it is expected that it will praise the success of the security forces because of its affiliation.

In brief, the above incident exemplifies the way that events and topics are covered in Iraq since each side prefers to show its own point of view. As a result, many Iraqi journalists have become polarised by following the editorial policy of their media outlets.

In writing this book, different research methodologies were employed, like quantitative and qualitative content analysis, participant observation, questionnaires, and interviews. US government confidential reports, classified materials from the National Security Archive, and Wikileaks cables were also used to enrich the information and strengthen the discussion.

Chapter 1 presents an overview of the Iraqi media from its beginning with an emphasis on the media during the Ba'ath Party's rule, whose inheritance can still be seen in Iraqi society. It was important to discuss the myth of the alleged first Iraqi newspaper *Jurnal Al-Iraq* (1816) and to investigate how this false idea originated. The second chapter offers new information and analysis on the way that the Bush Administration misused and misinterpreted two articles from Iraqi newspapers to strengthen its claim that Iraq was linked to Al-Qaeda. Appendix I contains extracts from two newspapers, *Babil* and *Al-Nassiriah*, which were used to strengthen this Al-Qaeda claim. Chapter 3 discusses US efforts to form the Iraqi media before the 2003 invasion, which ultimately created a sectarian media. Chapter 4 discusses the current Iraqi media and the Iraqi government's efforts to control it. The fifth chapter deals with the rules governing the coverage of election news in Iraq, whereas Chapter 6 focuses on the way that four Iraqi TV channels (those cited in page 3) covered the 2010 general election. Finally, the book offers a second appendix that contains a comprehensive inventory of Iraqi satellite channels based on my personal observation and monitoring.

1
Iraqi Media: The Beginnings

In this section, a brief overview of the Iraqi media is presented in order to give the reader an idea of the major landmarks in the history of the different media channels in Iraq. The discussion below is mostly focused on the Iraqi press that was the dominant medium in the 19th and early 20th centuries. I classify the Iraqi press into six distinct stages according to the nature of the media and the relevant political environment:

(1) the beginnings until the reactivation of the Ottoman Constitution (1863–1908);
(2) the relative freedom after the revival of the constitution until the establishment of the Iraqi state (1908–1921);
(3) the beginning of the partisan press until Rashid Ali Al-Kaylani's failed revolt (1921–1941);
(4) the totalitarian press with varying degrees of media freedom (1941–2003);
(5) the sectarian and plural press (2003–2007);
(6) the totalitarian press (2008–ongoing).

Phase I

In the 19th century, Iraqi newspapers witnessed a modest development that mostly ebbed due to the political and cultural limitations that were imposed by the Ottomans who occupied the country at that time. Iraq is believed to have had the first Arabic newspaper, *Jurnal Al-Iraq*, which was established in Baghdad in 1816 during the rule of the Mamluke ruler Dawood Pasha (1767–1831). This ruler made positive changes to the country and tried to develop its infrastructure.

The newspaper he allegedly founded was published in Turkish and Arabic and was distributed to important figures and military leaders. It was hung on the walls of the Ottoman administrative headquarters, which were called Al-Saray, in Baghdad (Butti 1955, p. 10; Al-Rawi 2010, p. 11). However, no copies of this newspaper are available today and there is no concrete evidence to support the idea that it really existed. Razuq Eissa, who was the first Iraqi writer to make this claim, reportedly relied on the accounts of some Western travellers, like J Baillie Fraser (1783–1856) and Anthony N Groves (1795–1853) (Eissa, 1934). Yet he did not specify the traveller's name, the book he cited, or the page number from which this claim was borrowed. Unfortunately, many other writers referred to Eissa's claim without challenging it by cross-checking the references he cited. Al-Hassani did doubt the existence of this newspaper as there were no records of it in the Ottoman Archives or the British Museum (1969, p. 3). Besides, the works of these travellers contain no reference to any newspaper or publication that was issued during this time in Iraq. In 1816 the British traveller James Silk Buckingham (1786–1855) visited Baghdad, but he never referred to any publication that was in circulation (Buckingham 1827). Other Western travellers and residents – like Sir Robert Ker Porter (1777–1842), Claudius James Rich (1787–1821), James Raymond Wellsted (1805–1842), and Lieutenant William Heude, who visited Baghdad in 1817 – made no reference to any newspaper or book published in Baghdad. There is only a reference to a lithographic printing press in Groves' *Journal of a Residence at Bagdad During the Years 1830 and 1831* (Groves 1832). It seems that he ordered this printing press from Bombay, and it arrived in Basrah around July 12, 1830. As a missionary, he wanted to use the printing press to publish Christian books, saying: 'we hope to find most useful for us in our present position' (p. 22 and p. 76). It is not clear what happened to the press. Since it is believed that Dawood Pasha bought the printing press that published his book on Iraq from the East India Company (Al-Rawi 2010, p. 150), which originally brought Groves' press from Bombay, it is possible that Dawood Pasha used Groves' press to publish Iraq's first printed book, which is cited below.

On the other hand, Eissa mentioned that the first printing press introduced into Iraq was brought, in 1821, into the Shiite city of Kadhmiah in Baghdad. Hence, it was not possible for any newspaper to have been published in 1816. This press was called Dar Al-Salam, and it printed the first book in Iraq, entitled *Dawhat Al-Wizaraa fi Tarikh Waqai' Al-Zawraa*, which was written by Rassul Hawi Al-Karkukli. A Persian man called

Mirza Mohammed Baqir Al-Taflisi was in charge of copying it in his own handwriting (Eissa 1926, p. 206). Although Eissa mentioned the year 1821 as the date when the first printing press was introduced into the country, Ya'qbub Sarkis refuted this claim because there was no evidence (1955, pp. 269–270). Other sources indicate that it was only in 1830 that the lithographic printing press Dar Al-Salam first operated in the country (Albi 1981, p. 167; 'Afas 1985, p. 39; Khalil 1985a, p. 314). It seems that the confusion was caused by the nature of *Dawhat Al-Wizaraa's* book, which chronicled the daily events that occurred during the rule of Dawood Pasha. This was probably the reason behind Eissa's misunderstanding that *Jurnal Al-Iraq* was a separate newspaper rather than being a reference to the history book of *Dawhat Al-Wizaraa* itself.

Indeed, the Iraqi press was associated with the introduction of the printing machines that were under the total control of the Ottoman government. However, religious groups, like Iraqi Jews and Christians, were interested in importing the printing press mainly for religious reasons. Iraqi Christians, for example, were more active in printing their religious books than all the other groups in Iraq. The Dominican Fathers in Mosul bought their first printing machine in 1856 (Butti 1926, p. 150). In 1860 they imported a newer machine from Paris with the help of the Orient Missionary Society. This cost 6000 francs (ibid., pp. 151–152). Three years later, the Chaldean Printing House was established in Mosul to publish more sermon books (Mahmood 1971, p. 20 and p. 22; Khalil 1982, p. 5).

Furthermore, Moses Baruch Mizrahi, an Iraqi Jew, imported a privately owned printing machine in 1863 which published religious books in Hebrew. The first Iraqi newspaper is believed to have been a Hebrew one that was owned by Mizrahi and was called *Ha-Dover* or *Dover Me-sharim* (1863). It stopped in 1871 after publishing 17 issues (Khadduri 1979, p. 205; *Encyclopedia Judaica* 2007, vol. 16, p. 497; Hakak 2009, p. 143).

Finally, Persians living in Iraq were also active in publishing books. One of the first lithographic presses was introduced in 1856 and it published only one book during the rule of Mohammed Rashid Pasha (Hilmi 1913, p. 309; Butti 1926, p. 150). In 1861, Mirza Abbas brought another lithographic printing press from Iran that was called the Kamil Al-Tabrizi press (Hilmi 1913, p. 306).

It is worth mentioning that Iraq did not witness a regular Arabic newspaper until the reign of the Ottoman ruler Midhat Pasha (1822–1883). During his rule, the first official Iraqi newspaper, *Al-Zawraa*, was published, and copies of it are still available today. It first appeared on June 15, 1869, a date which later became the yearly anniversary of the

Iraqi press. It was printed by the Wyliah Printing House, where the press was designed to operate by steam (Hilmi 1913, p. 304). The newspaper used to be published in four pages: two pages in Arabic and the other two in Turkish (Al-Rawi 1978, p. 8). *Al-Zawraa* was published for 48 years, during which time 2607 issues were produced, and it stopped on March 11, 1917, when the British occupied Baghdad. In Mosul, another official newspaper, *Mosul*, was established in June 1885, while Basrah city had its own paper, *Basrah*, which first appeared in December 1889. Yet all of these newspapers were mere mouthpieces for the Ottoman government.

Instead of Baghdad, the first Iraqi magazine was published in Mosul and was called *Eklil Al-Wurood*, established by the Dominican Fathers in January 1902. It was a religious magazine produced on a monthly basis (Al-Hassani 1957, p. 25; Mahmood 1971, p. 37; Ibrahim 1976, p. 209). It was made available in three languages: Arabic, Chaldean, and French (Khalil 1985b, p. 335).

It is important to note that the Iraqi press did not develop rapidly in its first phase, mainly due to the severe press restrictions imposed by the Ottoman authorities. For example, during the rule of Sultan Abdul Hamid II (1842–1918), freedom of the press was greatly limited in the entire Ottoman Empire because of the sultan's fear of the power of the Fourth Estate. He made some ridiculous restrictions, such as banning the publication of any reference to assassination attempts against foreign monarchs or riots and protests organised in foreign lands since 'our peaceful and honest people must not hear such news' (Butti 1955, pp. 138–140). Also, words like 'Ermenistan' (Armenia), 'strike', 'revolution', 'socialism', 'dynamite', 'chaos', 'toppling a monarch', 'fighting', 'Bosnia', 'Hersek', 'Macedonia', 'Crete', 'Cyprus', 'freedom', 'equality', 'basic law' (constitution), and 'homeland' were strictly banned from being used in newspapers and other publications (ibid.; Said 1970–1971, p. 339). The circulation of foreign journals was also limited if not banned. Indeed, the few Iraqi newspapers that were published in the late 19th century were closely monitored by the Ottoman authorities.

Phase II

The second stage in the Iraqi press began after the Young Turk Revolution in 1908, during which the Ottoman sultan restored the 1876 constitutional monarchy. More liberties and press freedoms were enjoyed due to the positive political change. Immediately after the Ottoman reformation, Iraqis suddenly had 25 newspapers and magazines (Khalil

1982, p. 37); more than 70 newspapers and magazines were published in Iraq within three years. The first private Iraqi newspaper was established on August 6, 1908 and was entitled *Baghdad*. It was owned by Murad Sulaiman (Butti 1972a, p. 20). The majority of these new publications were based in Baghdad, including *Al-Raqib* (1909), *Sada Babil* (1909) and *Al-Najah* (1910), which was known for its pan-Arab and pan-Islamic tendencies, and the newspaper *Al-Nahdha* (1913).[1]

Also, private publishing houses spread quickly in Iraq at this time, such as one in Mosul that began working in 1910 (Khalil 1985b, p. 321). Still, there were few publishing houses available in comparison with other Arab countries, like Lebanon, Egypt and Syria. Due to the lack of publishing houses in Baghdad, the political newspapers used to appear on a weekly basis (Butti 1976).

However, one of the negative consequences of this sudden proliferation of newspapers and magazines was the fact that many unqualified Iraqis started publishing without any planning. Many publications ceased to exist after only a few issues because they did not sell well (Butti 1955, p. 21). Another widespread shortcoming was that many publications became vehicles for publishing personal insults wherein obscene language was occasionally used (Al-Tikriti 1969, pp. 59–60). Despite these problems, the Iraqi press at that time did not witness a sectarian rhetoric like the one that characterised the Iraqi media after 2003. This honeymoon period did not last long since the Ministry of Interior in Istanbul feared such kinds of freedom; it cancelled most of the licences, leaving only three newspapers and two magazines (Butti 1955, pp. 22–23; see also Khalil 1985b, p. 339).

One of the advantages of that time was the formation of some nationalist political groups, such as the Freedom and Coalition Party in Baghdad and the secret Al-Alam Society in Mosul that opposed the Ottoman's pro-Turkish stances and consolidated the role of Arabs in the country (Azzildin 1976, p. 3; Khalil 1982, p. 8).

With the beginning of the First World War, British forces occupied Basrah in the south from November 22, 1914, during which time they controlled all the publishing houses, bought all the private printing presses and cancelled the licences of all the available newspapers (Barakat 1977, pp. 69–70; Al-Rawi 2010, p. 113). The Ottomans did the same thing in Baghdad and Mosul, except for one private newspaper in Baghdad that sided with them – *Al-Zuhoor* (Butti 1976, p. 43). In other words, the two occupying forces that took control of Iraq had opposite agendas but shared the same media policies of controlling all publications, restricting press freedom and silencing the opposition.

With the new British occupiers, *Al-Awqat* in Basrah was first published in 1915 and continued until 1921. It appeared in four languages: English, Arabic, Turkish, and Persian, and mainly took its news from Reuters. The newspaper attacked the Germans and the Ottomans. Probably its most notable editor-in-chief was Sulaiman Faidi.

The British authorities established several other newspapers in the cities they occupied, such as *Al-Arab* and *Al-Awqat* in Baghdad and *Najma* in Kirkuk. *Al-Awqat* first appeared on January 1, 1918, and advocated the policies of the British forces in Iraq. It remained until March 18, 1928. On June 23, 1918, the British forces began publishing a weekly newspaper called *Dar Al-Salam* in Baghdad, which later became a literary magazine. In Mosul, the British established *Mosul* newspaper for the same purposes. It was first published on November 15, 1918.

A couple of years passed, after which anti-British sentiment grew in the country due to the disappointment that Iraqis felt towards the British, who had initially promised them independence and freedom from the Ottomans. This kind of frustration and disappointment was echoed in the Iraqi press. For example, the newspaper *Al-Lissan*, first published in July 1919, was the first Iraqi publication that called for a revolution against the British forces. Its two editors were Antoine Luqqa and Ahmed Izzat Al-Adhami. After announcing the British mandate over Iraq on April 26, 1920, Iraqis started to attack the British authorities directly. Indeed, the mandate and the criticism published in the Iraqi press created a popular opinion against the British which ultimately led to the 1920 Iraqi Revolution, during which Sheikh Mohammed Baqir Al-Shabibi published the paper *Al-Furat* in Najaf in August 1920. Together with *Al-Istiqlal*, which was printed in two different versions in Baghdad and Najaf, these newspapers published the detailed news on the revolution and the speeches of its leaders (Butti 1968, p. 38).

During the British occupation, other newspapers flourished, such as *Sada Al-Haqiqa*, *Al-Iraq*, and *Al-Sharq*. The latter was published by the British on August 30, 1920, and stood against the 1920 Iraqi Revolution, but it only lasted two months. Further, the first issue of the daily *Al-Iraq* was published on June 1, 1920, and was owned by the famous Iraqi journalist Razuq Dawood Ghanam. It also supported the British forces against Iraqi insurgency. The newspaper remained in circulation for 12 years, after which Prime Minister Nouri Said revoked its licence.

Other journals and magazines appeared in the Iraqi governorates, like *Al-Nadi Al-'Almi* (1919) in Mosul (Iraqi National Library and Archives 2011e) and *Mira't Al-'Iraq* (1919) in Basrah (Iraqi National Library and

Archives 2011f). This stage in the Iraqi press ended with the formation of the Iraqi state in 1921 and the appointment of Faisal I as King of Iraq.

Phase III

The third stage in the Iraqi press was probably the most liberal and democratic in the history of Iraq. It started with the official declaration of the Iraqi state, though the British remained in control of the country that was under their mandate. This phase ended in 1941 after the failed revolt led by Rashid Ali Al-Kaylani. After ratifying the July 2, 1922, decree, political parties were allowed to function and the partisan press was formed.[2] During this time a new newspaper was published under the title the *Iraqi Government Gazette*. Under that name it lasted only two years and was published in English and Arabic. Its name was changed to *Al-Waqai' Al-Iraqia* on December 8, 1922 (Al-'Adhami 1972, pp. 41–52; Al-Rawi 1978, p. 26). It is still published by the Iraqi government to announce new laws and decrees, making it the longest-surviving publication in Iraq's history.

Contrary to prevalent views that Iraq did not witness any kind of democratic rule before 2003, Dawisha argues the opposite, stating that the period between 1921 and 1958 was one of the most liberal phases, during which political parties were free to voice their concerns and criticise the government (Dawisha 2005). The period between 1941 and 1958 witnessed major developments in terms of education, economy, and well-being that were also reflected in the quality of the media produced. Hanna Batatu states the following regarding this period:

> Baghdad throbbing with a vigor long unknown, a middle class in continuous growth and already intensely articulate, a modern education still meager in content but extending in bounds, paved roads, railroads and air services gradually spanning more and more of the country, a commerce still hesitant but in a lively mood.
>
> (2004, p. 78)

However, since the early 1930s there had been a negative influence on the Iraqi press caused by Prime Minister Nouri Said as he opposed any kind of government opposition voiced in the press. Government pressures on the press and political parties probably reached their climax in 1949 with the crack down on the opposition (Fawzi 1986, p. 8). Though the first Iraqi press law was signed by Said himself, decreed in 1931, he was against the freedom of the press from the beginning (Shukur 2010).

The law Said signed was shortly followed by another regulation (Decree No. 57 of 1933) during Rashid 'Ali Al-Kaylani's premiership. Al-Kaylani was more liberal than Said, and all of the 25 newspapers whose licences had been revoked during Nouri Al-Said's rule returned to work. The 1993 law stated that the government had no right to cancel the licence of any newspaper except by a court order. Yet, there were still strict regulations to be followed. For example, Article 12 mentioned that the interior minister could warn the publication's manager if it published anything that:

1. Destabilises the internal and external security of the state.
2. Causes hatred and animosity among the people and its classes in a way that disturbs security.
3. Affects the brotherly relations between Iraq and foreign countries.
4. Breaches the mores and ethics.
5. Contradicts the truth in order to agitate the public opinion.

(Iraqi Publication Law 1933)

Most of the political parties that were established during this period started to produce their own newspapers. For example, *Al-Ikha' Al-Wattani*, first published in 1931, was sponsored by Akha' Al-Wattani, the political party led by Naji Al-Sweidi, Rashid 'Ali Al-Kaylani, and Ali Jawdat Al-Ayubi. Also, Al-Nahdha, a party established in 1922 and led by Amin Al-Jarjafji, published *Al-Nahdha* in 1927. Al-Wattani had its own publications, such as *Sada Al-Wattan* and *Al-Thabat*. In 1930 it published its own paper, *Sada Al-Istiqlal*. Finally, the Ahali Group, formed in 1931 under the leadership of Abdul Fattah Ibrahim, Muhammed Hadid, Abdul Qadir Ismael, and Hussein Jamil, published *Ahali* in 1932. This later became the 'most prominent daily paper in the country because the members of the group co-operated actively in the editing of the paper and contributed articles which had a wide influence in Baghdad' (Khadduri 1951, p. 72).

During this period a new trend in the Iraqi press emerged that was represented in the popularity of sarcastic newspapers like *Kanas Al-Shawar'*, which first appeared on April 1, 1925, and whose editor was a famous Iraqi Christian writer called Mikhail Taisi (Butti 1976, p. 154). It ceased publication on December 2, 1926 after its owner suffered an assassination attempt because he wrote a book that was labelled by some Muslim scholars as 'atheistic'.[3] Another popular newspaper, *Habazbuz*, appeared on September 29, 1931 (Butti 1955, p. 121). It was owned by Nuri Thabit and lasted for a long time, with 302 issues being published over the years (Al-Rawi 1978, p. 26). Yet it is important to note that the first sarcastic newspaper that appeared in Iraq was published in Basrah on November 21, 1909 and was called *Marqa'ah Al-Hindi* (Butti 1976, p. 147; Al-Jubouri 1986, p. 22). Others were published in Baghdad, such as *Khan Al-Dahab* (1911), *Al-Bulbul* (1911), and *Al-Dhara'if* (1924) (Butti 1976, p. 149; Al-Jubouri 1986, p. 22).

In relation to the Kurdish press, one of the first newspapers published in Kurdistan was *Bank Kurdistan*, and it appeared in Sulymaniah on August 2, 1922. It was followed by the *Ruzi Kurdistan* newspaper, which was first published on November 15, 1922. In Erbil, monthly magazine *Kirmanji* was first published on March 25, 1926 and edited by Hussein Huzni Mukirani (Khalil 1985b, p. 342).

The Iraqi press enjoyed a relative freedom that culminated in the events of 1941. In April of that year a group of Iraqi officers revolted against the monarchy and demanded complete independence from British domination. The action was led by four military officers and their attempt was called the Golden Square coup. When the revolt failed, Iraq suffered more press restrictions that varied in intensity, but the media began to be mere tools used by the consecutive national governments. During the revolt, some Iraqi publications stood with the rebels – such as *Al-'Alam Al-Arabi*, *Sut Al-Shaab*, *Al-Sijil* (Basrah) magazine, *Al-Tayarah*, and *Al-Majalah* (Al-Rawi 1978, pp. 35–57), as well as the newspaper *Al-Bilad* (Butti 1968, p. 120).

During the first months that followed the 14 July Revolution of 1958 which toppled the monarchy, several newspapers were published, such as *Al-Akhbar*, *Al-Hurria*, *Al-Yaqadha*, *Al-Jamhurriah*, *Sawt Al-Ihrar*, *Al-Thawrah*, *Al-Zaman*, *Ittihad Al-Sha'ab*, *Al-Ihali*, and *Khah Batt* (Kurdish). Among the new features introduced were the investigative reportages accompanied by photos, and brief editorial articles that were first written by Abdul Jabbar Wahbi in 1959 (Butti 1972b, p. 36 and p. 38).

Other media developments included the announcement of the December 12, 1954 Publication Law that imposed more restrictions on newspapers and their ownership. Unfortunately, the Iraqi Journalists Syndicate assisted in ratifying this new law as it was always a tool manipulated by consecutive governments (Hasoon 2007).

Turning to other media channels, Iraqi radio was established in the 1930s. It was always linked to government control since Iraq did not have private radio stations (except after the US invasion of Iraq in 2003). The first radio transmission in Iraq was on March 22, 1932, between 08:30 and 10:30, and the first scheduled radio programme published in the newspapers was on January 27, 1935 (Al-Rawi 1992, p. 28 and p. 31). Yet the official beginning of Baghdad Radio was on June 10, 1936 (ibid., p. 37), and it was supervised by the Iraqi Telegraph and Mail General Administration (Boyd 1982, p. 400).

Interestingly, King Ghazi of Iraq (1912–1939) was very interested in radio channels. On June 15, 1937, he established Al-Zuhoor Radio Stations, which consisted of three stations – two of them located at royal palaces in Baghdad (Al-Rawi 1992, pp. 10–11). He used to broadcast news and speeches in Arabic and English. Then in 1943, Al-Zuhoor started broadcasting in three languages – English, Hindu, and Polish – owing to the presence of large numbers of foreign experts and workers from countries that speak these languages (ibid., p. 90). The King used to supervise and purchase the radio equipment himself, and he dealt with an American telecommunication company called Hallicraft. His radio messages broadcast his pro-Nazi stances and his desire to annex Kuwait with Iraq – an idea that was allegedly welcomed by some Kuwaiti youth (ibid., p. 13).

Other landmarks in the history of radio in Iraq include the establishment of Kurdish Radio, which started transmitting in 1939. On February 1, 1959, Turkomen Radio was established, and on April 4, 1965, the Iraqi Armed Forces Radio was formed. After the 1967 War, a new Iraqi radio was established called Al-Zahf Al-Muqadas ('The Sacred March'), but it did not last long (Al-Rawi 1992, p. 52).

Before the fall of the monarchy in Iraq, a 'radio war' was waged between Egypt and Iraq because of their conflicting polices (Boyd 1982, p. 401). Gamal Abdul Nasser was against the Baghdad Pact, which he saw as a threat to his regime and dominance in the region. Abdul Nasser established the Voice of the Arabs, which transmitted from Cairo alongside a clandestine radio service called Radio Free Iraq – both of which called for a toppling of the monarchy.[4] On the other hand, Iraq was aided in its anti-Egyptian and anti-Saudi propaganda by the UK and US governments, which supplied it with the necessary radio equipment and training (Vaughan 2002). Later, Iraq managed to jam the transmission of the Egyptian radio stations and transmitted a radio programme called *Voice of Truth*, which attacked Egypt and its leadership (Al-Rawi 1992, p. 50). Malcolm Kerr identified this period as the 'Arab Cold War', which lasted even after the formation of the republic in Iraq (1971).

As for Iraqi TV, it started broadcasting in 1954 from a mobile station originally imported by the British company Pye. Hence, Iraq became the first Arab country to have a TV station. However, regular transmission of news and programmes only started on May 2, 1956 (Boyd 1982,

p. 111; Al-Rawi 1992, p. 103 and p. 106; de Beer and Merrill 2004; Rugh 2004a, p. 2; Al-Rawi 2010, p. 11 and pp. 201–202). When Iraq's TV station was inaugurated by King Faisal II, only 120 TV sets were sold to Iraqis (Al-Rawi 2010, p. 202). On November 18, 1967, Kirkuk TV station was inaugurated, transmitting in Arabic, Kurdish, Turkomen, and Syriac. Indeed, the development of Iraqi TV was rather slow due to budget constraints and the rapid political changes.

Among the landmarks of Abdul Karim Qassim's reign (1958–1963) was the founding of the INA in 1959 (Al-Rawi 2010, p. 116). Also, Iraqis watched the Mahdawi trials on TV, in which official figures from the monarchy era were shown and tried. The motive was to 'allow viewers to see that the new government is prosecuting those suspected of wrong doing' (Boyd 1982, p. 406). In fact, the TV presentation of the trials was similar to the way in which senior Iraqi Ba'athists and officials were tried by the Iraqi government after 2003. In the two cases, the Iraqi judges made public statements that denounced the former government, while they intentionally humiliated the defendants to show off their authority.

The Iraqi media during the Ba'ath rule, 1968–2003

When the Ba'ath Party took control of the country in 1968, the state-control of media channels intensified – especially with the beginning of Saddam Hussein's rule in 1979. Inspired by the communist model, Saddam Hussein wanted to shape Iraq's media in a way that guaranteed the state's manipulation of it at the expense of objectivity. Aumente et al. (1999, p. 51) confirmed that the goal of objectivity as a non-partisan ideal was largely discarded in Eastern Europe during the communist reign since it was regarded as an 'enemy of "truth"'. The role of the media was to serve the state, and journalists were viewed as mere tools to 'facilitate this objective' (1999, p. 189). The authors describe the kind of journalism prevalent in Eastern Europe as follows:

> It was mostly a 'see, they are wrong, again', or a 'here's the real truth' approach to journalism. A journalism of information with a measure of objectivity and verifiability, a journalism of systematic inquiry and informed opinion was not to be found or only rarely found in any East/Central European or USSR media...'.
>
> (1999, p. 152)

The case of Eastern Europe and the former Soviet Union is relevant to this study because Saddam Hussein's Iraq was somehow shaped by similar socialist and anti-imperialists slogans.

Yet, major developments in Iraq occurred during this era for three main reasons:

(1) the Ba'ath Party made use of the extra oil revenues that were generated after the 1972 nationalisation of oil;
(2) the party's policy to expand its ideology to the Arab homeland made the Iraqi government think of ways to reach the Arab masses and develop its communication facilities; and
(3) the introduction of modern mass-communication technologies made the Arab world closer than before.

In relation to the first point, former Iraqi Minister of Information Abdul Ghani Abdul Ghafur gave some figures that showed the disparity between the budgets of Iraqi radio and TV channels before and after 1968. For example, the budget allocated to radio and TV in 1973 was 4 million dinars (approximately 12 million dollars), while it was 650,000 dinars (approximately 1,950,000 dollars) in 1968. The INA's budget was 135,000 dinars in 1968 (approximately 405,000 dollars), yet it reached 900,000 dinars (approximately 2,700,000 dollars) in 1973 (Abdul Ghafur 1974, p. 98). We will first have a look at the nature of Saddam Hussein's media policy.

During the Ba'ath rule, the media were generally shaped by the government's policies. Social and moral values and norms, such as the famous 'Faith Campaign'[5] in the 1990s, were all dictated to the public via the mass media. Thompson (1990) asserts that ideology is a 'meaning in the service of power' (p. 7); hence the official media are part and parcel of the political system controlling the country. The media become a mere tool to convey the ideology of the ruling political party, especially in totalitarian states like Iraq before 2003.

Foreign journalists were not free to move and report in the country unless they were accompanied by government minders, who were mostly from the intelligence apparatus. Yet the condition of the media in Iraq before 2003 was not unique in the Arab world because many Arab countries followed the same strict media policy (Ayish 2002, p. 138). For example, Rugh, in his work on the Arab media, described news presentation in Arab media as being politically biased because they were generally utilised by different Arab governments to serve their political interests (Rugh 2004a, p. 17).

According to the United Nation's *Arab Human Development Report*, there are unified features that characterise the Arab media because their 'communication policies' are similar. Most Arab governments 'employ media channels for political propaganda and entertainment, at the expense of other functions and services' (UNDP 2003, p. 65). The general characteristics of Arab media are authoritarian; uni-dimensional, in the sense that the media 'discourse mostly excludes the other point of view, keeping it away from the public mind'; and official, as most media channels wait for the official line before reporting events or never report an event unless told to by the concerned officials (UNDP 2003, p. 62).

To understand the media policy, it is important to have a closer look at the way that the media were viewed by the authorities at this time. Iraqi Minister of Information Lattif Ansaif Jassim, who held this office during the Iran–Iraq War, repeatedly emphasised Saddam Hussein's famous speech, which addressed a group of journalists working for Dar Al-Jamahir at the end of 1979, saying: 'We tell you to write without limitation or hesitation or fear and whether the state is satisfied or not with what you say' (Jassim 1990, p. 152). This statement indicates the double standards held by Hussein towards the media since the reality was something completely different. Hussein himself was believed to have given an order when he was deputy president that 'programs should not concentrate on "sad" or "negative" aspects of Iraq and that programs should strive to be more entertaining and happy' (Boyd 1982, p. 403). Hussein was described in a Reporters Sans Frontières' (RSF) report as a 'predator of press freedom' who controlled the media with 'an iron fist and has given them the single mission of relaying his propaganda' (2003a, p. 3 and p. 1). Many communication experts and politicians in the West regarded his media as mere propaganda, whereas the Iraqi government thought of it as a vehicle to educate the public and convey facts. Within such a contradictory way of interpreting the nature of the media, one has to be careful in assessing media messages. What William Hatchen and James Scotton said about media messages is true here: 'one person's truth is another person's propaganda, and vice versa' (2007, p. 15).

Jassim directly and indirectly oriented Iraqi journalists to become tools used by the government to strengthen its position and policy. During the inauguration of the new headquarters of the Iraqi Journalists Syndicate on April 30, 1989, he said:

> We will not direct this or that journalist to write in a certain way, but we direct writers to put the interests of the homeland and the [revolutionary] process above all considerations. This is important in order to avoid making a political mistake and or a mistake that might anger this or that foreign country. These are basic principles followed

by journalists rather than editorial lines dictated by the parties that control the press and media

(Jassim 1990, p. 190).

Jassim wanted Iraqi journalists to practise self-censorship in order to avoid falling into trouble with the authorities. Within such an atmosphere, it was understandable that the majority of Iraqi journalists and writers were living in fear lest what they wrote was interpreted by a senior Ba'athist as 'anti-revolutionary'. Jassim himself acknowledged this fear when he once referred to a news conference held in the former Soviet Union to criticise an arms deal with Iran, but it was not covered by the Iraqi media. Instead, it was only published in a confidential bulletin, entitled *Al-Rassid*, which was circulated among senior officials (Jassim 1990, p. 218 and p. 227). Jassim commented: 'We have to make ourselves used to considering every piece of information except what touches the national and regional security' (Jassim 1990, p. 219). Other problems were related to the fear held by journalists that they must focus their attention on the official rather than the event covered. Jassim mentioned this issue by referring to a recurrent phenomenon: a certain state minister might inaugurate an art gallery, yet the only photos that appear in the newspapers are those of the minister, while the artist and his/her works are ignored (Jassim 1990, pp. 223–224).

It is important to note that the media policies followed in Iraq were based on the doctrines of the Ba'ath Party, which used to discredit and suspect any foreign news agency or journalist working in the country. Much of the jargon that evolved around a conspiracy woven against the Ba'ath Party was repeatedly used in the media, such as 'imperialist powers', 'colonialist aggression', and 'ugly occupation'. Bengio called these 'code words' and 'value loaded' expressions that were recurrent in the Iraqi media (1998, p. 9 and p. 10). Indeed, Saddam Hussein used the idea of a 'foreign conspiracy' threatening to destroy Iraq as a tool to unify the public and create an emergency state wherein more political, social, and economic restrictions could be freely applied (see, for example, Gray 2010). Abdul Ghani Abdul Ghafur, for example, objected to the concept of free media, claiming that 'liberal and destructive concepts that are advocated under the banner of freedom of the press together with the regressive intermediaries and foreign proxies continue spreading the spirit of despair and sluggishness among Arab citizens by what is published in the media' (Abdul Ghafur 1974, p. 57). The Ba'ath National Policy Convention, which was signed after 1968, mentioned that there must be a struggle against all the concepts, theories, trends, and methods that 'spread sectarianism, chauvinism, racism, regionalism, defeat, liberalism, and others that serve imperialism and its foundations' (ibid., p. 59). Ba'athists called for 'revolutionary media' to influence the Arab masses and ultimately help to achieve Arab unity. The media had to 'reflect the Revolution in a detailed, forthright, and innovative manner so as to become an inspiration for the masses and the educated elite not only in Iraq but in the Arab homeland [as a whole]' (ibid., p. 104). In fact, there were serious dangers in advocating such media rhetoric because other Arab leaders were not pleased with the idea that Iraq would lead the Arab masses. Sultan Qaboos of Oman once revealed that 'Iraqis... had arrogantly fancied themselves as the leaders of the Arab world. Consequently, Oman's relations with Iraq had never been very strong' (Wikileaks 2008f).

During the economic sanctions that started in 1990 and lasted more than ten years, the Iraqi media rhetoric intensified its presentation of Western schemes and conspiracies against the 'Ba'ath Revolution' that were designed by 'the American imperialists' who were 'out to punish Iraq as a nation' (Bengio 2000, p. 94).

After 1968, Iraqi TV remained under the same state management with stricter monitoring and censorship. During this period the government exercised full authoritarian control over the production and flow of the mass media. The programmes were characterised as 'heavily political', for media officials devoted a major 'time to documentaries about the progressive stance taken by the government' (Boyd 1982, p. 113; Sinjari 2006, p. 479). Some media scholars categorised the Iraqi media during Hussein's rule as 'Marxist–Leninist', since 'the media were subordinate to state interest and were harnessed to serve only one political party, Ba'ath' (Kim and Hama-Saeed 2008, pp. 579–580).

In particular, TV was closely monitored by media officials and employees to filter what was aired. I spent months working as a freelance translator at the headquarters of the Iraqi TV station in Baghdad in 1996 and 1997. During that time the Directorate of Monitoring and Translation had a noticeboard upon which instructions were given to the employees who checked everything that was aired on TV. Aside from political discussions, sexual scenes, and religious controversies that must be deleted, one of the striking directives was to cut any illustration of food because the government did not want Iraqis to see varieties of fruits and meat during the economic sanctions. The government used to distribute food rations through the UN Oil-for-Food Programme, during which Iraqis used to get the same kinds of cheap, and in many cases expired, food every month. In this context, Ofra Bengio was right in saying that Saddam Hussein 'tried to inculcate patience...(*sabr* in Arabic – an oft-praised Islamic value) in the Iraqi people and manipulate it for his political purposes especially to encourage his much-abused populace to withstand the post-1990 sanctions' (2000, p. 92). Also, the noticeboard mentioned that any reference or scene that encouraged pregnancy must be deleted. This shows that the government was facing great difficulties in coping with the increasing demands of the Iraqi population living under an embargo. Due to the threats of punishment, such as imprisonment or even torture, the staff who were checking TV series and movies paid extra care to the deletion of any potentially 'suspicious' materials.

In general, no criticism against the country or the government was allowed in Iraq at this time. The Revolutionary Command Council (RCC) decreed order No. 840 in 1986, stating that 'any person who insults or criticises the President, his entourage, the Ba'ath Party, the RCC, or even the government' faces a death penalty. In terms of press freedom in 2002, Iraq ranked 130 out of the 139 countries around the world that exercised media restriction, and it was in the top ten of 'countries that were hostile to the media and journalists' (RSF 'Press Freedom Index' 2002b; RSF Report 2003a, p. 2). As the government closely monitored the media, whatever was published was immediately investigated by government officials, which is in contrast with what has happened in Iraq since 2003, according to an Iraqi journalist (Kim and Hama-Saeed 2008, pp. 585–586).

In relation to Iraqi TV, the Education Television Station became operational on June 17, 1971, and it worked in co-ordination with the Iraqi Ministry of Education (Al-Rawi 1992, p. 121 and p. 144). In 1972 a new TV station (Channel 7), which worked as part of Baghdad TV, was formed (Abdul Ghafur 1974, p. 39). Starting from November 10, 1973, the hours of transmission were reduced in order to 'enable the citizens to have enough rest and assist them to work actively in the next day' (Al-Rawi 1992, p. 111). Baghdad Cultural TV was formed in the 1990s, and was later turned into Baghdad Satellite, whose headquarters in Baghdad were bombed during the 2003 US-led invasion of Iraq. At the beginning of the second millennium, there were only four official TV channels: two Iraqi National channels, Iraqi Satellite TV, and Ashabab (Youth) TV. A couple of years before the Iraq War, the Iraqi Ministry of Information offered a wireless subscription to more than a dozen Arab TV channels, but the service stopped after the occupation in 2003. Satellite TV reception was strictly banned because information censorship was not possible: any individual caught having a satellite dish was either fined or imprisoned for a few months. State control of the media means that messages must be directly controlled by the government and facts are sometimes distorted, such as was the case in the Iraqi media coverage of the 1973 Arab–Israeli War (Rugh 1975, pp. 312–315).

However, the situation in Iraqi Kurdistan was different. The number of partisan Kurdish TV channels exceeded 20, broadcasting from the northern region of Iraq in which the Kurds had their own relative independence from the capital, Baghdad, after 1991 (RSF 2002a, p. 2). Media personnel in Kurdistan were first called 'mountain journalists' because they worked in the 1990s propagating against the central government and encouraging Kurds to join the *Pashmerga* – the armed militia.

All media outlets, from 1991 until the present day, are affiliated with Kurdish political parties, especially the Patriotic Union of Kurdistan and the Kurdistan Democratic Party. The only independent newspaper, *Hawlati*, which was established in 2000, faces great pressure from regional government as some of its journalists were jailed for 'covering controversial stories' (Axe 2006). On July 20, 2010, another Kurdish paper, *Rozhnama*, published an article that accused the ruling Kurdish parties of profiting from millions of dollars from smuggling oil to Iran. As a result, the Kurdish regional government filed a defamation lawsuit against the newspaper and demanded 1 billion dollars in compensation, which is regarded as the largest in the history of Iraq (JFO 2010). The case remained in an Iraqi Kurdistan court and was used as a warning for other Kurdish oppositional newspapers that periodically receive defamation suits. For example, the editor-in-chief of *Livinpress* magazine in Kurdistan, Ahmed Mira, had two libel suits against him and was arrested in June 2011 for criticising Kurdish Minister of Natural Resources Ashti Hawrami (*Kurdnet* 2011).

Furthermore, there were more than seven main daily newspapers, including *Al-Iraq, Al-Jamhuriah, Al-Qaddisiah, Al-Thawra, Babel* (Arabic and English versions), *Baghdad Observer* (English), and *Al-Ba'ath Al-Riadhi* (sports); a few government and privately owned weekly newspapers – *Al-Musawr Al-Arabi, Al-Zawra', Al-Iqtisadi* (economics), *Nabdh Al-Shabab, Al-Ra'i, Al-Zamen, Uruk Al-Siahiah* (tourism), *Al-Ittihad, Al-Maw'id, Alwan, Sawt Al-Talabah,* and *Al-'Illam* (issued by the Department of Communication at Baghdad University); some magazines – *Alif Baa', Wa'i Al-Umal, Al-Mar'ah, Al-Shabab, Ishtar, Al-Rafidain, Al-Kawthar, Al-Rasheed, Majalati* (children), and *Al-Mizmar* (children); and a handful of newspapers in other governorates – *Sawt Al-Ta'mim* in Kirkuk, *Al-Nassiriah* in Dhi Qar, *Nainawa* in Mosul, *Basrah, Al-Furat, Al-Jana'in* in Babil, *Sawt Al-Qadissiahtayn, Wassit, Al-Anbar,* and *Tikrit*. Aside from publishing books, the Ministry of Culture in general was responsible via its different directorates for publishing some literary and academic journals, such as *Al-Aqllam, Al-Thaqafah Al-Ajnabiah*, and *Afaq Arabiah*.

Oddly enough, media experts have not pointed out the relative freedom that the weekly private newspapers enjoyed during Saddam Hussein's rule. These publications, which can be regarded as Iraq's former 'yellow journalism', started to criticise some government practices and officials (without mentioning their names) since the government thought of offering channels to vent frustration due to the pressure and hardship of living under the economic sanctions (see one example in Daragahi 2003). Very few Iraqi journalists were able to criticise the government in a direct way. Dawood Al-Farhan, for example, wrote a series of articles in *Alif Baa'* magazine that were entitled *'Balad Sa'id, Balad Nazil'* ('One Country Up, One Country Down') in which the writer sarcastically compared Iraq (going down) and Japan (going up). As a result, he was imprisoned for his cynical views and was later pardoned by Hussein. Others, like cartoonist Mu'yad Ni 'ma, 'drew fire for his cartoons, which always pushed the edge of what was tolerated in the press' (Wikileaks 2005f).

In relation to radio developments, Voice of the Masses radio was established on May 1, 1970, with an emphasis on the issues related to the Iraqi armed forces. In 1974 it started broadcasting for 24 hours a day, but from 1976 the radio became focused on Arab regional issues rather than local ones (Abdul Ghafur 1974, p. 39; Al-Rawi 1992, pp. 74–75). Voice of the Masses stopped broadcasting a few days after the beginning of the Persian Gulf War of 1991, as it was merged with Baghdad Radio (Al-Rawi 2010, p. 200).

On June 1, 1972, live radio transmissions from Baghdad Radio started making more listeners tune in. During the Iran–Iraq War, the Iraqi government utilised all its resources to counter the Iranian propaganda and that of the Iraqi opposition parties, like the Shiite Supreme Council of the Islamic Revolution in Iraq, whose members used to operate in Iran. In the 1980s, Iraq dramatically increased its radio transmission: about 244,000 hours were broadcast at an average of 120 hours each day from September 4, 1980 to September 4, 1986 (Al-Rawi 1992, p. 58). Iraqi journalists were involved in the war either as soldiers or as media personnel. For example, there were 700 INA workers before 1980, but only 246 journalists, editors, and reporters worked for the INA during the war as others served in the army (Jassim 1990, p. 227 and p. 226).

As part of the Ba'ath Party expansionist policy discussed above, Iraq intensified its efforts to spread the Ba'ath ideology with covert radio transmission, making Iraqis 'the most enthusiastic supporters of non-official radio in the Arab World' (Boyd 1982, p. 404). Among the radio channels established were Voice of Arab Syria (1976); Voice of the Arabian Peninsula People (1973–1975), which was anti-Saudi Arabia; Voice of the Eritrea Revolution; and Voice of Egypt Arabism (1979). Throughout the programmes aired, the Iraqi government wanted to say that 'Iraq, and Ba'ath philosophy, should lead the Arab World' (Boyd 1982, p. 405). After the end of the Iran–Iraq War in 1988, Saddam Hussein became more enthusiastic about spreading his pan-Arabism policy, making some Arab Gulf countries fear his ambition. As a result, Saudi Arabia urged Iraq to sign a non-aggression agreement in March 1989 (Farouk-Sluglett and Sluglett 1990, p. 24), just about a year before Iraq invaded Kuwait.

As for the Internet, it was only introduced into the country in early 2000, making Iraq one of the last countries in the world to have it. It was supplied to the Iraqi public with very limited access because it was prohibited to have unmonitored communication with the outside world. For example, ordinary Iraqis could not use Yahoo and Hotmail email systems because they were restricted. The only legal email account had to be created via uruklink.net, which was the official Internet provider. A few days before the onslaught of the military operations on Iraq in March 2003, the official website of the Iraqi government was hacked, seemingly by US hackers, and an anti-Ba'ath announcement was posted. At this time there were around 45,000 Internet users, most of whom were government officials (OpenNet Initiative 2007, pp. 1–2).

After the invasion of Kuwait and the bombing of the main TV and radio stations around the country, significant deterioration in the media field as a whole occurred due to a lack of necessary funds and the required human resources. As a reaction to this reality, Uday Saddam Hussein, who was once the chairperson of the Iraqi Journalists Syndicate, established his own *Babil* (Arabic and English versions) and *Ba'ath al-Riadhi* (sport) newspapers with up-to-date news, as well as producing *Shabab* (Youth) radio and TV channels that used to broadcast Western pirated movies and programmes to provide a link for Iraqis to the outside world.

Due to Saddam Hussein's foreign policy, many neighbouring countries had clandestine radio stations transmitting to Iraqis. Saudi Arabia, for example, established radio station Voice of Iraq, on which Georges Mansour, an exiled Iraqi journalist, worked (RSF 2003b, A new but fragile freedom). Later, Mansour worked for the Iraqi Media Network in post-2003 Iraq. Also, Iran was very active in supporting anti-Saddam radio and TV channels, such as SCIRI's Voice of the Islamic Revolution in Iraq, which later became Voice of the Rebellious Iraq. Syria was also involved in its support of clandestine radio stations, such as Voice of Iraq (Al-Rawi 2010, pp. 196–200).

Despite all the aforementioned facts, Iraqi media before the Iraq War never witnessed any kind of sectarian rhetoric, religious discrimination, or racist remarks because these practices were strictly prohibited by the law. Differences between religious and ethnic groups existed, but they were 'rarely articulated in official, public debate, nor used as a basis by politicians or religious and community leaders to criticize the others' (Al-Marashi 2007, p. 97). For example, the terms 'Shiites' and 'Sunnis' were never used (Bengio 1985, p. 13). Even the surnames of Iraqi officials were not disclosed so as to avoid suggesting their religious or racial origins (ibid., p. 14), which was part of a decree issued in 1978 (Davis 2005, p. 327). In fact, Iraq is ethnically and religiously very rich, having Muslims (Shiites and their various doctrines, and Sunnis), Christians (Chaldians, Assyrians, Armenians, etc.), Sabians, Yezidis, and Jews, among others. There are also many different ethnicities, like Arabs, Kurds, Turkomen, Persians, Anglo-Indians, and so on. In fact, Saddam Hussein was aware of the sensitivity which accompanies the issue of sectarianism, especially as Iran waged a fierce propaganda campaign during the Iraq–Iran War to win over Iraqi Shiites. Hence, Shiite political parties and flagellation ceremonies were banned, but the Iraqi government used to air speeches by famous Shiite clerics during certain religious events in order to address more Iraqis.

On the other hand, Hussein's government prohibited Sunni fundamental movements, like the Saudi-backed Wahabism/Salafism and the Muslim Brotherhood. Many official books were published and TV shows aired to counter any extreme religious propaganda coming from abroad. As for the Kurds, the Iraqi government stood against Kurdish race chauvinism, fearing the instability and disunity that it might cause in the country. However, there were many Kurdish language publications, and the language itself was taught in some high schools in Baghdad, unlike in some neighbouring countries where it was banned. In fact, Hussein's aim was to establish a secular political system to guarantee a secure and unified Iraq, and to avoid religious or ethnic rifts that would cost him lives, effort, and money.

According to Paragraph 200, Article 2 of the 1969 Iraqi Penal Code, 'any individual who encourages sectarian or religious differences and incites violence among the sects and ethnicities or creates grudges and hatred among the people of Iraq shall be punished by imprisonment of not more than seven years'. The temporary Iraqi Constitution decreed on June 16, 1970, also emphasised that 'any activity that aims at disintegrating the national unity of the masses or inciting sectarian and racial differences is strictly banned' (Al-Daqouqi 1986, pp. 240–241). Having in mind the strict observance of laws and the strong censorship, Iraqi journalists were not involved in these practices, at least not in public. Other media regulations include paragraphs 225, 226, 227, 433, 434, 435, and 436, which deal with defamation and insult in public. The punishment varies according to the case and its circumstances, ranging from imprisonment of not more than seven years to fine payments. These strict rules meant that journalists had to be very careful what they wrote. A senior Iraqi journalist compared the post-2003 media in Iraq with that during Saddam Hussein's rule, saying:

> Definitely there is more press freedom now [post-Saddam], but the question is, who cares about the media reports? During the Saddam era, every single word of a journalist had to go through censorship, but there was (constant) monitoring by the government as to what was reported in the newspapers. If a certain establishment were criticized, the Baathist government would immediately investigate and correct the problems. But these days, the government rarely does anything about what the media reported.
>
> (Kim and Hama-Saeed 2008, pp. 585–586)

In a basic questionnaire designed and distributed in 2011 to six Iraqi journalists who worked before 2003, the respondents agreed on the main features of the Iraqi media during Hussein's rule. For example, three out of five respondents said that their main concerns and fears were related to their safety and security, while two mentioned that their concerns were connected to their welfare. Only one journalist did not answer this question. Two journalists mentioned that they had experienced a security incident which was linked to their profession. Though the nature of the incidents was not clarified, most Iraqi journalists who committed mistakes, whether intentionally or not, were usually punished or humiliated. Also, only two out of six journalists published an article that criticised either the government or its officials. In relation to the journalists' welfare, five out of six respondents mentioned that the salaries given to journalists were 'not at all' enough for them. Only one journalist said that the salary was 'somehow' enough. This is mainly due to the hardship that Iraqis in general had to go through during the economic sanctions. All of the respondents mentioned that they had to work a second job to make ends meet. Three of the respondents said that the alternative jobs were not related to the media field. Unexpectedly, four out of six respondents mentioned that there were journalistic principles, like balance, objectivity, and impartiality, followed at the time. I assume that the respondents are fully aware of the nature of these media terms, since five out of six of them hold PhD degrees in media and communication. Besides, four respondents mentioned that they had media training in different areas prior to 2003 which was mostly organised by the Iraqi Journalists Syndicate. One of the most striking answers was related to the editorial control of the publications. Five respondents agreed that their editor used to give the journalists the freedom and capacity to produce news. Only one respondent mentioned that Iraqi journalists received the news from INA without having the necessary freedom to write original news reports.

In brief, Iraqi journalists did not have the freedom to freely express their opinions because of the nature of the former regime. Due to the nature of the one-party rule, journalists were financially encouraged and professionally required to write about the positive achievements of the government rather than its negative policies. This was evident in the editorials written and the events covered. However, there were many exceptions that would have been ignored because they were not detected by the censorship radar. If someone was caught crossing the official line or disseminating banned information, both of which were known to every Iraqi journalist as not allowed, he/she would be imprisoned or tortured. As for gatekeepers, they were greatly pressurised to make sure that no critical views were communicated to the public.

2

US Propaganda Efforts to Wage a War on Iraq: The Case of *Nassiriah* and *Babil* Newspapers

Amid the neo-conservative Bush Administration's efforts to find evidence that linked Iraq to Al-Qaeda and the 9/11 attack, some US officials misled the American public into believing that Iraq was a serious threat to US national security and to the whole international community. One of the key pieces of evidence cited by some US officials is an editorial published in *Nassiriah* newspaper, whose distribution was mainly limited to Nassiriah city. Its author, Naeem 'Abd Muhalhal, a literary figure from the Sabaean religion, wrote a fantastical literary account in which he prophesied that Osama Bin Laden might attack the USA.

After the US-led occupation of Iraq in 2003, another article, published on November 14, 2002, in the *Babil* newspaper, was wrongly interpreted by a US judge in order to connect Iraq with Al-Qaeda amid the escalating criticism about the legality of the war on Iraq and the lack of evidence with regard to Iraq's alleged weapons of mass destruction (WMDs). This chapter shows how US officials intentionally planted scare stories in the Western media by misinterpreting the two articles in order to make a connection between 9/11 and Iraq. Before discussing the two articles, we need to have a better understanding of the context that surrounded the US (dis)information efforts to wage a war on Iraq.

It has been proven that prior to the 2003 war, Iraq possessed no WMDs and had no links with Al-Qaeda. This is according to the Duelfer Report carried out by the multinational Iraq Survey Group, the Senate Select Committee on Intelligence reports in 2004 and 2006, and the 9/11 Commission Report in 2004.

Yet the efforts to wage a war on Iraq and remove Saddam Hussein go back to October 31, 1998, when President Bill Clinton signed the Iraq Liberation Act. This law was preceded by providing Iraqi opposition parties with $5 million on May 1 of the same year. This included media assistance to 'such organizations for radio and television broadcasting by such organizations to Iraq' (The National Security Archive 1998; US Congress 1998). Clinton emphasised the importance of waging a media campaign in 1998 against Saddam Hussein's regime, since the US government was supposed to 'work with Radio Free Iraq, to help news and information flow freely to the country' (The National Security Archive 2001a).

When President George W Bush was elected, the efforts to wage a war on Iraq greatly intensified. According to former Treasury Secretary Paul O'Neill, Bush planned the war on Iraq within days of assuming office by instructing his aides to look for any kind of justification. A few hours after the 9/11 attack, Secretary of Defense Donald Rumsfeld instructed the Pentagon lawyer, Jim Haynes, to discuss with Paul Wolfowitz, Deputy Secretary of Defense, ways of linking Saddam Hussein and Osama Bin Laden (The National Security Archive 2001b). And a day after the 9/11 attack, President Bush asked Richard Clarke, his chief counter-terrorism advisor, to search for any relation between Iraq and 9/11, saying: 'See if Saddam did this . . . See if he's linked in any way' (The 9/11 Commission Report 2004, p. 334). On the same day, Wolfowitz formed the infamous Office of Special Plans (OSP) to 'shape public opinion and American policy toward Iraq' (United States Department of Defense, Inspector General 2007, p. 3). It was directed by Abram Shulsky, who previously worked for the National Strategy Information Center.

OSP was run by the Deputy Undersecretary of Defense, William Luti, and worked in co-ordination with the Undersecretary of Defense for Policy, Douglas Feith. Rumsfeld mentioned that OSP's aim was to 'search for information on Iraq's hostile intentions or links to terrorists' (Hersh 2003). Secretary Colin Powell asserted that Wolfowitz was more enthusiastic about attacking Iraq than the other US officials. 'Paul was always of the view that Iraq was a problem that had to be dealt with.' Making use of the 9/11 events, Wolfowitz 'saw this as one way of using this event as a way to deal with the Iraq problem' (The 9/11 Commission Report 2004, p. 335). In other words, 9/11 was used as a pretext to invade Iraq and all the intelligence efforts had to be directed at linking Iraq with Al-Qaeda, even if this entailed spreading false statements (as will be discussed below).

The OSP supplied the Bush Administration with false intelligence that only served to find a link between Iraq and Al-Qaeda. Lieutenant Colonel Karen Kwiatkowski, who worked for the Pentagon's Near East and South Asia unit in 2002, mentioned how OSP planted fearful stories

in the media, saying: 'It wasn't intelligence, – it was propaganda....
They'd take a little bit of intelligence, cherry-pick it, make it sound much
more exciting, usually by taking it out of context, often by juxtaposi-
tion of two pieces of information that don't belong together' (Dreyfuss
and Vest 2004). Among the false charges made against the government
of Iraq was Saddam Hussein's effort to possess uranium tubes from
Niger. This claim was based on 'forged documents, – documents that the
CIA, the State Department, and other agencies knew were fake nearly
a year before President Bush highlighted the issue in his State of the
Union address in January 2003' (ibid.). Among the interesting things
that Kwiatkowski highlighted in her revelation was that OSP hired an
intelligence officer called Navy Lieutenant Commander Youssef Aboul-
Enein, an Egyptian-American who worked as a special assistant to Luti.
'His job was to peruse the Arabic-language media to find articles that
would incriminate Saddam Hussein about terrorism, and he translated
these' (ibid.). Aboul-Enein's work seems to be of interest here because it
is likely that he translated one of the articles discussed in this chapter.
Despite Aboul-Enein's work being cross-checked by intelligence experts,
the translation he 'produced found its way directly into speeches by
Bush, Cheney, and other officials' (ibid.). Kwiatkowski summed up her
experience at OSP by saying that: 'While the people were very much
alive, I saw a dead philosophy – Cold War anti-communism and neo-
imperialism – walking the corridors of the Pentagon' (Kwiatkowski
2004).

Among the grave shortcomings of OSP intelligence efforts was its
main reliance on tips from Ahmed Chalabi's Iraqi National Congress
(INC) members. INC, an Iraqi oppositional party, was funded and supervised by the CIA to find ways to topple Saddam Hussein's regime. It is
well known now that Chalabi's group supplied most of the lies about
Iraq's WMDs. Despite the harsh criticism Chalabi got for providing false
intelligence, he justified the fabrications he disseminated by saying:
'As far as we're concerned, we've been entirely successful' in toppling
the Ba'ath regime (*The Washington Times* 2004).

It is beyond the scope of this chapter to discuss the Bush Administration's dissemination efforts to mislead the public, as other works
have carefully investigated them (for example, see Messing 2004; Miller
2004; Prados 2004; Ahmed 2005). The Center for Public Integrity made
a timeline for the false statements made by the Bush Administration
about Iraq's link to Al-Qaeda and the 9/11 attack. The report shows that
935 lies were communicated to the public in the two years that followed
9/11; most of the false statements were made in February 2003 (140 in
that month).[1] There were at least 532 'separate occasions' during which

Bush and his aides made these false statements. President Bush alone lied 232 times about Iraq's alleged WMDs and made 28 false statements on its link to Al-Qaeda (Lewis and Reading-Smith 2008). US Secretary of State Colin Powell made several false statements, too. The most significant one, which was communicated at the UN, was probably the allegation that Iraq had WMDs. Powell later regretted making such a false accusation, saying: 'I'm the one who presented it to the world, and (it) will always be a part of my record. It was painful. It is painful now' (*The Associated Press* 2005).

After the initiation of the 2009 Chilcot Inquiry by former British Prime Minister Gordon Brown, more revelations appeared about the way that the USA and the UK had planned together to attack Iraq and about the extent of the two countries' knowledge of Iraq's presumed WMDs. Similar to the US agency OPS, the British Operation Rockingham, which operated as an 'interface with MI5, MI6, GCHQ, and Defence Intelligence did similar things to prepare the public for a war on Iraq' by selecting favourable pieces of information (Clark 2005, p. 6).

British Foreign Secretary Jack Straw mentioned that in December 2001, a report by the Joint Intelligence Committee revealed that Iraq had 'no responsibility for the 11 September attacks and no significant links to Usama bin Laden' (Straw 2010, p. 3). Also, British chief of intelligence Eliza Manningham-Buller, who was head of MI5 between 2002 and 2007, said that British and US intelligence agencies found no connection between Iraq and the Al-Qaeda group. In March 2002, Manningham-Buller wrote a letter in which she revealed that there was 'no credible intelligence that demonstrates that Iraq was implicated in planning the 11 September attacks' (Biles 2010). It seems that Bush Administration officials were determined to wage a war on Iraq long before 2003 and that 'intelligence and facts were being fixed around the policy', according to the July 2002 Downing Street memo (Vannatta 2006). One of the main reasons behind the war appeared to be related to a personal animosity between Bush and Hussein. In a letter from Political Director Peter Ricketts to Jack Straw, on March 22, 2002, Ricketts mentioned the following: 'US scrambling to establish a link between Iraq and Al Aaida [sic] is so far frankly unconvincing. To get public and parliamentary support for military operations, we have to be convincing that: the threat is so serious/imminent that it is worth sending our troops to die for.' Ricketts concluded that all the warmongering efforts seemed to be caused by a 'grudge between Bush and Saddam' (Foreign and Commonwealth Office 2002). Besides, British MI6 chief Sir Richard Dearlove said that 'Bush wanted to remove Saddam, through military action, justified by the conjunction of terrorism and WMD' (Cabinet

Minutes of Discussion 2002). On January 31, 2003, British Prime Minister Tony Blair met with President Bush to discuss Iraq. In their two-hour meeting at the Oval Office, Bush revealed that he did not need a second UN resolution to initiate the war, 'even if international arms inspectors failed to find unconventional weapons'. The two leaders admitted that no WMDs had been found in Iraq, so Bush suggested other ways to provoke a war, such as painting a 'United States surveillance plane in the colors of the United Nations in hopes of drawing fire, or assassinating Mr. Hussein' (Vannatta 2006).

Furthermore, the Chilcot Inquiry exposed other pieces of information, such as the fact that Blair's aides prepared plans of what is needed in 'sensitising the public'. This included the need to initiate a 'media campaign to warn of the dangers that Saddam poses and to prepare public opinion both in the UK and abroad' (UK Cabinet Office 2002, p. 10). One of the most famous false statements made by Blair was that the Iraqis were able to deploy WMDs within 45 minutes.

As a reaction to the US–UK media efforts to link Iraq with Al-Qaeda, the Iraqi government tried to show its sympathy for the 9/11 victims. Saddam Hussein delivered a speech on Iraqi TV in which he denounced the assault, criticised Islamic extremism, and related the 9/11 attack to the US foreign policies in the Middle East that were 'biased'. Tariq Aziz, Iraq's former Foreign Minister, recalled how Saddam Hussein reacted after the 9/11 attack, saying: 'We were against that at the time, but we were not speaking to the US government. Saddam Hussein called me and said he would like me to write a letter to Ramsey [Clark, a former US attorney general] and say that we condemn the attack. I did that' (Chulov 2010). In their US detention after 2003, Saddam Hussein mentioned that he 'wrote editorials against the attack, but also spoke of the cause which led men to commit these acts'. Further, Tariq Aziz said that he wrote personal letters to two senior US figures that 'served as informal means of communications for Iraq to denounce the attack' (United States Department of Justice 2004, p. 2).

As part of the US attempt to link the Ansar Al-Islam group, which operated in Kurdistan, to Iraq, Tariq Aziz gave a press conference in Baghdad prior to the 2003 war in which he revealed that the Iraqi government opposed the Islamic militant group and even gave weapons to a Kurdish faction, Kurdistan Democratic Party (KDP), in order to expel its members from the region. Yet, the Iraqi media efforts to stop the upcoming assault did not seem to make any difference to US–UK policy towards Iraq.

Following the Bush–Blair policy to find an excuse to wage a war on Iraq, many media fabrications were designed by the CIA to distort and direct the public into believing that Iraq was utterly evil. For example, the White House ordered the CIA to counterfeit an old handwritten message dated July 1, 2001, from Tahir Jalil Habbush Al-Tikriti, the head of Iraqi intelligence during Saddam Hussein's rule (Suskind 2009). In this letter, Al-Tikriti revealed a 'short resume of a three-day "work programme" [Mohamed] Atta had undertaken at [the Palestinian] Abu Nidal's base in Baghdad' (Coughlin 2003). The US government presumably awarded $5 million to Al-Tikriti, who disappeared after the US-led invasion on Iraq in 2003, in order to silence him, and arranged for his resettlement in nearby Jordan. This handwritten message was exclusively given to a British newspaper, *The Telegraph*, which published it at once (Suskind 2009). Though it was not executed, another attempt to mislead the public was designed by the CIA by making a 'sex gay tape' showing Saddam Hussein having sex with a teenage boy (Harris 2010). Added to the other false claims made by the US government that Iraq was linked to Al-Qaeda was the allegation based on articles published in two Iraqi newspapers, which will be discussed below.

The Iraqi newspapers

The first Iraqi newspaper tackled in this chapter is called *Nassiriah* (Muhalhal 2001). It was a local weekly newspaper issued in the Dhi Qar governorate that was mostly distributed in the southern city of Nassiriah (for a translation of the article, see Appendix I).[2] Its editor-in-chief, Sabbah Nahi, was the Baghdad correspondent of the Saudi-owned network MBC and later worked on Al-Arabyiah channel in Dubai, UAE. Nahi, who was the newspaper's honorary editor-in-chief as he was stationed in Baghdad, stated that the article published in its July 21, 2001, edition by Naeem 'Abd Muhalhal was a literary one rather than political, as the writer himself was a poet and a literary figure (telephone interview with Nahi, 2011). Muhalhal wrote in his weekly column 'A Spot of Blue Ray' about Osama Bin Laden's threat (for the original article in Arabic, see Image 1 in Appendix I). In a highly decorative style, he fantastically predicted that Bin Laden might attack the White House and the Pentagon based on his latest threats that were aired by Al-Jazeera TV. It seems that OSP, with the help of Ahmed Chalabi's group, found the article and made use of it in linking Iraq with Al-Qaeda and 9/11, claiming that Saddam Hussein was aware of the attack beforehand. The translated version of the article reached Senator Ernest Fritz Hollings, a Democrat from South Carolina, who used it on September 12, 2002, during his speech in the Senate. Hollings claimed that the article gave clear evidence about Iraq's link to terrorism, and he interpreted the sentence of attacking the 'arm that is already hurting' to the assault on the World Trade Centre, while a reference to Sinatra's song – New York, New York – was explained as an indication of the attack on New York City (for a full translation of the article, see Appendix I). The article's author was accused of being an 'Iraqi operative' working for Saddam Hussein's intelligence.

After Hollings' speech, a US law firm, Kreindler & Kreindler, filed a suit against the government of Iraq demanding more than $1 trillion on behalf of 9/11 victims, citing the article as 'one of the key pieces of evidence', and that the 'Iraqi leader Saddam Hussein apparently praised this writer on September 1, 2001' (Thompson 2004, p. 325). Jim Kreindler, who is described as a 'super lawyer', stated that Muhalhal 'had advance knowledge of bin Laden's plans and that "Iraqi officials were aware of plans to attack American landmarks"' (Marrs 2006, p. 207).

In reality, Muhalhal was never praised by Saddam Hussein as the US lawyer claimed (personal correspondence with the author, 2009). Yet, the Iraqi authorities felt concerned about the US accusations, so they questioned Muhalhal about his article but found nothing that was suspicious (telephone interview with Nahi, 2011). It seems that the Iraqi government did not bother to write a rebuttal because they either felt that no tangible outcome would be reached or they believed that the allegation and the article were so absurd that they did not require any response. On March 22, 2006, Muhalhal wrote an article in the *Azzaman* newspaper (Baghdad edition) in which he defended his position and elaborated on the *Nassiriah* newspaper article, saying: 'The article was simple and clear. As he was interviewed on Al-Jazeera channel, I read in Bin Laden's eyes that he was hiding something for America. Five weeks later, the ill-fated September approached and the two towers threw their rubbles on Kabul and Baghdad' (Muhalhal 2006). After the US invasion of Iraq in 2003, Muhalhal, who lived in Nassiriah city as did many other members of the Mandean religious group, was advised by some friends to head to the nearest US Army base in his city in case there was some confusion about his article. Muhalhal went with Amir Dushi, a translator and a friend, and met the US commander who asked him a few questions. By the end of the meeting, the US commander laughed and declared that the article was only a writer's intuition (Muhalhal 2006). If Muhalhal's article had been seriously considered as a key piece of evidence to indict Iraq, its author would have been immediately arrested and imprisoned.

Though Hollings apologised later for supporting the war in Iraq, he did not refer to the *Nassiriah* newspaper in his apology. He mentioned the following in his written statement: 'I was misled. Saddam Hussein was not reconstituting a nuclear program, and in no way was he connected to 9/11. There were no terrorists in Baghdad, no weapons of mass destruction, and Saddam was no threat to our national security. Iraq was not a part of the war on terrorism.' Hollings concluded that 'President Bush has misled us into Iraq' (Hollings 2003).

The second newspaper tackled is *Babil*, which was owned by Saddam Hussein's son Uday (for the original article, see Appendix I).[3] When Gilbert S Merritt, a federal appellate judge from Nashville, visited Iraq around June 2003 together with 13 other law experts, he was given the November 14, 2002, issue of *Babil*. In this issue, the newspaper published a list of names entitled 'List of Honour' with a subheading that reads: 'This is a list of men, The Men,[4] so that our great people can view them' (*Babil* 2002, p. 2). Merritt recounted that an Iraqi lawyer called Samir, with whom he worked, asked whether a 'list of the 600 people closest to Saddam Hussein would be of any value now to the Americans' (Merritt 2003). The US judge welcomed the idea and told him that President Bush and his aides claimed that a relationship existed between Iraq and Al-Qaeda. The Iraqi lawyer responded: 'Well, judge, there is no doubt it exists, and I will bring you the proof tomorrow' (ibid.). On the following day, the list was translated, especially a sentence stating that someone called Abdul Karim Mohammed Aswad was the Iraqi 'official in charge of regime's contacts with Osama bin Laden's group and currently the regime's representative in Pakistan' (*Babil* 2002). Samir and his colleague Zuhair described to the judge what happened the day that the newspaper was published: 'Samir bought his paper at a newsstand at around 8 a.m. Within two hours, the Iraqi intelligence officers were going by every newsstand in Baghdad and confiscating the papers. They also went to the home of every person who they were told received a paper that day and confiscated it.' Merritt concluded that the list provided a 'strong proof that the two [Iraq and Al-Qaeda] were in contact and conspiring to perform terrorist acts' (ibid.).

Some US writers and supporters of the war on Iraq used the aforementioned article to argue that Iraq was actually linked to Al-Qaeda. For example, Stephen Hayes wrote in the *Weekly Standard* that the list published in *Babil* 'appears to confirm U.S. allegations of links between the Iraqi regime and al Qaeda. It adds one more piece to the small pile of evidence emerging from Iraq that, when added to the jigsaw puzzle we already had, makes obsolete the question of whether Saddam and Osama bin Laden were in league and leaves in doubt only the extent of the connection' (2003a). In a subsequent article, Hayes further analysed the list in an attempt to find more clues. On *Babil's* first page, a picture of Osama Bin Laden was published that was taken from an interview on Al Jazeera channel. Hayes tried to link between the 'picture of Osama bin Laden speaking, next to which was a picture of Saddam and his "Revolutionary Council", together with stories about Israeli tanks attacking a group of Palestinians' (2003b). It seems that Hayes consulted with US 'analysts' who expressed some doubts about the list's authenticity, but they concluded that Uday Saddam Hussein did in fact publish the list 'without realizing he was publicly linking his father to Osama bin Laden' (2003b).

Unfortunately, Hayes' 'analysts' did not want to investigate the claims of the Iraqi lawyer and the US judge who believed him, but they rather took what was published at face value. In fact, the 'List of Honour' was originally published by Ahmed Chalabi's London-based oppositional newspaper, *Al-Mu'tamar*, under the title 'List of Dishonour', with a subheading that reads: 'Stop Harming the Citizens'. The list was published in batches in 2001 (Al-Mu'tamar 2001a and 2001b) and on the website of the INC, which was headed by Chalabi (*Iraqi National Congress* 2001).[5] It included the names of senior Iraqi officials, Saddam Hussein's inner circle, and ardent supporters of the Ba'ath Party, and Chalabi incorporated some of his WMD and Al-Qaeda allegations in the list. Since the names listed were those regarded as regime supporters by the opposition, Uday Saddam Hussein took pride in them and 'honoured' them by publishing the list as it appeared without altering a word. As for the claim that Iraqi intelligence members were involved in confiscating the newspaper, it is neither practical to go to every house nor reasonable to do so. I had a copy of the newspaper at that time, just like many other Iraqis. The list became a sensational topic because it was the first time that such information had been openly published; many people found it interesting to go through the names of their friends, neighbours, relatives, or managers in order to see their ranking by the Iraqi opposition. If an official's name was published, it meant that he was a true nationalist because he supported Saddam's regime and stood against its enemies.

Ironically, it seems that US officials used the two Iraqi newspapers to suggest that Iraq acknowledged its link with Al-Qaeda and 9/11, which would only lead to war and the country's destruction. War critics and political analysts never questioned these facts; instead, the two articles were regarded as important pieces of evidence to link Iraq with Al-Qaeda. Implicitly, the allegations suggest that Iraq had the most liberal media in the world since all state secrets were presumably disclosed to Iraqi citizens. This contradicted all the previous assessments on Saddam Hussein's media, including the one made by the US Department of State before the war, stating: 'Iraq suffers under the Ba'athist regime of Saddam Hussein, the worst example of information deprivation of citizens anywhere in the world' (The National Security Archive 2002a, p. 2). During the Ba'ath rule, any release of governmental statistics or figures had to be approved by the Ministry of Information. 'Official information was closely guarded and a number of criminal law provisions were enacted to penalise the disclosure of official information' (Article 19 2004, p. 6). Also, International Media Support published a report prepared by one of Iraq's oppositional figures during the reign of Saddam Hussein in which the media scene was described as follows: 'Iraqis, and the media in particular, lived within a secretive world that denied Iraqis from their fundamental right to information. In that secret world, Iraqis didn't have any idea about the most important issues that constituted turning points in their lives and had a crucial importance to them' (Al-Jezairy 2006, p. 4). The only explanation for this contradiction is similar to what Kwiatkowski described as cherry-picking information for the sake of waging a war.

As a result of media manipulation and the dissemination of false statements, such as the discussion on these two Iraqi articles, the US government managed to convince the public that Iraq was an imminent threat to world peace and that it was linked to Al-Qaeda and 9/11. Osama Bin Laden and Saddam Hussein became associated in the US official rhetoric in the war efforts to build a case against Iraq (Althaus and Largio 2004). Yet the continuous US–UK media hammering sensitised the public, who remained convinced that Iraq was partly or mostly responsible for the 9/11 attack even though contrary evidence had already been published. A poll survey conducted by CBS News in autumn 2002 showed that 51 per cent of US citizens believed that Saddam Hussein was involved in the 9/11 attacks. After a short period, another survey carried out by the Pew Research Center mentioned that two out of three US citizens were certain that 'Saddam Hussein helped the terrorists in the September 11 attacks' (Solomon and Erlich 2003, p. 43). Other poll surveys conducted after the US invasion still showed that the US public was convinced that Saddam Hussein aided Al-Qaeda. In late 2003 the figure decreased to less than 50 per cent (Everts and Isernia 2005), but many Americans still believe that Iraq was associated with Al-Qaeda and its attack on the USA.

3
The US Role in Shaping Iraq's Post-2003 Media

After the Anglo-American invasion, the US neo-conservative administration established the Iraqi Governing Council (IGC) in July 2003. It included 25 members selected for their ethnic and religious origins; it was the most obvious sign of the USA's political separatist strategy. As a result of the new political reality, the Iraqi media was divided along ethno-sectarian lines that were the result of previous policies followed by the US administration. This chapter discusses the USA's media policy prior to and after its invasion of Iraq, which played a part in enhancing and encouraging the sectarian divisions in Iraqi society. This policy was mainly carried out by sending biased media messages through the state-run Iraqi Media Network (IMN) and other US-aligned channels, and by allowing militant voices from different Iraqi sides to wage a war of words without interfering. In fact, the only time that US officials interfered was when they were criticised by Iraqi media outlets. When the US invasion occurred in 2003, Iraqis were amazed to read about and listen to the words 'Shiite' or 'Sunni'; this was the new media reality that they faced. Since the media scene is a direct reflection of the political reality in Iraq, it is important to discuss the political developments after the US invasion.

The new political scene

When the US Army invaded Iraq there was no clear or comprehensive planning for what would come after the military operations. This fact led the country into chaos. First, the looting occurred, mostly sanctioned by a US Army that only shielded the Iraqi Ministry of Oil and ignored the rest of Iraq's infrastructure such as the other ministries, universities, libraries, and museums (Baker et al. 2010). But what was striking was the way that the US administration tried to rule the country and create a political system that would ultimately segregate the society. It theoretically divided the country into groups, sects, and ethnicities following the 'divide and rule' strategy. The formation of the IGC was the first step. Afterwards, the Iraqi Constitution of 2005 came, co-written by US experts (Wong 2005a); the constitution opened the door for the idea of federalism and a possible future division, especially for the Kurds in the north and the Shiites in the south. Indeed, the US government 'created institutions based on sectarianism in its reconstruction of Iraq' (The Saban Center for Middle East Policy 2007).

Furthermore, several US politicians were in favour of dividing Iraq into three separate states. For example, Leslie Gelb, president emeritus of the Council on Foreign Relations, suggested a complete division after the beginning of the war. The Fund for Peace propagated a 'managed partition' in the same year (Baker 2003/2007). Further, US Vice-President Joe Biden, and the then-chairman of the Senate Foreign Relations Committee, called for a 'soft partition' of Iraq in 2006 (Joseph and O'Hanlon 2007). During Biden's visit to Iraq as vice-president in July 2009, some Iraqi politicians feared the dire consequences of his old proposal of dividing the country into Kurdish, Sunni, and Shiite parts. For instance, the Sunni Arab politician Osama Nujaifi warned that Biden's proposal would have driven the country into 'bloodshed and wars between the sects over borders and resources, to the persecution of minorities and all kinds of problems' (Sly 2009).

In fact, Paul Bremer, Iraq's civil administrator, and his aides wanted to mould Iraq following the example of Lebanon, which had witnessed a long and bloody civil war in the 1970s and 1980s. 'Quotas are obligatory; power is rigidly contested on sectarian and ethnic lines. Deadlock often ensues, with each community seeing politics as winner-takes-all. It is resolved only when a kingmaker's pressure finds a last-minute solution' (Shadid 2010). The various politico-religious parties played a damaging role in polarising Iraqis, which was directly reflected in their different partisan media channels. Unfortunately, the Bush Administration and the Department of Defense ignored a report written by the US Department of State on January 28, 2003, in which the sectarian issue was raised in the discussion of 'Administrative Arrangement for Holy Sites':

> Iraq is a secular nation, there is no need to emphasize and signify religion through institutions; this is a sensitive matter and needs no intervention. Why making changes to a system that has been

functioning for hundreds of years. At this critical time, why open the door for religious unrest and sacrifice the unity of Iraq?

(The National Security Archive 2003)

Ismael and Fuller (2009) and Visser (2007/2008) argue that the US administration intended to weaken and control Iraq by manufacturing sectarianism and encouraging schisms. As a result of US policy, the Iraqis became more attached to their sect and ethnic origins.

Furthermore, the threats of and attacks by Al-Qaeda and groups like it against Iraqi Shiites on one hand, and the Mahdi Army and Badr Brigades' death squads against Sunnis on the other hand, deepened the sectarian divisions. Arab Sunni fighters who were associated with Al-Qaeda infiltrated Iraq from Jordan, Saudi Arabia, and Syria after the US invasion. They played a dangerous role in igniting sectarian tension by legitimising the killing of Shiites, whom they regarded as *Rawafidh* (those who refuse to follow orthodox Islam) (Rosen 2006b). The main reason behind this kind of hatred was the fact that those Arab fighters did not have direct contact with Shiites, unlike the Iraqi Sunnis who have lived alongside Shiites for more than a thousand years. Furthermore, sectarianism was greatly enhanced with the sudden return of thousands of Iraqis from neighbouring countries, especially Iran. Many of these Shiites were expelled by Saddam Hussein because they were originally Persians (*taba'iah*), so they returned carrying a great deal of animosity towards the Ba'ath rule and against Sunnis in general, who were regarded as *Nawasib* (those who hate Prophet Mohammed's descendants).

Indeed, the culmination of this sectarian tension occurred after the bombing of the holy Shiite shrine in Samaraa on February 22, 2006. The destruction of the shrine was allegedly conducted by an Al-Qaeda group to ignite a civil war that would increase the group's power and authority by drawing more Sunni fighters and financial supporters seeking protection. After February 2006, the internal conflict in Iraq reached a level that can be termed as civil war. It entailed 'the hardening of ethno-sectarian identities, a sea change in the character of the violence, ethno-sectarian mobilization, and population displacements' (National Intelligence Estimate 2007, p. 7).

At this stage, the Shiite militias that were in control of the Ministry of Interior were largely responsible for the killing of Sunnis. James Downley, a US Army commander in Dura district in Baghdad, recalled the 'liquidation missions' that were routinely conducted by the Shiite-run Iraqi police forces whom he described as 'sectarian murderers'. Downley confirmed that the Iraqi police were present in his area 'to kill the people who lived there' (BBC Two 2010, part 2). Furthermore, H R McMaster, a US Army commander who was later positioned in Afghanistan, mentioned that Shiite government ministers, such as the ministers of the interior, agriculture, education, transportation, and health, were complicit in the sectarian killings, which became 'platforms from which Shiite militias would launch attacks against Sunni Arab community' (BBC Two 2010, part 2). Despite the fact that the US Army was aware of these mass killings, no serious and immediate action was taken to stop the slaughter. The famous British journalist, Robert Fisk, went even further by accusing the US Army of indirectly supporting the Shiite militias:

> Who runs the Ministry of Interior in Baghdad? Who pays the Ministry of the Interior? Who pays the militia men who make up the death squads? We do, the occupation authorities. I'd like to know what the Americans are doing to get at the people who are trying to provoke the civil war. It seems to me not very much.
>
> (Jones 2006)

Unfortunately, the US Army did not play its expected role in calming down the situation between the two sects since it merely observed from afar. The award-winning journalist Nir Rosen depicted this gloomy picture about the situation in Iraq in late-2006, where Shiite militias were 'running their own secret prisons, arresting, torturing, and executing Sunnis in what was clearly a civil war. And the Americans were merely one more militia among the many, watching, occasionally intervening, and in the end only making things worse' (2006a). In its report on the Shiite death squads, the UK's Channel 4 revealed that the mass killings in 2006 were 'happening under the eyes of US commanders, who seem unwilling or unable to intervene'. As a result, US forces were 'complicit with the murderers because they ordered their men not to talk' (Channel 4 2007). Finally, former Deputy Chief Constable of South Yorkshire Police, Douglas Brand, said he had voiced his concerns about the death squads many times: 'Probably ten times a day to whoever would listen, usually two star Generals and above'. He even spoke directly to US Defense Secretary Donald Rumsfeld, 'But I sensed the subtleties were not understood and if there were consequences down the road, that's something the Iraqis were going to have to handle themselves' (Channel 4 2007).

This scene reflected the irresponsible stance taken by the US administration towards Iraq's internal problem, which was a direct consequence of the occupation and its inept policies. The former vice-chair of the

US Army Defense Staff, General Jack Keane, revealed that in 2006 the US Army 'made a conscious decision not to protect the [Iraqi] population'. The reason given by Keane was that the 'security situation in Iraq by late 2006 was the worst it had ever been and it was getting worse by the day – that was the reality' (Collyns 2010). As a result of this US policy, 'Iraqis were being abandoned', as Keane stressed. He pointed that the priority was to 'transition to Iraqi security forces as quickly as possible. Major vulnerability of that strategy was no where in there was a plan [sic] to protect the population' (BBC Two 2010, part 2).

The US academic Daniel Pipes bluntly emphasised in March 2006 that the US Army should avoid any kind of interference in the Shiite–Sunni conflict. 'Fixing Iraq is neither the coalition's responsibility nor its burden.... Americans, Britons and others cannot be tasked with resolving Sunni-Shiite differences, an abiding Iraqi problem only Iraqis themselves can address' (Pipes 2006). Even the British Army in the South remained inactive towards the crimes committed by the Shiite Mahdi Army against Iraqi citizens. During 2005 and early 2006 there was an escalation of violence in southern Iraq, especially in Basrah. But it was 'only when the activities of Jayish Al-Mahdi began to affect the British soldiers directly that they acted' (BBC Two 2010, part 1).

Surely the Iraqi media, which is the product of this new political reality, played a role in widening the sectarian rift. Partisan and official media messages that directly and indirectly associated the crimes committed during the Ba'ath rule with Arab Sunnis, though most Ba'ath party members were Shiite, played another role in dividing Iraqi society.[1] Several Shiite figures, such as Abdul Aziz Al-Hakim and his aid Jalal Al-Deen Al-Sagheer, were instrumental in agitating the Shiite public against Sunnis. On the other hand, critical statements against the Shiite-dominated Iraqi government made by Harith Al-Dhari, the head of the Sunni Muslim Scholars Association, and Adnan Al-Dulaimi, the former head of the National Accord group, worsened the situation between the two Iraqi sects.

It is correct to mention here that the differences between the Iraqi sects and ethnicities were in existence long before the US presence. However, there was an obvious harmony among the different sects even before the establishment of the Iraqi state in 1921. Gertrude Bell, the British Oriental Secretary, advised the following in 1916: 'there has never been jealousy or bitterness between the two branches of Islam [Sunnis and Shiites] in the Iraq, and whatever changes the future may bring it should be the first care of the ruler of the country to preserve that fortunate condition' (cited in Kedourie 1988, p. 252). All the previous rulers of Iraq were cautious when the issue of sectarianism was raised. Robert Fisk confirmed that 'Iraq is not a sectarian society, but a tribal society. People are intermarried. Shiites and Sunnis marry each other' (Jones 2006). A former prime minister of Iraq, Ayad Allawi described how Iraqi political leaders who were originally appointed by the US administration carried this kind of sectarianism. They together with a 'blurred vision of the United States, has created, has exaggerated the creation of Sunni, Shiite and Kurd'. Allawi confirmed that before 2003, 'Iraq was not sectarian – only now is it becoming sectarian. And the sectarianism is only among the elite, the political elite, not within the people of Iraq' (Shadid 2011, MM38). Indeed, the US occupation did not create these differences, 'but facilitated all of it, giving space to the region's worst impulses' (Shadid 2009).

Indeed, the US inaction towards the conflict was a direct reason behind the escalation of violence. This was also accompanied by a complete carelessness from an Iraqi government led by two Shiite prime ministers who both belonged to the Dawah Party: Ibrahim Al-Ja'afari and then Nouri Maliki from May 2006. The obvious reason behind the Iraqi government's failure to act was the fact that it was too weak to act independently since it took its popular support from the Mahdi Army and other militant Shiite groups. After President Bush's refusal to have Al-Ja'afari as prime minister, Maliki was selected, but he was also criticised by the US administration for his weakness in confronting Muqtada Sadr and disbanding his armed militia that was responsible for most of the sectarian killing and civilian displacement (Beehner 2006).

With the escalation of the sectarian violence, organised Shiite death squads roamed the streets and began arresting Sunni men. After a few days, the dead bodies of those men were thrown onto the streets bearing signs of severe torture. At least 100 dead bodies were found each day and taken to Baghdad morgue. Despite the fact that Maliki pledged to crack down on these death squads, very little action was taken. The Islamic Supreme Council of Iraq by its control of the Ministry of Interior and the Mahdi Army, was involved in these squads, and they both supported Maliki's election as prime minister.

When US forces raided a stronghold for one of these squads, Maliki immediately protested in the media, stating that these actions were illegal and conducted without his approval. A US diplomat complained by saying that 'every time' US forces 'strike against the Mahdi Army, they are publicly scolded by the Iraqi prime minister' (Gosh 2006; Kukis 2006). However, Maliki would not react in the same manner if a US attack was directed at Sunni areas. Mohammad Shaboot, the government appointed editor-in-chief of *Al-Sabah* newspaper, refers to his disappointment with TV channel Iraqia because it was established to represent all Iraqis, saying: 'It was supposed to be fair, and address all the people of Iraq, but so far it hasn't succeeded in achieving this unique goal' (Roug 2006).

As a reaction to the unprecedented number of people killed and the growing criticism against Maliki's policy, President Bush sent US Security Advisor Stephen J Hadley to Iraq in late 2006 to investigate the nature of the violence. He concluded that Maliki had a 'narrow Sadrist political base' which blinded him from taking any reconciliation policy. Hadley sums up the condition by saying:

> Reports of non-delivery of services to Sunni areas, intervention by the prime minister's office to stop military action against Shia targets and to encourage them against Sunni ones, removal of Iraq's most effective commanders on a sectarian basis and efforts to ensure Shia majorities in all ministries – when combined with the escalation of Jaysh al-Mahdi's (JAM) [the Arabic name for the Mahdi Army] killings – all suggest a campaign to consolidate Shia power in Baghdad.
>
> (*The Australian* 2006)

The United States Institute of Peace team, 'The Iraq Study Group' headed by James Baker, published its report in December 2006. In the report the Iraqi government was defined as 'sectarian, and key players within the government too often act in their sectarian interest. Iraq's Shia, Sunni, and Kurdish leaders frequently fail to demonstrate the political will to act in Iraq's national interest, and too many Iraqi ministries lack the capacity to govern effectively' (Baker et al. 2006, p. 15). Furthermore, reports were published about government corruption, placing Iraq as one of the top kleptomaniac states of the world in which petty bribery is widespread practice, according to Transparency International (2009).

Despite all the calls by US politicians to replace Maliki, the prime minister pursued his sectarian policy throughout 2007. The US Senate Armed Services Committee Chairman Carl Levin made a trip to Iraq in August 2007 and observed similar policies to the ones seen by Hadley. Besides, Maliki established the Office of the Commander-in-Chief, which overruled the ministries of interior and defence and followed hard-line sectarian policies (Damon 2007). In October 2006, Bush warned that Iraq could slide into chaos if its leaders did not work together, and threatened to take some extra measures: 'We're making it clear that American patience is not unlimited' (Reuters 2006).

Colonel Mansoor, the founding director of the US Army and Marine Corps Counterinsurgency Center, revealed that it was only when General David Petraeus became the commander of US forces in Iraq in January 2007 that a change in policy occurred: 'The strategy emphasized protecting Iraqi civilians instead of simply killing bad guys.' This change meant an additional 30,000 soldiers in Iraq, which was known as the US forces 'surge'. After agreeing to form the anti-Qaeda *Sahwa* (Awakening) forces, largely from the members of the Sunni insurgency and the break-up of Shiite militias, the violence started to ebb (Levinson 2010). Before the surge, the US Army was focused only on fighting insurgents and other suspects who might attack US soldiers. For example, the spokesperson for the Iraqi Army, General Qassim Atta, revealed in 2009 that an insurgent fighter called Yasser Al-Takhi, who belonged to the Sunni *Jaish* (Army) Mohammed, was caught and confessed to raping and killing the female Iraqi correspondent Atwar Bahjat, who worked for TV channel Al-Arabiya . Al-Takhi was twice arrested by US forces in Iraq – in October 2003 and at the end of 2006. However, he was released both times because, according to Atta, 'the Americans only investigated him for attacks against them' (Agence France Presse 2009). In brief, the US Army had a role in facilitating the tension and hatred between the two sects by its inaction, negligence, and carelessness. Before further elaborating on the post-2003 media scene, we need to discuss the US media plan for Iraq in early 2003.

The Rapid Reaction Media Team

The US government was involved in propaganda activities in Iraq long before the 2003 invasion; its aim being to counter the communist threat from the Soviet Union and the pan-Arab nationalism of Gamal Abdul Nasser (Vaughan 2002; al-Rawi 2012). In the 1990s, the US government focused its propaganda against Iraq to topple the Ba'ath regime. A great deal of money was channelled through the media outlets of some Iraqi opposition groups, such as Ayad Allawi's Iraqi National Alliance (INA) and Ahmed Chalabi's Iraqi National Congress (INC). These propaganda activities intensified with the approach of the war.

As part of the effort to topple Saddam Hussein, Bill Clinton's administration provided 5 million dollars for 'desks, computers and fax machines needed to equip an office and begin spewing out pronouncements' against the Iraqi government. These activities were mainly run from Iraqi Kurdistan, which enjoyed US protection (Myers 1999, p. 5). According to INC's old website, Chalabi's group had a newspaper, *Al-Mu'tamar*, and radio and TV stations called *Hurriah* TV (Liberty). (See Chapter 2 for more details on Chalabi's newspaper.[2]) The CIA was reported to have provided 10–15 million dollars a year to INC to finance their operations, including the distribution of 'propaganda' (Fedarko 2001).

As for Allawi's INA, it was first funded by the British MI6, but the CIA took over in 1995. The group ran its media activities from Amman, Kurdistan, and London by publishing a newspaper called *Baghdad* and broadcasting over radio station *Al-Mustaqbal* (future) (Curtius 2004; Drogin 2004; INA n.d.). Other groups – such as the Iraq Foundation, whose former Shiite board member Laith Kubba became the Iraqi government's spokesperson in 2005 – received huge funds in 2003 from the US National Endowment for Democracy (NED), amounting to 1,648,914 dollars. In 1998, the group that published the *Iraq Newsletter* received 265,000 dollars from NED (Hanieh 2006). It is worth noting that NED had a huge yearly budget from the US Congress, and it partly worked with the CIA to serve clandestine objectives around the world through its projects of democracy (Blum 2003).

In October 2002, amid the preparation to wage a war on Iraq and change its political system, the Bush Administration established the Office of Special Plans (OSP) as part of the Department of Defense (as discussed in Chapter 2). OSP was also partly responsible for forming a new face for the Iraqi media together with the Pentagon's Special Operations and Low-Intensity Conflict Office, which specialised in psychological warfare (Battle 2007; Lobe 2007). As a result of the work of these two bodies, the Rapid Reaction Media Team (RRMT) was formed in mid-January 2003 before the invasion. Working under Paul Wolfowitz was Douglas Feith, Under Secretary of Defense for Policy, who was later in charge of the plans for post-war Iraq, including the White Paper project.

In fact, Feith's involvement in Iraq goes back to the 1990s. Together with other analysts, he wrote a report entitled *Clean Break* in 1996 for Israel's Prime Minister Benjamin Netanyahu, in which he mentioned the need to topple Saddam Hussein's government and divide the Arab world in order to serve the interests of Israel (Borger 2003). The report also mentioned that post-Saddam Hussein Iraq might be plagued by the rise of sectarianism, leading to a possible political division in the country. Clearly, the policy of divide and rule was on the back of those analysts' heads when they wrote their report (Zunes 2006). In his autobiography,

Feith admitted that he had pointed out the possibility of 'some serious problems' such as 'sectarian violence, power vacuum' after the invasion. In another context, he clearly mentioned that 'we warned about rioting, looting, sectarian fights...' (Feith 2009, p. 275 and p. 363); however, little if no action was taken by the US administration to prevent the looting and sectarian fighting.

Later, the RRMT formed the nucleus of the IMN, whose establishment was supervised by the media development department of the Office of Reconstruction and Humanitarian Aid (ORHA), led by Bob Reilly (Hassen 2006). Reilly, the director of the US government radio station, Voice of America, was known to be an 'outspoken right-wing ideologue' who worked in the 1980s as a 'propagandist in the White House for the Nicaraguan contras' (Dauenhauer and Lobe 2003).[3] Reilly ORHA reported directly to Douglas Feith, 'receiving very broad policy goals, objectives, and policy direction' (United States Department of Defense, Office of the Inspector General 2004, p. 1).

The RRMT's main task was to initiate a ' "quick start bridge" between Saddam Hussein's state-controlled media network and a longer term "Iraqi Free Media" network in post Saddam era' (United States Department of Defense 2003, p. 1). With an initial budget of 49 million dollars, the media project was greatly significant because it set out the whole strategy on the ground. For instance, the document suggested different themes for broadcasting, such as: 'De-Ba'athification program'; 'Recent history telling (e.g. "Uncle Saddam", History channel's "Saddam's Bomb Maker," "Killing Fields" '; 'Environmental (Marshlands re-hydration)'; 'Restarting the Oil'; 'War Criminals/Truth Commission'. Later, these themes became recurrent on the official Iraqi channel Iraqia TV. In addition, programmes were proposed to be executed by RRMT, such as: 'Political prisoners and atrocity interviews'; 'Saddam's palaces and opulence'; WMD disarmament' (ibid., p. 3). Again, these shows were made into documentaries and repeatedly aired on different Iraqi state-aligned TV channels. Also, the document stated the need to '[i]dentify/vet US/UK/Iraqi "media experts team" such as Siyamend Othman; Hussein Sinjari' (ibid., p. 2). On April 20, 2004, the US Coalition Provisional Authority (CPA) appointed Siyamend Othman, a Kurd, as the CEO of the Iraqi National Communications and Media Commission, which became the first Iraqi media regulatory body (Coalition Provisional Authority 2004).

In fact, the White Paper was written by two US agencies that were directly involved in propaganda for the US government. One of them was the Science Applications International Corporation (SAIC), which works closely with the CIA. It was assigned by the Pentagon to form a 'government in exile', including five Iraqis to run the new media channels (Chatterjee 2004). Douglas Feith was a former SAIC vice-president, and it had close connections with Ahmed Al-Chalabi (Alexander 2004). Later, SAIC's Corporate Vice-President for Strategic Assessment and Development, Christopher Ryan Henry, also worked for the Pentagon as deputy under secretary of defense serving with Feith (Dauenhauer and Lobe 2003). At one stage, SAIC hired David Kay, Iraq's weapons inspector, as its vice-president; Kay, who was commissioned by the CIA to head Iraq's weapons programme, urged the US administration to wage a war against Saddam Hussein because of the alleged weapons of mass destruction (WMDs) (Chatterjee 2004).

Among ORHA's pre-war activities was the organisation of the 'Inter-Agency Rehearsal and Planning Conference' held on February 21–22, 2003. The experts participating in the conference agreed that 30 days were needed for the 'indigenous media' to be 'on the air-presenting vision of a new Iraq' (ORHA 2003, p. 9). The estimated budget allocated for restructuring the Iraqi media was 55 million dollars (ibid., p. 7). ORHA's original idea was that Iraq would become a democracy, and 'within 12 months, reconstitute indigenous Iraqi media as a model for free media in the Arab world' (ibid., p. 45). It seems that ORHA's main aim behind forming the new Iraqi media was to assist 'CENTCOM's mission to stabilize Iraq' (ibid., p. 46). In other words, the new Iraqi media was designed from the beginning to become a propaganda tool for the US forces. Due to security reasons, ORHA decided to manage the Iraqi media in the first phase of the invasion. The other aims of this new media were as follows:

> Iraqi media coverage (via satellite TV) of what the US military has found in Iraq; inform the international community; inform the Iraqi public about USG [United States Government]/coalition intent and operations; stabilize Iraq (especially preventing the trifurcation of Iraq after hostilities); provide Iraqis hope for their future; begin broadcasting and printing approved USG information to the Iraqi public very soon after cessation of hostilities; help justify USG actions.
>
> (ibid., p. 47)

SAIC received 108.2 million dollars to run IMN, including a TV and radio station and *Al-Sabah* newspaper (Haner 2004). After the 2003 invasion, the most prominent Iraqi exiles who worked for IMN were: Shameem Rassam, herself an SAIC subcontractor (Barker 2008, p. 120); George Mansour; Alaa Fa'ik; Ahmed Al-Rikabi; Isam Al-Khafaji; and Eyman Thamer, who was relocated to Kuwait by SAIC before the invasion (Wikileaks 2006d). Indeed, the Iraqi media was formed to strengthen US control over the country and to increase the public acceptance of its actions, despite the pretence that IMN was to be an independent media body. The White Paper, for instance, mentioned the need to have 'hand-selected US-trained Iraqi media teams imme-diately in-place to portray a new Iraq (by Iraqis for Iraqis) with hopes for a prosperous, democratic future, will have a profound psychological and political impact on the Iraqi people' (United States Department of Defense 2003, p. 1). These Iraqi media experts were supposed to work as the cover or '("the face") for the USG/coalition sponsored informa-tion effort' (ibid., p. 2). This technique was later literally followed by the US Army on the ground as shown below.

Most importantly, RRMT highlighted the importance of devising a divided Iraqi media, representing the three major parts of Iraqi society: Shiites, Sunnis, and Kurds. Although the report claims that the Iraqi media have to work on 'stabiliz[ing] Iraq (especially preventing the tri-furcation of Iraq after hostilities)' (ibid.), there is an indication that the US government wanted to stress the 'internal divisions' within Iraqi society (Battle 2007). For instance, the document proposes printing an Iraqi newspaper 'with section for...Shia news, Kurd news, and Sunni news' (United States Department of Defense 2003, p. 2). Indeed, this policy foreshadowed the events that followed during which the Iraqi media became characterised by ethno-sectarian orientations.

As well as the controversial White Paper project of the US Department of Defense, it is important to mention the Department of State's pre-war efforts with regard to the Iraqi media and Saddam Hussein's regime. It, for example, established the Economic Support Funds for Iraq as part of Clinton's Iraq Liberation Act efforts and donated 68 million dollars from 1999 to 2002 to support the Iraqi opposition and the investiga-tion into the Ba'ath regime's war crimes. From this amount, 16 million dollars was given to Chalabi's INC (p. 5). Less than a month after 9/11, the Department of State organised more than 200 Iraqi experts in different fields into 17 working groups to set Iraq's future strate-gies in the following areas: 'public health and humanitarian needs, transparency and anti-corruption, oil and energy, defense policy and institutions, transitional justice, democratic principles and procedures, local government, civil society capacity building, education, free media, water, agriculture and environment and economy and infrastructure' (Hassen 2006). In relation to the Iraqi media, the Free Media Working Group (FMWG) was formed, but its members held a single meeting in February 2003 (Institute for War and Peace Reporting 2003) because the Department of Defense's contractor, SAIC, later used the experts for its own Iraqi media project.

Though the recommendations of FMWG were basically ignored by ORHA, its report is important, for it presents a realistic account of what the Iraqi media was and should be like in the future since it was mainly written by Iraqi experts who knew the situation and the culture in Iraq better than the US. The FMGW report predicted a reality that occurred after the occupation: 'the worst offenders among the Ba'ath-journalists will leave the scene, the others will fight to demonstrate and defend the cultural capital they think they possess' (The National Security Archive 2002b, p. 1). As part of the De-Ba'athification policy, which was the first order taken by the CPA on May 16, 2003, any senior member of the Ba'ath Party was expelled from his work and his rights were removed. In fact, most of them were either killed, imprisoned, or forced to leave the country.

One of FMGW's recommendations that was followed by the Department of Defense was the dissolution of the Iraqi Ministry of Information after the war; a decree which was issued on May 23, 2003, by Paul Bremer (Coalition Provisional Authority 2003/2002). The United States Institute of Peace made the same recommendation in February 2003 (Jennings 2003, p. 12). However, the order to dissolve the Ministry of Information was an obvious step in the process of De-Ba'athification since such ministries were 'primarily tools of authoritarian regimes' (Price 2007, p. 9).

Among the points stressed by the Department of State, but not followed by the Department of Defense, was that the US government should not be involved in any propaganda efforts and should act sincerely in reconstructing the Iraqi media to serve Iraqis, stating: 'We do not need to fabricate lies and false information. We should rely on presenting in a very reliable manner the facts that will serve to enhance the image and reputation of the Iraqi people and their aspiration for peace and progress...' (The National Security Archive 2002b, p. 3). Despite the efforts of the Department of State to set a serious future plan for the Iraqi media, the Bush Administration decided that ORHA, which later became the CPA, should take over the responsibility of planning and implementing future Iraqi projects. The following section will discuss the US Army's media role in Iraq.

The US Army and Iraq's media

In its counterinsurgency manual, the US Army stresses the importance of the information battle that goes along with military operations. It states that 'Information Operations' are instrumental in winning the war since 'the decisive battle is for the people's minds' (US Army Field Manual 2006). The US Army also runs its famous Psychological Operations (PSYOP), which is defined in one of its manuals as:

> ....planned operations that convey selected information and indicators to foreign audiences to influence their emotions, motives, objective reasoning, and ultimately to influence the behavior of foreign governments, organizations, groups, and individuals. The purpose of psychological operations is to induce or reinforce foreign attitudes and behavior favorable to the originator's objectives [US government].
>
> (US Army Field Manual 2003, pp. 2–3)

But perhaps the most important objective for PSYOP is 'projecting the image of US superiority' (ibid.). To achieve the aims mentioned above, the Pentagon spends hundreds of millions of dollars a year to produce and disseminate pro-US media messages.

Shortly before and during the invasion, the US Air Force, stationed in neighbouring Arab countries, dropped 36 million leaflets over different regions in Iraq between October 2002 and March 2003. These leaflets were regarded as the best means to infiltrate the Iraqi Army and introduce ideas that might demoralise Iraqi soldiers. The US government felt that the leaflets were influential in winning the war (Clark and Christie 2005, p. 152). Also, many Iraqis who had email accounts supplied by the Internet government provider uruklink received anti-Saddam emails, apparently from US sources, in January 2003. It was revealed that the Department of Defense was responsible for these emails, which promised 'to protect those who cooperated and their families, but threatening to treat as war criminals those who "took part in the use of these ugly weapons"' (Caterinicchia 2003). Even some official Iraqi websites, like those of the ministries of culture and information, were hacked, and anti-Ba'athist statements that called for the fall of the regime were posted on them.

During the war, the USA started airing a TV/radio station to the Iraqi public on March 20, 2003, from a US aircraft called Commando Solo (Dauenhauer and Lobe 2003). The channel, called Towards Freedom, was run by the Foreign and Commonwealth Offices of the UK's public diplomacy department (APFW Report 2003, p. 27; McCaul 2003), and there was a daily hour of unedited material dubbed into Arabic, mainly borrowed from CBS, ABC, Fox News, and NBC (Byrne 2003; IWPR 2003). The channel was received by Iraqi National TV's 1 and 3 frequencies, but its reception was extremely bad and its Arabic was of a non-Iraqi dialect (Knights 2003). Furthermore, the US government operated a clandestine radio station called Radio Tikrit in February 2003, which was aimed at discrediting Saddam Hussein's government and calling upon Iraqi soldiers to throw down their arms and withdraw during the military confrontation (BBC News 2003a). As for the UK government's media efforts, it sponsored 10,000 copies of a newspaper published in Kuwait to be distributed in Basrah after the invasion (IWPR 2003). During the war itself, more propaganda efforts were exerted to influence the Iraqi public and project a positive image of the occupation to make it appear as liberation.

In December 2003, the US Army operated an American Forces Network radio station for its forces in Iraq. It was called Freedom Radio, and the first song aired was Paul McCartney's 'Freedom'. Transmitting on FM airwaves, the radio station closed down on September 23, 2011, in preparation for the US forces withdrawal from Iraq by the end of 2011 (Keyes 2011).

When the US Army invaded Iraq it started to study how to penetrate the newly established Iraqi media to guarantee that 'friendly' channels would cover its activities. Yet, this also entailed monitoring and censoring Iraqi channels. For example, David Petraeus, the US military commander in Mosul in 2003, considered sending a US officer with a translator to the local TV station to monitor the programmes. Petraeus confessed that he was after censorship: 'you can censor something that is intended to inflame passions'. In fact, the US commander feared that the speeches of some local politicians might incite violence against his soldiers; some Iraqis are 'opposed to what we're doing and are willing to do something about it' (Pincus 2003). As a result, one of Petraeus' female officers objected and reminded her commander about the right to freedom of speech; she was then exempted from her duties and sent home. Petraeus preferred to close down the TV station because of its 'predominantly non-factual/unbalanced news coverage' represented in airing some programmes from Al-Jazeera TV (Jayasekera 2003b). He clearly admitted that there was 'editorial control' over the programmes, saying: 'what we are looking at is censorship, but you can censor something that is intended to inflame passions' (Pincus 2003).

After the invasion, US PSYOP officers DeCarvalho et al. (2008, p. 91) mentioned that an Iraqi media section was formed by their department to monitor the media, send press releases, and establish good relations with more than a dozen Iraqi media outlets. Following the advice given in the White Paper project, DeCarvalho et al. revealed that the best way to address the Iraqi public was to make Iraqis themselves speak on behalf of the US government, thus: 'putting an Iraqi face on the story; an Iraqi reporter talking to fellow Iraqis has a much greater effect on the psyche than if a coalition reporter told the story' (2008, p. 92). It is important to note here that the US Army supported Iraqi media channels that covered its activities in a favourable manner, which is part of its communication strategy. However, it obstructed the work of other media outlets that sought to remain distant. In this regard, independent Iraqi TV journalist Abdel-Hakim (pseudonym) revealed the difficulties faced by his colleagues, saying that 'U.S. forces often tell such journalists they are not allowed to cover certain events', but 'if they insist, they have been known to be arrested or killed'. In the same context, 'journalists working for television stations directly supported by coalition forces have been given permission to cover the same events' (Allen 2006). For example, the staff of the government-owned Iraqia TV were allowed special access to the Green Zone,[4] where the CPA conducts interviews with US officials and covers press conferences. The only Arab journalist who was permitted to be present during George Bush's formal meal in Baghdad in 2003 was from Iraqia TV, and John Nicols noted that IMN covered the event as excitedly as other US TV channels (Nicols 2003).

Furthermore, Colonel Thomas M Cioppa (2009) mentions that the US Army in Iraq used the strategic communication approach, which entails 'monitoring, measuring, analyzing, and assessing' (p. 27) media messages to understand the Iraqi and Pan-Arab media in relation to the events taking place in the country. Cioppa claims that the aim behind their project is to 'promote Iraqi security, political and economic progress, refute inaccurate and misleading reporting, and develop Government of Iraq (GoI) strategic communication capability to do the same, in order to minimize the effects of sectarianism and advance political reconciliation in Iraq' (p. 27). However, it is not clear how the strategic communication approach tried to 'minimize' the effect of sectarianism, as the emphasis is on how the Iraqi and Arab media depict US forces and how to establish timely and effective contacts with these channels. There is no reference to stories or reports that promote unity among Iraqis. Instead, Cioppa defines 'good news' stories (p. 32) as those related to 'progress and stability' in the country, which is directly connected to the US 'positive' presence in the country.

On the other hand, news reports in 2005 revealed that the US Information Operations Task Force, with the help of a US contractor Lincoln Group, were engaged in 'planting' 'storyboards' in the Iraqi press. Iraqi journalists who expressed their willingness to help the US military were paid 400–500 dollars on a monthly basis to write favourable articles in the Iraqi media. As a result of the money spent, more than 1000 articles were planted in several Iraqi newspapers, like *Al-Mu'tamar*, *Al-Mada*, and *Addustour*. These newspapers agreed to publish the articles in return for money paid by the US contractor, ranging from 40 to 2000 dollars. IMN's TV channel Iraqia aired anti-violence advertisements that were sponsored by this media group too (Mazzetti and Daragahi 2005).

The aim of this 'dubious scheme' was to 'burnish the image of the US mission in Iraq', 'trumpet the work of the U.S. and Iraqi troops, denounce insurgents and tout U.S.-led efforts to rebuild the country' (White and Graham 2003, A01; Gerth 2005; Mazzetti and Daragahi 2005). However, the Pentagon did not regard these activities as illegal as they targeted a foreign audience. According to the US Army, the term 'merchandising' was introduced, which means that a PSYOP's officer was allowed give gifts to journalists and others to polish the image of the Army. 'The best way of disseminating a message might be to print it on a matchbox, a toy, a novelty, or a trinket. A soccer ball marked "Gift of the United States" and given to a schoolboy might get the message of American friendship across more effectively than any conventional medium' (US Army Field Manual 1994, p. 9–9). Despite the harsh criticism from different media organisations, the US government's media efforts continued and greatly expanded in 2008. With a budget of 300 million dollars, the project was supposed to run for three years to 'produce undercover news stories, entertainment programmes and public service advertisements for Iraqi media in an effort to "engage and inspire" the local population to support United States policy'.

The contractors involved in these 'media services' – SOSi, Lincoln Group, MPRI and Leonie Industries – were supposed to plant '30- and 60-minute broadcast documentary and entertainment series' on different Iraqi TV channels (Young and Pincus 2008, A01). Most importantly, the storyboards were classified in a pattern that resembles the White Paper project; for example, each story 'had a target audience, "Iraq General" or "Shi'ia," ' with a dominant 'theme like "Anti-intimidation" or "Success and Legitimacy of the ISF" '(Gerth 2005). Indeed, the huge sums of money invested in spreading propaganda revealed the fact that the US forces in Iraq were facing great troubles in communicating with the public and persuading them to accept their views. One US military official pointed out in 2007 that the 'coalition's PSYOP avowals have become so cloying they no longer possess any credibility' (DeCarvalho et al. 2008, p. 88). Hence, the US military hired companies specialising in public relations to sort out this troubling issue, as mentioned above.

Up until 2007, the media division of the US military in Baghdad managed to disseminate positive stories about coalition activities to many radio stations, TV channels, and newspapers. Close co-ordination was established with the Iraqi media, including 27 newspapers, 13 TV stations, 11 radio stations, and a large number of websites (DeCarvalho et al. 2008, p. 90 and p. 91). Also, the 101 Airborne Brigade stationed in Mosul supported different Iraqi newspapers by supplying them with 'some equipment, like computers, as well as offering journalistic courses'. A brigade commander also offered 800 dollars for every newspaper published in the city (al-Jezairy 2006, p. 15). In the south, two US soldiers from the Department of Defense Arabic translator group, one of whom is of Iraqi origin, established an Arabic newspaper in May 2004 called *The Voice of the Euphrates*, to be disseminated to the Iraqi public (Mink 2004). In Baghdad's Shiite Sadr City, Army Sergeant Alan Coffman initiated his 'radio in a box' project in which a 'playlist of Iraqi pop garnered from local CDs and – inserted between songs – pro-American messages translated into Arabic' were broadcast (Marra 2009). At the beginning Coffman did not reveal the real source of the radio, but he later announced it to the public, saying: 'We wanted to make it as much like an Iraqi station as possible' (ibid.). This kind of media campaign was surely focused on presenting 'positive news' about the US military and mostly refrained from mentioning other serious concerns to the public.

When General David Petraeus became the commander of the Multi-National Force in Iraq in February 2007, he confirmed to his commanders that 60 per cent of the conflict was information, but it had to be disseminated to the public (Cioppa 2009, p. 27). As a result of his emphasis on the 'information war', the US Army established the MNFI-Iraq YouTube channel in March 2007.[5] Also, a new media database, the Iraqi/Pan-Arab Database (IPAD), was created in September 2007 to monitor more that 160 Iraqi and Arab media outlets. The work of IPAD developed and by May 2008 it had more than 15,000 references (Cioppa 2009, p. 30).

As for the themes of these US public-service programmes and advertisements, they were mainly focused on countering the Al-Qaeda threat; warning people from joining armed groups, encouraging Iraqis to vote in the elections and to establish reconciliation. There is an apparent connection between the US and Iraqi strategic interests in these themes, especially those dealing with fighting Al-Qaeda and, to a lesser extent, opposing the Shiite militias supported by Iran. Due to the airing and publishing of several advertisements on Iranian intervention in Iraq, the Iranian Embassy in Baghdad wrote a protest letter addressed to the editor-in-chief of the *Addustour* newspaper because it ran many advertisements that implicated Iran in the spread of violence in the country (Journalistic Freedoms Observatory 2008; YouTube 2009b).

To sum up, the US government carried the banner of media freedom and democracy and hailed the new regime that it brought to Iraq, but it worked in the opposite direction, serving and protecting its own interests. Indeed, the US/UK authorities used a double-standards policy when dealing with the Iraqi media. On the one hand, they claimed to be advocating a free and independent media that could become a model for democracy in the Middle East. On the other hand, they curbed media freedom under different pretences (Rugh 2004b). In this regard, Al-Qazwini affirms that the US authorities followed 'their own agenda, paying lip service to the concept of a proper public broadcasting system, while doing what they feel is good for the Coalition, not for the Iraqi people' (2004).

International media support

Some international media organisations worked on their media plans for Iraq even before the military operations officially ended. It is not clear whether they acted alone or were motivated by the US government, since the documents released by the National Security Archive clearly emphasise involving international media organisations in the Iraqi media. In all cases, the UN is mandated to work under international law in occupied countries, and UNESCO is the organ for implementing any media project together with the United Nations Development Programme. After the war about 20 media organisations were involved in the Iraqi media and they shared information so as not to duplicate their efforts (Jayasekera 2003a).

The first media organisation involved was the London-based Arab Press Freedom Watch (APFW), which held a discussion in September 2002 in London on the Iraqi media after the overthrow of Saddam Hussein. Another APFW meeting in which the Iraqi media was discussed was in May 2003 in Cairo, with the involvement of some Iraqi journalists (APFW Report 2003, p. 2).

Other organisations that participated in developing the Iraqi media include: Index on Censorship, International Media Support, the International Federation of Journalists, Internews, Index on Censorship, Alliance Internationale pour la Justice, the Institute for War and Peace Reporting (IWPR), and Article 19. Before the official end of military operations, 20 media organisations met on April 24, 2003, in London to discuss the future of the media in Iraq. Among the participants were representatives from the Baltic Media Centre, BBC World Service Trust, Danish School of Journalism, European Journalism Centre, International Research & Exchanges Board (IREX), the International Federation of Journalists, Internews International, Internews Europe, Media Action International, Media Diversity Institute, Open Society Institute, Press Now Foundation, US Committee for a Free Press in Iraq, and World Association of Newspapers (International Media Support 2003).

Between June 1 and 3, 2003, the US Department of State, through *Internews*, organised a conference in Athens, Greece, to discuss the future of Iraqi media and to propose a code of conduct; however, the event took place without the presence of 'indigenous' Iraqi journalists (Price 2007, p. 7). A total of 75 media experts from 21 countries attended the meeting. Ironically, some CPA experts, who were involved in writing the new media codes, were not aware of this conference – according to spokesperson for the coalition Naheed Mehta – while Department of State experts did not know about the CPA's new media decrees (Daragahi 2003). This lack of co-ordination was reflected in the level of confusion at the time of restructuring the new Iraqi media.

At the Athens conference, an Iraqi Media Law Working Group was formed and co-chaired by the Shiite Iraqi exile Hamid AlKifaey, who became the spokesperson for the IGC in 2003. The conference advocated new rules to be applied with this motto: 'A Law to Promote, Protect and Regulate Free, Independent, Pluralistic Media During the Transition to Democracy'. During the conference, the establishment of the Interim Media Commission, which later became the Communications and Media Commission (CMC), and a 'Press and Broadcast Council' were suggested (*Internews* 2003). The organisers suggested having an IMN representative, and Bob Reilly promised to take its proposals to Baghdad; however, he later abandoned the proposed suggestions due to the Department of Defense's control of IMN. The aim of this gathering was stated in its report: 'To achieve a free, independent and pluralistic Iraqi media that promote and protect freedom of expression in a democratic society' (World Free Press 2003), which literally followed what the Pentagon designed in its White Paper project.

In fact, *Internews*, which did not have an operational office in Iraq, received 160,359 dollars from US international development agency USAID in 2003 to work on developing the Iraqi media (USAID Report 2004).[6] Between August 16, 2004, and June 30, 2007, USAID sponsored the Iraq Civil Society and Independent Media project, spending 57,104,492 dollars. Part of this project was 'developing a professional independent media sector' (USAID 2007). Before the Athens conference *Internews* held a meeting in Cairo, in co-ordination with Cairo Institute for Human Rights Studies (CIHRS), to prepare a draft media law to submit at the conference. CIHRS, which worked on translation and technical issues for the Athens conference, was mainly funded by NED, getting 160,000 dollars from 1994 to 1999 alone (National Endowment for Democracy 2004). It is important to note that USAID continued its support for the Iraqi media after the US invasion in 2003. For example, it assisted in forming the National Iraqi News Agency (NINA) to replace to the infamous INA of Saddam Hussein's rule. In 2006, the US Ambassador to Iraq, Zalmay Khalilzad, was pleased to know that more than 100,000 visitors viewed NINA's website every month and that the website had a 'link with BBC Arabic news' (Wikileaks 2006b).[7] In his overall account of the achievements of the US government, Khalilzad bragged:

> Since April, 2005 over 1,000 Iraqi journalists and managers have received technical training from USAID on investigative journalism and strategic management. Over two hundred journalists have received informal training by working with MNFI [Multi-National Force–Iraq] and Embassy press officers, and up to 100 have participated in ... exchange programs in the U.S. and the region.
>
> (ibid.)

The US Embassy in Baghdad was also active in assisting Iraqi journalists; for example, it supported the Iraqi media organisation, the Journalistic Freedoms Observatory (JFO), in different ways, such as training journalists, capacity building, and holding a 'Press Courage Awards Ceremony' on December 6, 2009, to reward Iraqi journalists who had risked their lives to uncover government corruption and wrong practices in the society (Wikileaks 2009h and 2009b).

Furthermore, in 2004 the IWPR received 109,000 dollars from NED to 'strengthen the independent media sector' in Iraq (Democracy Projects Database 2004). However, the activities of the IWPR were always shown to be an initiative from the organisation itself rather than funded from another side. According to NED's records, about 325,000 dollars was given between 2003 and 2005 to Iraqi media outlets and publications and about 105,000 dollars to other projects that involved the media and publications (Barker 2008, p. 122).

The US government supported other non-governmental organisations (NGOs) in 2002/2003 as part of the Middle East Partnership Initiative (MEPI). As a result, MEPI established two bureaus in the Arab world – one in the UAE and the other in Tunisia (Sakr 2006, p. 3). Also, the Index on Censorship organisation was partly funded by the British Foreign Office's Human Rights Programmes Fund to support a group of Iraqi journalists to write reports that would later be published online and on paper (Jayasekera 2003a).

It is important to note here that the UAE government supported the US efforts in rebuilding Iraq, especially during the first phase of the occupation. Some of the efforts were focused on the media sector. For example, the UAE and US embassies in Baghdad invited ten Iraqi journalists to the UAE from September 25–30, 2004, to attend a workshop entitled 'Effective Use of the Internet for Journalists' (Wikileaks 2004b). Besides, in August 2005 the BBC World Service Trust started TV and radio station Al-Mirbad in southern Iraq where British troops were stationed. The UK's Department of International Development gave 11.81 million dollars to cover the station's expenses for two years, after which it had to search for funding from other sources (Cochrane 2006). Other expenses came from the UAE Sheikh Mohammed Bin Zayed Al Nahyan, ruler of Abu Dhabi, to fund the construction of studios in the southern Iraqi city of Basra. Al-Mirbad had about 150 staff who were locally employed and trained by the BBC World Service Trust (BBC World Service Trust 2006).

The support for international media organisations continued throughout the years that followed the invasion. For example, the United Nations Development Fund for Women supported the establishment of Al-Mahaba Radio for Iraqi women, with a budget of 500,000 dollars as of January 2005. The radio aired its programmes for about eight hours a day and discussed women's issues. It is regarded as the first women's radio station in Iraq and the Arab world (Wong 2005b). Also, in 2010, the US Department of State supported two media organisations, IWPR and IREX, via its Bureau of Democracy, Human Rights, and Labor. A two-day conference was held in Erbil on September 27 to investigate how Iraq could make use of new technology, information, and e-governance, which included training sessions on managing blogs and 'visualising information' (IWPR 2010).

Sensing the important role of the Iraqi media, UNESCO held a conference in Paris on January 8–10, 2007. The conference, which was entitled

'Freedom of Expression and Media Development in Iraq', witnessed the participation of 300 people, including 200 Iraqi media personnel and 20 Iraqi MPs. Some of the main topics of discussion at the conference were the challenges of the civil conflict in post-2003 Iraq and the means of making IMN an independent media body by being 'politically, financially and editorially independent of the Iraqi Government' (UNESCO Conference 2007; Wikileaks 2007a). In the following year, UNESCO held another meeting in Amman, Jordan, where 37 Iraqi journalists signed a professional code of conduct to develop the professional level of journalism and encourage pluralism in the media (UNESCO 2008).

Finally, other countries offered their assistance to train Iraqi journalists and support the Iraqi media, mostly to improve their images and win supportive voices. For example, the Jordanian government sponsored a three-day 'Media Training Workshop' in Amman between October 6 and 8, 2003. The theme of the workshop focused on the 'Relations between Journalists and Media Officials'. Twenty journalists from Iraq, Palestine, and Jordan were invited to attend; among them, five Iraqi journalists (Wikileaks 2003). Furthermore, the Italian state-sponsored network RAI invited ten journalists and technicians from IMN for training in January 2004. Interestingly, the Italian Ministry of Foreign Affairs organised and sponsored the training course, yet it asked RAI to keep the training issue a secret from the press without giving any justification (Wikileaks 2004a). Also, the Czech NGO People in Need (PIN) supported a training programme in 2006 for Iraqi journalists in Amman, Jordan. After the training, PIN paid the journalists money for every article they published in local Iraqi newspapers. The Czech Ministry of Foreign Affairs and PIN wanted to co-operate with the US government to further assist Iraqi journalists (Wikileaks 2006f).

On the other hand, there seems to be some kind of duplication and a lack of co-ordination among the international media organisations, as well as the relevant UN agencies. For example,

During the 2007 UNESCO conference cited above, an Iraqi participant pointed out that he had lately witnessed in Amman 'three different UN and UN agency-sponsored training programs, all concerning media in Iraq'. Ironically, these training sessions were 'held in the same hotel with none of the meeting organizers aware of the fact that other UN groups were present' (Wikileaks 2007a). This kind of confusion is understandable since most of these organisations had the funding and wanted to spend the money without much prior planning. The result was to be expected – many Iraqi journalists who did not have the right contacts were marginalised, whereas other fortunate ones got several training opportunities.

In brief, some international media organisations worked closely with the US authorities, who were mostly funding media projects to monitor the development process and build a new Iraqi media. The co-operation was meant to ensure that Iraqi journalists got a high standard training, but it was also used by the US authorities to suggest that a great new change had occurred in the media sector. Whether by US authorities or international organisations, millions of dollars were spent after 2003 on improving the Iraqi media. However, what has been achieved is minimal in comparison to the money spent and the effort exerted.

4
The Iraqi Media after the US-Led Invasion

This chapter discusses the changes that occurred to the media sector after the US-led occupation of Iraq. It seeks to give the reader an understanding of the different types of influence that shaped the Iraqi media after 2003, and offers some analyses and conclusions on the general media trends that are prevalent in today's Iraq.

After the 2003 occupation of Iraq by US-led forces, a transformation occurred in the Iraqi media. The first phase of the post-invasion media (2003–2007) is more or less similar to the change that occurred to the Iraqi press after the 1908 Ottoman reformations, in four major areas:

(1) Prior to both 1908 and 2003, there were strict laws wherein civil liberties were harshly curbed. As a result of the political change that occurred, Iraqis vented their anger, frustration, and aspirations in the newly established publications.
(2) Many newspapers and magazines were established within a short period of time and most of them ceased to exist after a while because they did not sell well.
(3) Many newspapers and magazines were run by unqualified people who made use of the relative freedom given by the Ottomans or the US authorities.
(4) Many writers used insults, obscene language, and directly attacked other people and political parties.

It is important to note here that the research for this chapter made extensive use of US cables leaked by Wikileaks because of the important and relevant information that they contained. The Iraqi journalists and media experts who freely expressed their views to US officials gave an accurate and unflattering picture of the Iraqi media that they would never have exposed otherwise for fear of being attacked or even killed. The following section offers a discussion on the nature of the post-2003 Iraqi media.

The new Iraqi media scene

As stated in Chapter 3, the new political reality in Iraq drove the country to obvious divisions; accordingly, the media became divided along ethno-sectarian lines. Tens of political and religious parties established their own newspapers and later radio and TV stations, but the new media scene was characterised by its partisan nature, with clear ethnic and sectarian orientation. As mentioned earlier, the different Iraqi politico-religious groups had in most cases conflicting agendas and ideologies that played a negative role in further dividing the different sects and ethnicities. With the sudden appearance of hundreds of newspapers and tens of radio and TV channels post-2003, Iraqis started consuming the media that fit into their religious, ethnic, or political backgrounds.[1] This is also the case in the USA, where TV audiences are heterogeneous according to their preferred political trend (Morris 2007).

These Iraqi politico-religious parties had certain ideologies that were mostly sectarian in nature. Accordingly, the media messages that were sent were loaded with harmful effects. Hall (1985) suggests that journalists working in different media channels are influenced by their own ideology even if they have not noticed or have not acknowledged it as they are 'inscribed by an ideology to which they do not consciously commit themselves, and which, instead, "writes them"' (p. 101). van Dijk (1998) stressed that ideologies can distinguish between the different groups in a given society, and they mostly determine how 'groups and their members view a specific issue or domain of society' (p. 65). Indeed, the partisan media in Iraq was instrumental in forming and unifying the ideology of the different segments in the society because it was their main source of information.

According to the agenda-setting theory, people get to understand the world around them and the issues covered through the perspective of the media since 'citizens deal with a second-hand reality, a reality that is structured by journalists' reports about these events and situations' (McCombs 2004, p. 1). In other words, the media sets its own agenda (Iyengar and Kinder 1987; Entman 1989) and shapes certain beliefs (Krosnick and Kinder 1990). If certain issues are continuously repeated in the media, they become more important for the public. 'The agenda of the news becomes, to a considerable degree, the agenda of the public'

(McCombs 2004, p. 2). However, when certain issues are related to the people's core beliefs, like their religion and creed, the issues start to have much more importance and influence over the way that people behave (McCombs 2004, p. 138). In this case, the media can have a very effective role in driving the people towards certain actions. For example, during civil wars the media are known to assist in justifying 'mass violence' through the 'constructions of ethnophobia' or sectarian animosity; the media are used to 'escalate hatred and spread fear against one another' and as a 'centerpiece of the struggle between factions' (Erni 2005).

In the case of Iraq's media, it was an integral part of the conflict. It created a great deal of confusion, chaos, and risk for all the journalists involved (see, for instance, Al-Qaisi and Jabbar 2010). Paul Cochrane (2006) described the new reality as the 'Lebanonization' of Iraqi media channels since Lebanon and Iraq became similar in their political and media experiences:

> the political and social sectarianism of Iraq is, like the multiple political party scene and media landscape, a very new arena that will no doubt change alongside political developments. Channels may fare as their political backers do, sink or swim. But with no effective or impartial national public TV channel – the moribund TeleLiban is hardly watched, and Al Iraqiya favors Iraq's Shiite government – both Lebanon and Iraq's media will remain driven by sectarianism.

Cochrane drew some similarities between the two countries, for he stressed the pluralistic nature of the media, and most importantly its negative role in disintegrating the society, especially when the rhetoric is loaded with sectarian language and unsubstantiated slurs. In this regard, Roug (2006) gave the example of the Shiite Al-Furat TV, which is backed by the Islamic Supreme Council of Iraq (ISCI). The channel used to air messages about the Shiites' need to stand up for their rights after the bombing of the Samaraa Shrine, indirectly inciting violence against Sunni Arabs. On the other hand, the Sunni Baghdad TV that is sponsored by the Iraqi Islamic Party started to air programmes on the atrocities committed by the government-backed Shiite militias against Sunnis (Roug 2006). Also, Al-Marashi (2007) referred to the controversial Sunni Al-Zawraa TV channel, which used to air footage of Iraqi insurgent groups fighting against coalition forces. The channel used to attack the Shiite-led government and called for the attacking of its officials for being backed by Iran and the USA. Al-Marashi confirms that 'Iraq's ethno-sectarian media are providing the psychological groundwork for bitter divisiveness and conflict' (p. 99). Besides, Iraq's partisan press was loaded with a sectarian spirit. Since newspapers carry more details, graphic images, and can be easily circulated, they played an important role in dividing the society. In this connection, Professor Hamida Smessem, former dean of the Communication College at Baghdad University, mentioned that these 'newspapers need to be organized.... They're hurting each other with these words' (Daragahi 2003). Former director of the Iraqi Media Network (IMN), Ahmed Al-Rikabi, revealed in November 2006 that 'We are witnessing a civil war. And this civil war is conducted by different religious groups and different political groups. And of course, the media is an extension of this sectarian violence we are witnessing today' (CNN Broadcast 2006).

Other observers blame foreign powers of being behind the media war. The US Ambassador to Iraq, Zalmay Khalilzad, clarified that the reason behind the increasing number of local and foreign media channels operating in Iraq was because of the country's 'importance to the global economy, global religion, and regional politics', making it an 'automatic draw for anyone with a message' (Wikileaks 2006b). For example, Ibrahim Al-Saidi, Radio Baghdad's manager, confirmed that several Iraqi media outlets that were engaged in inciting sectarianism since 2003 carry foreign agendas, but he did not specify which countries were involved (Al-Qattan and Juma'a 2006). Many Iraqi experts think that Iran and Saudi Arabia are the main instigators of sectarian hatred in Iraqi society by their direct and indirect support of certain media channels and political parties. For example, in November 2008 a US cable from its embassy in Baghdad cited Ibrahim Al-Saraji, head of the Iraqi Journalist Rights Defending Association, and other journalists, who claimed that they 'perceived growing Iranian influence in Iraqi media and accused Iran of bribing journalists, making payments to media organizations, and implementing a strategy to infiltrate all news agencies' (Wikileaks 2008b).

The dilemma for Iraqi journalists

Due to the lack of security and the necessary infrastructure that was destroyed in the war, Iraqi journalists at this time, who were mostly new to the profession with no media background, were 'not always professional' (Wikileaks 2009b) since they mostly followed 'confused, mediocre journalistic standards' in reporting (Kim and Hama-Saeed 2008, p. 581). Mahmoud Bachari, an Iraqi journalist living in Basrah, pointed out that many new journalists in his city 'got their jobs through connections or as favors. Most had little or no experience in the field before being hired' (Wikileaks 2010a). Bachari's observation does not only apply to Basrah; it can be found in the rest of the country, even in Kurdistan where Kurdistan Democratic Party (KDP) or Patriotic Union of Kurdistan (PUK) connections play an important role in the recruitment process. Indeed, this phenomenon is a manifestation that no radical change has occurred in the Iraqi media since Saddam Hussein's Ba'athist rule and journalists would gain more benefits.

Surely, having many unqualified journalists increased the confusion in the Iraqi media. Yet Iraqi journalists largely felt powerless and isolated, and it was extremely difficult to report objectively on the conflict as many were kidnapped, detained, or murdered. In fact, there was a 'whole collection of forces working to undermine one of the pillars of Iraq's emerging democracy, its free press' (Isakhan 2008, p. 12). The pressures mainly came from coalition forces, Iraqi government officials, powerful political parties, insurgent groups, religious leaders, and armed militias, and sometimes foreign intelligence officers. As a result, many Iraqi journalists became polarised either towards their sect, race, or religion to seek protection or win the favour of their party or community leaders (Al-Rawi 2010).[2] In Iraq's media today, 'any media person who belongs to a party must support the party's opinions', according to Falah Al-Thahabi and Rafel Mehdi from the US-funded channel Al-Hurra TV (Wikileaks 2007d). A report written by a US official positioned in Basrah, after a meeting with Bachari, revealed the following:

> [Iraqi] journalists are paid by political parties, businesses or wealthy people to run specific stories or cover certain events. [Bachari] added that the government is a big source of revenue for media outlets because it pays journalists to cover specific stories. PRT staff witnessed this pay-for-play practice several months ago, watching as the media advisor to the governor openly passed out envelopes of money to journalists at the end of a joint Governor/Prime Minister press conference. Positive coverage by a journalist generates more coverage requests and thus more revenue from the government. As a result, many journalists, editors, and media outlets are reluctant to criticize the government in their stories.
>
> (Wikileaks 2010a)[3]

Furthermore, Bashar Manadalawy, deputy head of the Journalistic Freedoms Observatory (JFO), asserted in 2009 that the Iraqi government office is used for 'manipulating journalists with job promises if they agree to work' for a state-sponsored media channel (Wikileaks 2009b). In fact, this method is similar to the one used by the Ba'ath regime during Saddam Hussein's rule; journalists who praised the president and his 'heroic', 'brave', and 'genius' achievements were given monetary rewards and sometimes cars or plots of lands.

In relation to the security risks faced by journalists, Al-Thahabi asserted that 'most of the threats comes from religious parties', and mentioned that the Shiite Thar-Allah militia and the Iraqi Hezbollah group directly threatened him after criticising them (Wikileaks 2007d). In one incident dealing with the state-sponsored Al-Fayhaa newspaper in Babil governorate, a US official wrote the following:

> [The newspaper] recently carried an article detailing the Mahdi Militia abduction of a music shop owner from his hospital bed. Two days later, grenades were thrown at Al-Fayhaa's offices and the newspaper quickly printed a retraction and Mahdi Militia's version of the incident.... Since then, Al-Fayhaa has prominently carried articles about Muqtada al-Sadr's activities.
>
> (Wikileaks 2006d)

Media freedom in the rest of Iraq's governorates is not different from what happens in Baghdad. For example, the US official positioned in Basrah pointed out that 'religious and political groups, backed by militias, seek to influence journalists. The threat against them is high, and several have been killed in the past year' (Wikileaks 2006e). In Salahadin governorate, journalists are pressured by insurgent groups in order to be silenced. For example, Muhammed Hussein, who works for the US Army-funded Free Iraqi Radio, mentioned in 2008 that he had to change his phone number three times due to the threats he had received. Hussein believes that three-quarters of the Iraqi journalists working in the governorate must have a 'protector' such as a 'tribal leader' or a 'government official'. Accordingly, the journalist must write favourably about his/her 'protector' (Wikileaks 2008e). Similar media restrictions are found in Iraqi Kurdistan. For example, 23-year-old Kurdish journalist and blogger Sardasht Othman was kidnapped in 2010 in the Kurdish city of Erbil and his body was found a few days later in Mosul. Othman's articles were mostly critical of Masud Barazani's regional government. Some of Othman's friends believe that Kurdish officials might have been angered by a piece he wrote for the online Kurdistan Post in which he mentioned that the only way to climb the ladder in the society was by marrying the daughter of the president (*The Associated Press* 2010b). Other Kurdish journalists were either beaten, blackmailed, or pressured to stop writing critical articles (*Agence France Presse* 2011). US officials working in northern Iraq met with several Kurdish journalists who expressed serious concerns over their safety. They mentioned that the two main Kurdish parties, the KDP and the PUK, together with Iranian intelligence, did not like to have any kind of criticism of them published. Some of the details presented to the US officials contained the names of Kurdish party members who were thought to be implicated in the murder of some local journalists (Wikileaks 2008d).

Censorship remains a fundamental issue since most journalists still practise self-censorship for fear of being killed. For example, it is still 'unthinkable' to criticise political or religious leaders like Muqtada Sadr (Kim and Hama-Saeed 2008, p. 588) or the grand four Shiite Ayatollahs in Najaf. Firas Al-Hamdani, an Iraqi journalist, confided to a US official in 2007 that he 'cannot write articles about militias, although he feels he can write very freely about PM Maliki' (Wikileaks 2007d). However, this media situation radically changed from 2008 onwards.

In 2011, Hadi Al-Mehdi, who had a weekly radio programme called 'To Whoever Listens' in which he directly criticised government corruption and injustice, was killed at his apartment. Al-Mehdi was instrumental in gathering public support via his facebook page to hold protests against Maliki's government, but he was later imprisoned and severely tortured during his detention. Despite the continuous threats he received, he never ceased working and attacking the government. On September 8, 2011, gunmen carrying silenced pistols killed Al-Mehdi in Baghdad and then fled (Gowen and Alwan 2011; Yahya 2011). During a meeting between US Embassy officials in Baghdad and seven Iraqi journalists from different media channels in 2007, a discussion on the challenges facing Iraqi journalists was made. They mentioned various 'threats they have experienced in connection with their employment, including one instance of kidnapping. They have coped with threats in different ways such as self-censoring, going into hiding, and in some cases, applying for refugee status in the U.S.' (Wikileaks 2007d). There are other risks to Iraqi journalists if they dare to criticise some sides; these threats come from many, such as 'ministry officials', 'provincial governors', 'representatives of parliamentarians', and the 'Iraqi police' (ibid.; Wikileaks 2008e).

As for the ordinary Sunni Arabs who have no armed protection, it is also 'unthinkable' to criticise Al-Qaeda or any Iraqi insurgent groups because of the repercussions involved. For example, Essam Al-Rawi, a senior member of the Sunni Muslim Scholars Association, was allegedly assassinated by Al-Qaeda in Baghdad in October 2006. The assassination occurred one day after he had stated to Al-Arabiya channel that establishing a so-called an Islamic state in Iraq, which was Al-Qaeda's aim, was far-fetched due to the political and social reality in the country.

Other ways of silencing journalists are libel suits, or just the threat of filing them, as elaborated below. This is usually practised by senior Iraqi officials like Maliki, Talabani, and Barazani. The Iraqi Journalist Rights Defense Association mentions that there were 39 libel suits against Iraqi journalists in 2009, and the number of cases dramatically increased to 55 in the first ten months of 2010 (Human Rights Watch 2011, pp. 42–43). Mu'aid Al-Lami from the Iraqi Journalists Syndicate revealed in April 2010: 'Before 2008 things were different – killing was the preferred method of silencing journalists in Iraq. Today it's with lawsuits' (ibid., p. 43).

Ironically, some Iraqi journalists found it 'safer' to attack US forces and point out their mistakes and shortcomings because they did not usually assassinate journalists for voicing their opinions; the worst that might happen was detention.[4] This claim does not mean that the US-led forces in Iraq have not harmed journalists; Reporters Without Borders mentions that 'at least 19 journalists' have been killed [by multi-national forces], comprising 9 per cent of the estimated 230 journalists and media professionals who have died in Iraq since 2003. In all the cases, the US army claimed that such incidents were due to 'accidental fire' or 'collateral damage' (RSF 2010).

On the other hand, many Iraqis worked with foreign news agencies as stringers and fixers whose duties increased due to the deteriorating security situation and the 'impenetrable political and cultural environments' (Wikileaks 2006b). They used to translate, generate stories, fix appointments, find suitable interlocutors, arrange for cars, hotels, and transportation, assess the security situation, film events, and conduct interviews (Palmer and Fontan 2007, p. 10; Murrell 2010, p. 131). As a result, many foreign journalists who 'rely on Iraqi legwork' started to 'add flavor with "stand ups" from (relatively safe) hotel balconies' (Wikileaks 2006b). In many cases they managed to substitute foreign journalists themselves and became correspondents sent to cover the news in other countries (Palmer and Fontan 2007, p. 12).

It is indeed right to say that the US-led invasion and its aftermath brought with it new freedoms of expression and some other benefits for Iraqi journalists, such as lively interaction with international media organisations/Western journalists and a huge salary scale improvement. The new political system created an atmosphere wherein people started to publish newspapers freely, express their opinions in the media without fearing for their lives, and watch satellite TV channels with no restrictions. For many Iraqis, both men and women, this media reality opened new frontiers from which they could declare their views and criticise opinions (Prusher 2003a).

Also, the number of Internet users increased with the opening of Internet cafés and the availability of wireless local subscription. By the end of 2004, the number of Internet users in Iraq reached around 50,000, and by July 2006 more than 170 Internet cafés were functional (OpenNet Initiative 2007, p. 2). Mainly based on facebook subscribers, Internet World Stats calculated in June 2011 that about 860,400 Iraqis were using the Internet with a penetration rate of 2.8 per cent of the total population (Internet World Stats 2011). This is the lowest percentage in the Middle East region, even in relation to countries like Yemen. This is mainly due to the continuous disruption of the electricity supply, the lack of stable governmental Internet services, the relatively high costs, and poor maintenance.

One of the positive signs for the Iraqi media was the media conference organised by the Iraqi Journalists Syndicate and the International Federation of Journalists. Held in Baghdad on May 23–24, 2009, it was the first international media gathering in Iraq since 1995, indicating that some security improvements had been achieved. The aim of the conference was to 'develop a challenging vision that breaks with the past and clearly defines the role that media and journalism should play' in the new Iraq (International Media Support 2009).

Iraqi Media Network and sectarianism

On March 19, 2003, US-led coalition forces started operation 'Iraqi Freedom', and on May 1, 2003, US President George W Bush announced the end of the military operations. US and other coalition forces became the occupying powers, according to United Nations Security Council Resolution 1483. The first US Civil Administrator, General Jay Garner, was appointed before the war as head of the Office of Reconstruction and Humanitarian Aid (ORHA) and started working from Kuwait, but he did not stay long in office.

As mentioned in Chapter 3, ORHA was responsible for forming IMN based on the White Paper project. It was established as a public broadcasting channel, like the BBC and PBS, independent from the government and any other side. However, very few Iraqis were involved in its planning process, mainly due to the deteriorating security condition. As for the Iraqi Governing Council members who work from the fortified Green Zone, they were mostly busy with their 'own survival and succession' and lacked the motivation and interest to discuss the future of Iraq's media (Price 2007, p. 15).

In relation to media development, Garner confirmed that he was 'instructed by Secretary of Defense Donald Rumsfeld to ignore the "Future of Iraq Project" proposed by the US Department of State' (Rieff 2003, p. 28). This was part of the lack of co-ordination between the US Departments of State and Defense, as mentioned in Chapter 3. As mentioned in Chapter 3, the Department of State hired Iraqi exiles to work as media experts. One of the Iraqis involved was Isam Al-Khafaji, who became the first IMN member to resign because of its unclear objectives, stating:

> [b]itter disputes between the defence department and the state department continue to affect the situation. Even though Bremer has the formal authority within Iraq, it seems like each and every decision must go back to Washington, and we are the victims of indecision.
>
> (Al-Khafaji 2003)

Due to the delay in initiating the work of IMN by the Science Applications International Corporation (SAIC), Garner, in an interview with the BBC in May 2003, expressed his 'disappointment' with the absence of a national media channel, saying: 'I want TV going to the people... with a soft demeanour, programmes they want to see' (BBC News 2003b). Some criticism was directed at Garner himself and his short term of service, claiming that 'Jay [was] not relating' to the Iraqi public. As a result, President Bush nominated Margaret Tutwiler, the US Ambassador in Morocco, and an ex-Department of State Spokesperson, to take control of the Iraqi media with the assistance of ORHA (Claypole 2003). In another interview, after leaving his post, Garner confirmed that the US government did a 'bad job' of communicating with Iraqis, who ultimately resorted to watching Al-Jazeera instead (*Redorbit.com* 2003).

After the removal of Garner, ORHA was dissolved and President Bush appointed Paul Bremer as the head of the newly formed Coalition Provisional Authority (CPA) and Civil Administrator for Iraq. Bremer assumed his office on May 12, 2003. According to Order 2 issued on May 23, the Iraqi army, the national security and intelligence bodies, and the Ministry of Information were all dissolved. This decision created an unprecedented high unemployment rate, led to a wave of anger and mistrust within Iraqi society, and encouraged the formation of various Sunni insurgent groups that opposed the occupation by different means, including the use of online media (International Crisis Group 2006; Kimmage and Ridolfo 2007).

Originally IMN was supposed to replace the Iraqi Ministry of Information. As for its hierarchical structure, it was led by Bob Reilly, a former director of Voice of America, who known for being a 'propagandist in the White House for the Nicaraguan contras' (Dauenhauer and Lobe 2003). Reilly worked with a defence contractor called Mike Furlong (Kuusi et al. 2003).

Later, IMN was run by John Sandrock, a SAIC employee, who reported to the CPA's director of strategic communication, John Buck. The latter, who directly reported to Paul Bremer, had a deputy called Dan Senor working as a White House liaison officer (BBC World Service Trust 2003). On April 10, 2003, IMN's radio aired its first programmes, and on May 13 the TV channel Iraqia started broadcasting with the help of 350 Iraqis; some of them came with the US forces (Dauenhauer and Lobe 2003).

SAIC, the Pentagon's contractor, received 108.2 million dollars to run IMN, which included a TV channel, a radio station, and *Al-Sabah* newspaper (Haner 2004). Despite having a 6 million dollar monthly budget (Williams 2003, A14), many problems occurred at Iraqia TV, such as only one studio being available (IMN, 'The Network: Its Beginnings and Establishments'), the incompatibility of equipment brought from the USA with the previous system, a lack of documentaries and films, and the low salaries given to local staff. IMN news director Ahmed Al-Rikabi, an exiled Iraqi journalist, revealed that in the beginning there was not enough furniture, so reporters had to sit and write 'reports on colleagues backs' (McCaul 2003). Furthermore, Internews Network's president, David Hoffman, described IMN as the 'worst mess I have ever seen in my life' (cited in Amos 2010, p. 22). In general, the US's first investment in the Iraqi media was both 'misdirected and misused' (Jayasekera 2004, p. 6).

Indeed, IMN was manipulated and fully controlled from the beginning of its establishment by the CPA, which used to dictate policies to be followed, such as dropping 'the readings from the Koran' and the ' "vox-pop" man-in-the-street interviews (usually critical of the US invasion)'. Due to Tutwiler's personal intervention, Hiru Khan, the wife of the current Kurdish President of Iraq Jalal Talabani, was told to review the Iraqi TV broadcast before airing it (Jayasekera 2003b; Claypole 2003).

Some programmes aired on Iraqia TV did not consider cultural and religious sensitivities, showing implicit sensual scenes. As a result, some leaders from the Shiite Islamic Supreme Council of Iraq which later became the Islamic Supreme Council of Iraq (ISCI), threatened to protest against this crucial matter and warned that a religious decree could be issued against IMN (Freedom House 2004, p. 5).

Also, the UK government, which provided technical support, programmes, and documentaries to help build IMN, undermined IMN's independence by its insistence on airing a one-hour daily programme called 'Toward Freedom', despite the objection of some IMN media staff (North 2003). Many IMN staff members felt disillusioned as a result of such overt interference. For instance, Don North worked for IMN for almost three months as a senior TV advisor and trainer. After leaving Iraq, he revealed how IMN became 'an irrelevant mouthpiece for Coalition Provisional Authority propaganda' due to its 'managed news and mediocre programs' (North 2003). IMN's original goal was to be 'an information conduit'; instead, it became 'just rubber-stamp flacking for the C.P.A.' (Opel 2003) because the US authorities could not 'resist controlling the message' (Democracy Now 2004). Furthermore, North claimed that the CPA made IMN a replica of Voice of America, indirectly suggesting the influence of Reilly. As a result, IMN's credibility was destroyed because of the CPA's 'incompetence and indifference' (Opel 2003). In his speech at the US Congress in February 2005, North revealed that several US officials stressed that 'we were running a public diplomacy operation' via IMN, which was given a 'laundry list of CPA activities to cover' (Margasak 2005).

Another media expert, Stephen Claypole, worked as an advisor for ORHA during April and May 2003, but he quickly left. He expressed his disappointment at the lack of professionalism and the favouritism that existed at the time. It seemed that the US authorities had 'direct control over the contents of the evening news', which undermined the early efforts of establishing an independent media (Claypole 2003).

Besides Stephen Claypole and Don North, a US manager of IMN's news department, Gordon Robison, worked there in late 2003. Robinson stressed that the CPA's editorial control over the Iraqia channel was overwhelming. In a TV show called 'Meet the Press', in which the CPA's administrator is interviewed by Iraqi journalists, Bremer's staff requested to choose the interviewers to make sure that they followed the CPA's line. Despite some resistance from the management, 'Bremer's staff retained the final say over who did or did not appear on the show' (Robison 2003, p. 6). Even the questions asked were supposed to be around reconstruction efforts and the positive aspect of the coalition presence in Iraq. When some journalists ventured to ask questions about the security situation, Bremer's assistants objected and 'mumbled', saying: 'that's not what this is supposed to be about' (ibid., p. 7). Afterwards, the show started involving officials other than Bremer, but the CPA's authorities dictated who could be interviewed and requested a 'firm idea what was going to be said beforehand' (ibid., p. 9).

Ahmed Al-Rikabi, who said the first words over Iraqi airwaves on April 9, 2003, sensed the grave task that IMN had, saying: 'We have a big responsibility. If you put the wrong message out, do things without feeling responsibility, your program might lead to civil war. You have to be careful, balanced' (McCaul 2003). Also, Jalal Al-Mashta, who first worked as editor-in-chief of Adnan Al-Pachachi's newspaper *Al-Nahdha*, was nominated as the general director of the channel Iraqia TV in May 2004, but he resigned after six months due to the lack of support and the CPA's influence over IMN (Haner 2004). Al-Mashta pointed out that 'the budget was being wasted on buying costly foreign programs while salaries were not being paid' (Price 2007, p. 17).

When SAIC's contract with IMN expired, and amid the criticism directed at it, another US military contractor, Harris Corporation, got involved in January 2004 with a 96 million dollar contract. Harris worked with the Lebanese Broadcasting Corporation, the Kuwaiti Al-Fawares media company, and also with Microsoft (Freedom House 2004, p. 5). According to Sherrie Gossett from Accuracy in Media, the aim of hiring another military contractor is to secure military and political gains as well as to 'quell unrest, win the minds of the people and combat anti-American propaganda from other sources' (cited in Haner 2004). In this sense, the CPA's control over IMN continued. Almost a year from the start of publishing the newspaper *Al-Sabah*, some of its staff members went on strike, in May 2004, because of the CPA's continuing editorial restraints (Freedom House 2004, p. 5).

Due to the presence of a Shiite majority who were mostly aligned to political parties (Levinson 2006), Iraqia TV started to show signs of bias. Al-Rikabi pointed out that IMN's one-sided policy would only lead the country towards anarchy: 'The people of Iraq, including the Sunni Muslims, are not about to turn against their liberators, but they are being incited to do so. These channels contribute to tension within Iraq. You need television at their level' (Oweis 2003). Salih Al-Mutlaq, a Sunni politician, agrees with Al-Rikabi and adds that aside from the prevalent political reasons, IMN has become 'another factor that is helping to turn Iraqi society into a sectarian society' (Levinson 2006). In June 2005, an official at the US Embassy in Baghdad described, in a cable sent to the Department of State, some kind of optimism about Iraqia TV:

> After almost two years of confusion, several hundred million dollars in investment, chaotic management, and Byzantine internal machinations, 'Al-Iraqiyya' – the television component of the Iraqi Media Network (IMN) – shows signs of finding its voice and projecting a populist 'Iraqi' message, even as technical capabilities deteriorate.
>
> (Wikileaks 2005b)

The first step taken by Iraqia TV was to broadcast the Shiite call of prayer (Oweis 2003) and to heavily cover the other Shiite sermons, flagellation events, and Friday prayer speeches, leaving the Arab Sunnis and Kurds without a voice. One of IMN's former board members, Fadel Jalal Mohammed, admitted in 2007 that the channel's 'coverage had been biased by, for example, giving live airtime to Shiite celebrations, while excluding similar coverage for other sects' (Wikileaks 2007c).

Second, Iraqia TV started highlighting the atrocities of the former Ba'ath regime by covering the crimes committed against the Shiites and Kurds in particular, implying that the Arab Sunnis were not affected by Saddam Hussein's regime. For example, emphasis was always placed on the mass graves in the mainly Shiite south, the 1991 Shiite uprising (Roug 2006), the Anfal campaign, and the Halabja attack against the Kurds. The fact that IMN is Shiite-dominated has definitely affected its neutrality. In 2006, US forces raided a hideout for militiamen and killed about 16 Shiite fighters who belonged to the Mahdi Army. Instead of showing it as the killing of terrorists, as it usually does when Sunni fighters are involved, Iraqia TV pictured the raid as 'the killing of unarmed worshipers in a Shiite Muslim mosque'. The camera focused on the dead bodies and interviews with Shiite politicians who criticised the US forces (Roug 2006). Hiwa Osman revealed that 50 per cent of Iraqis watch Iraqia TV, but he expressed his disappointment in the channel that turned out to be a 'propaganda tool for the country's leading Shiite politicians' (Levinson 2006). However, IMN and Iraqia TV rarely, if ever, mention the 1995 and 1998 Sunni Arab revolts of the Dulaimi tribe in Anbar region, the mass execution of senior Sunni Ba'ath Party members in 1979, and the arrest and execution of prominent Sunni religious clerics from the Muslim Brothers and salafi movements throughout the 1980s and 1990s.

Also, IMN aired a controversial programme called 'Terrorism in the Grip of Justice', which was also aired by Al-Fayhaa channel – an

Iraqi Shiite-oriented channel broadcasting from Dubai. The programme involved interviews with 'terrorists' captured by US forces and Iraqi security personnel shown on TV to confess their crimes without being tried by a judge or legal court. The UK's telegraph.co.uk described the 'intelligence successes' in Iraq by citing this show (2005). But there were clear signs of torture to be seen on the interviewees' faces, and they sometimes had difficulty talking. In addition, most of the suspects shown were Sunni insurgents, including some Arab fighters, but no Shiite militiamen from the death squads, the Mahdi Army or Badr Brigade were ever interviewed, though many were involved in sectarian killings and kidnappings. The programme, which was aired at 21:00 during Iraq's TV prime time, presented recurrent themes involving the implication of Al-Jazeera channel as a source of inspiration for those 'terrorists' in conducting their acts, or the accusation that Syrian intelligence was behind the insurgency in Iraq (Stalinsky 2005). There was no coincidence that these two themes were also what the US authorities used to cite to explain the source of violence in the country (Murphy and Saffar 2005, A18). In other words, there was an indication that most of these televised confessions were actually orchestrated to serve US and Iraqi official stances. Furthermore, 'Terrorism in the Grip of Justice' was hailed by some Iraqi Shiite politicians as evidence that the Ministry of Interior, headed by the infamous ISCI senior member Bayan Jabr Solagh, was able to perform its duties in the best manner. However, there were serious concerns about the channel because it bragged about showing people seemingly tortured and in grave suffering, and these concerns came at a time when the UN's special rapporteur on torture and cruelty, Manfred Nowak, described the human rights violations in Iraq as worse than during Saddam Hussein's rule and 'totally out of control'. Iraqi victims were mainly tortured in 'prisons run by US-led multinational forces as well as by the ministries of interior and defence and private militias' (BBC News 2006).

In some cases the Iraqia channel used to air false news, which enraged many Iraqis. For example, when Habib Al-Sadr was head of IMN in late 2007, the channel aired a news story that referred to the parliament's decision to build a defensive wall in the Shiite Kadhimiah city, allegedly to separate it from the Sunni Adhamiah city. As a result, the chairman of the Iraqi parliament, Mahmood Al-Mashhadani, was infuriated and stated the following:

> It [Iraqia TV] is not an Iraqi channel; instead, it works on a certain agenda to incite schism in the Iraqi society. Does the channel

serve our government or does it serve the hidden hands that firstly financed it and still control it! Sadr is always abroad, leaving the station to be run by illiterate and ignorant people. This is not news; it is a means of inciting sectarian tension. Is it an Iraqi channel or an American? There must be a policy to calm down the anger in the streets not to enrage the people against us because of superficial media.

(Al-Bayyna Al-Jadidah 2007)

As a result, Al-Mashhadani formed an investigation committee to be chaired by Baha' Al-Araji. Furthermore, Iraqia showed a report in June 2006 about a massacre conducted by Sunni militant fighters against a group of Shiite Iraqis celebrating a wedding party in Al-Dujail area. The channel narrated horrendous details of 70 men, women, and children being tortured and executed. The women were raped 'one after the other' including the bride, whose 'breasts were cut off before being killed'. However, independent media investigations revealed that no one in Al-Dujail area had ever heard about the incident and no one has claimed to know the relatives of the victims shown on TV. Besides, the Iraqi MPs who visited the area failed to meet any witnesses. Finally, the official story aired on Iraqia TV carried many other contradictions and discrepancies that were fully elaborated in a report prepared by the Arabic Service of Radio Netherlands (Radio Netherlands 2011).

Unfortunately, it seems that the managers of IMN wanted to depict scenes in which Iraqi Shiites were the victims of Sunni militant groups, especially in 2006 and 2007; this media policy only enhanced the sectarian spirit in the society. The media advisor to Iraq's president, Hiwa Osman, confirmed that Iraqia TV was meant to be a 'public service broadcaster' and provide a 'service for all the people, but they are providing a service only for certain people in government' (Levinson 2006). Osman refers to the channel's dependence on the Shiite political parties that run the political show.

It is important to note here that the CPA was complicit in IMN's efforts to create tension and schism between Sunnis and Shiites (see Chapter 3 for more details). Both shared the same rhetoric, though IMN would sometimes go a step further. To give a few examples, if the US Army captures a number of suspects from Sunni regions like Anbar, Mosul, or Salahideen, IMN would mention that a number of 'terrorists' had been arrested. When TV presenters made a reference to the US/UK military presence in Iraq, they used the term 'forces of liberation' instead of the internationally acknowledged term 'occupying powers' (Fisk 2003).

In fact, the word 'occupation' was banned in this media institution, and attacks conducted by insurgent groups against US forces were rarely covered lest they should agitate the public against the Americans (Sipress 2004, A15). Kareem Hammadi, a news editor at Iraqia, revealed that he used to highlight 'positive news' such as 'the liberation, freedom, electricity improvements and the capture of terrorists' (Redorbit.com 2003). It seems that the channel followed the same policy in 2005. A US official working for the Department of State bragged that 'the station's production values compare poorly with many of its competitors, but it offers something they do not (or do not wish to): undiluted positive messaging and an image of normalcy and self-confidence for the Iraqi people' (Wikileaks 2005b). Among the positive programmes aired on Iraqia TV were 'frequent paid public service announcements promoting Iraqi confidence and pride – produced by outside organizations' (ibid.). A US Embassy official in Baghdad wrote down this account in 2007; it was made by Iraqi journalist Asa'd Al-Rubaie, who worked as a correspondent and scriptwriter for the Iraqia channel:

> Al-Rubaie noted that some media workers at Al-Iraqiyya misunderstand the concept of public broadcasting and think that the station is supposed to promote the government; therefore, the network does not report on government failures, particularly due to interference from political groups – primarily Eitilaf, and specifically ISCI. While the staff includes Sunnis, Kurds, Christians, and Shi'a, he observed, 'The direction of Iraqiyya is in fact always praising Sh'ia'. Al-Rubaie also expressed frustration that he wanted to cover issues such as displacement and poverty accurately; however, his supervisor deleted many facets of his reports.
>
> (Wikileaks 2007d)

The emphasis on positive news, programmes, and coverage is, in fact, a shortcoming for an allegedly independent and objective channel that is supposed to reflect the facts as they are. For example, the Iraqia channel ignored the serious security and public-service issues because they were not in line with the CPA's media plan. Other incidents – like the Abu Ghraib scandal, the assaults on Falluja city and the high amount of radiation left there, the rape of 14-year-old Abeer Al-Jinabi and the slaying of her family in a Sunni area – received scant if no coverage by IMN. In fact, airing any kind of criticism against the Iraqi and US authorities was not part of IMN's policy.

Furthermore, IMN was treated by the CPA like a local US media outlet rather than a national Iraqi one; for instance, an Iraqi journalist working at Iraqia was invited to visit a US navy base in Basra to present a positive picture of the US protection activities in southern Iraq (NAVY mil. 2005). As a result of all these facts, many Iraqis viewed Iraqia as 'America Television' (Badrakhan 2006, p. 472), while IMN staff were looked upon by many Iraqis as agents and collaborators for the US and Iraqi governments. This fact probably explains why IMN suffered around 20 casualties between 2003 and 2010, which is the highest number of Iraqi journalists killed among all the other media outlets operating in the country (RSF 2010, p. 7). *Al-Sabah* newspaper's editor, Mohammed Shaboot, commented in 2006 on the Iraqia channel, saying: 'It was supposed to be fair, and address all the people of Iraq, but so far it hasn't succeeded in achieving this unique goal.... No one has invested in a real, nationwide Iraqi channel for all Iraqis' (Roug 2006). Indeed, the CPA allowed IMN to function freely though it knew about its biased and subjective coverage simply because it served its interests by covering and praising its activities.

In October 2003, the US Department of State conducted a poll survey to find out the popularity of Iraqia TV. Since 62 per cent reported that they had no satellite dish, they had to resort to watching Iraqi national TV, being the only national terrestrial TV available. However, the results showed that Iraqis with satellite TV access preferred to watch Al-Arabiya (37 per cent) and Al-Jazeera (26 per cent) rather than Iraqia TV (12 per cent) for Iraq's local news, mostly because these two Arab channels are the first to report breaking news. Also, 83 per cent of Iraqis surveyed mentioned that they had no difficulty receiving the TV signal for the Iraqia channel (Coalition Provision Authority 'TV Is a Crucial Information Source for Iraqis' 2003). Reporters Sans Frontières documented further views in one of its reports; most Iraqis interviewed regarded IMN as 'the American TV station' (RSF 2003b). Some analysts even believe that IMN's nature is an imitation of the former Iraqi national TV which functioned during the Ba'ath rule (Williams 2003, A14); hence, the media personnel who resigned from IMN felt that they could not work on establishing a free media outlet while confronted with CPA pressures.

In 2004, Article 19 wrote that IMN did not have a 'structural and organizational independence' from the CPA and recommended that 'the automatic regular appearances on IMN by CPA officials must cease immediately' (Article 19 2004, p. 38 and p. 6). Furthermore, it pointed out the fact that IMN was controlled by certain groups in Iraq (indirectly referring to Shiites and Kurds) whereas Sunnis were under-represented. Hence, IMN should be managed by a governing body that is 'broadly representative of Iraqi society' (ibid., p. 3). Despite all these shortcomings, and instead of solving the real problems, the CPA hired the services of a public relations company called J Walter Thompson to start a media campaign to persuade Iraqis that IMN's news is credible (North 2003).

Some Iraqi exiles praised the new media institution and regarded it as an independent one, although a great deal of criticism was directed at IMN by international media experts (as cited above). For example, Shameem Rassam, a former general director at IMN, said the following: 'We are independent in our editorial policy. Nobody dictates to us about what to do' (Sipress 2004, A15). The same view was adhered to by George Mansour, who succeeded Ahmed Al-Rikabi (RSF 2003b). After leaving IMN Mansour became the director of Christian TV channel Ishtar and was later appointed as Minister of Kurdistan Region for Civil Society Affairs. After a series of attacks on churches in Baghdad during July 2009, Mansour made a controversial declaration by saying that 'all Iraqi Christians have no choice but to leave and immigrate from the country' (*Al-Quds Al-Arabi* 2009).

After being asked about the poll surveys that indicated the position of the Iraqia channel, Alaa Fa'ik, who worked as second in command in the station, bragged: 'Now they are returning to us because they trust us to tell the truth' (Chatterjee 2004). Fa'ik probably referred to a national poll survey conducted in February 2004 that showed that more than 50 per cent of Iraqis had confidence in the Iraqia channel (Oxford Research International 2004). It is very clear that those media personnel were trying to give an opposite picture of what everyone knew as a fact, mostly because their main task was to safeguard US policies. In June 2005, an official at the US Embassy in Baghdad was pleased with Iraqia's new popularity among Iraqis, saying: 'All recent polling and anecdotal evidence continues to show "Al-Iraqiyya" as, currently, the most popular station nationwide' (Wikileaks 2005b).

Although there was an announcement to establish a 'free Iraqi domestic media' which can become a 'model in the Middle East where so much Arab hate-media are themselves equivalent to weapons of mass destruction' (United States Department of Defense 2003, p. 1), the US/UK governments had a contradictory policy because of disseminating propaganda to the Iraqi public. Indeed, the CPA planned to have an IMN that was independent and free from any political group, but the plan was destined to fail from the beginning because it remained on paper and was never put into action. In the following section, a discussion is made on the nature of the media rules introduced by the CPA in Iraq.

CPA media regulations

As part of President Bush's plan for Iraq's media, the US government aimed to 'support a free, independent, and responsible Iraqi media (including television, radio, and print) that delivers high-quality content and responsible reporting throughout Iraq' (Bush 2005). In February 2006, US Ambassador to Iraq Zalmay Khalilzad wrote a report on the Iraqi media that was sent to the Department of State. In this report he gives a rather positive account of the media, which is also characteristic of most of his reports on other areas, saying: 'Iraq has advanced light years beyond Saddam-era prohibitions on free speech.... In Iraq today, journalists frequently and openly criticize the government, ministers and senior officials with a freedom that is rare in the region' (Wikileaks 2006b).

During its work in Iraq, the CPA stated its commitment to 'creating an environment in which freedom of speech is cherished and information can be exchanged freely and openly' (CPA/ORD/10 June 2003/14). Paul Bremer, for instance, pointed out the disparity that existed between the Iraqi media before and after the war, saying: 'Under the last regime, it was illegal to criticise the government. Now you are free to criticise whomever or whatever you want' (Jayasekera 2003b). Hence, the original aim was to establish in Iraq the basis of democracy from which the process of democratisation in the Middle East could spread, and IMN was meant to be the model.

The CPA also appointed the British media expert Simon Haselock, whose assignment came from the British Foreign and Commonwealth Office. Haselock previously worked as a spokesperson for the Office of High Representative in Bosnia and as its media commissioner for a period before moving to Iraq (Price 2007, p. 7).[5] In June 2003 he drafted some media regulations that were similar to the ones available in Kosovo (Williams 2003, A14). As a result of Haselock's work, the CPA issued some regulations to organise the work of the Iraqi media, though it stated that the 1969 Iraqi Penal Code would still be applied (CPA/ORD/9 June 2003/07). In other words, the media laws followed by Saddam Hussein would be functional and valid during the CPA's authority. Even after Iraq gained independence and the issuance of the 2005 Constitution, the older laws remained in effect according to Article 130. Order 14, issued on June 10, 2003, under the title 'Prohibited Media

Activity', stated that media organisations are not allowed to publish or broadcast material that:

1. incites violence against any individual or group, including racial, ethnic or religious groups and women;
2. incites civil disorder, rioting or damage to property;
3. incites violence against coalition forces or CPA personnel;
4. advocates alterations to Iraq's borders by violent means; and
5. advocates the return to power of the Iraqi Ba'ath Party or makes statements that purport to be on behalf of the Iraqi Ba'ath Party.

The penalties for violating these regulations vary from being arrested to paying 1000 dollars. This order created a great deal of confusion among journalists because it did not clarify or give details, such as defining the word 'incites'; instead, the term remains vague up to this day, giving more liberty to the CPA, and later Iraqi officials, to issue arrest warrants and imprison journalists. The other significant issue is whether the US-sponsored IMN followed these regulations since its media outlets kept on calling for the elimination of Ba'athists from the society. In other words, it was calling for violence. However, it is not clear whether IMN played a role in instigating some groups to kill officials from the former government and senior Ba'athists after the occupation.

However, Order 14 was later applied to safeguard the CPA alone. Don North observed that US forces started to visit the headquarters of Iraqi newspapers that caused offence and damaged their properties. North even went as far as saying: 'If *The Washington Post* reported terrorist threats or bin Laden statements in Baghdad today, it would probably be closed down' (2004). Since the CPA was in charge of the country and the media sector, it became 'the judge and jury' (RSF 2010, p. 3) at the same time.

One of the first radio stations closed down by the CPA was *Sawt Baghdad* (Voice of Baghdad), only a month after its launch. It was affiliated with Mohammed Mohsen Al-Zubaidi, who announced himself Baghdad's ruler after the occupation, challenging the US authority over the country. The CPA claimed that the radio encouraged people to rob banks (RSF 2003b), though almost all the Iraqi banks were looted during the first days of the occupation under the eyes of US forces. On June 12, 2003, coalition forces closed down *Sada Al-Uma* (The nation's echo) newspaper in Najaf stating that it incited violence against coalition troops by inviting the people of Najaf to join the Sunni resistance in Ramadi city in Anbar province. The newspaper was run by the Shiite

Supreme Council for the Liberation of Iraq – one of the opposition groups that resisted Saddam Hussein's government and operated in the southern marshes (Barry 2003; Rohde 2003). Also, the CPA ordered the closure of *Al-Mustaqila* (independent) newspaper in July 2003 after it published an article 'proclaiming the killing of spies who cooperate with the United States to be a religious duty' (Freedom House 2004). However, the newspaper's editor-in-chief revealed that the article only quoted a religious cleric, and the piece was not solely written by a journalist from the newspaper (Brahimi 2003).

But probably the worst decision taken by the CPA was closing Muqtada Sadr's newspaper *Al-Hawza Al-Natiqa Al-Sharifa*. Sadr's hard-line Shiite movement strongly opposed the occupation. On March 28, 2003, US forces confiscated the weekly newspaper's last edition together with the editions of a quarterly journal called *Al-Mada*. The newspaper was accused of fermenting violence against US forces in Iraq, so its office was closed for 60 days. A letter was handed over to the newspaper's managers, detailing the situations where violations had occurred, such as the publishing of an article entitled 'Bremer Follows the Steps of Saddam' and another one which claimed that US helicopters fired rockets at an Iraqi police station. Following the closure of the newspaper, an insurrection erupted in almost all Shiite areas in the country (Rosen 2004a and 2004b).

Furthermore, the Iraqi Sunni preacher Ahmed Al-Kubaisi established a newspaper which he called *Al-Sa'ah* (The Hour), but the CPA authorities closed it down, despite the fact that he had obtained CPA permission to print it on June 12, 2003 (Abdel Majid 2007, p. 896). Al-Kubaisi was forced to leave the country after organising a joint Sunni–Shiite protest against the occupation in Adhamiah neighbourhood in 2003.

Non-Iraqi media channels were also subject to media restriction. For example, the Qatari-based Al-Jazeera and the Saudi-owned Al-Arabiya channels were closed for a month by the Iraqi Governing Council (IGC) for inciting violence in Iraq. Al-Jazeera was accused of presenting favourable news about Iraqi insurgent groups, whereas Al-Arabiya was blamed for airing an audiotape of one of Saddam Hussein's speeches (Freedom House 2004). In fact, the IGC could not possibly make any decision without being instructed by CPA officials, who were able to veto any of its verdicts.

Price (2007) observed that the CPA saw the media regulations as a 'military necessity' (2007, p. 16), which reflected the fear that US officials had of what is known as 'irresponsible journalism'. However, the CPA's fast and sometimes violent reaction towards any anti-US media outlet and its inaction towards other channels that incited violence and hatred against fellow Iraqi sects, groups, and religions show that the US administration was only concerned about its own safety and the security of its soldiers. Surely this careless and one-sided policy encouraged many Iraqi media channels, which were newly established, to be more polarised and extreme in their criticism and attacks against other fellow Iraqis because of the unlimited freedom given to them. Also, John Erni stressed that the CPA's media policies did not 'appear to be more egalitarian or less draconian' than those during the Ba'ath rule. By applying their 'heavy-handedness' policy, the CPA officials were 'preserving the old culture of totalitarianism. Concepts of freedom, fairness, pluralism, and even human rights might be perceived as empty promises, or worse, as codes of neo-colonialism' (Erni 2006). Indeed, the US authorities in Iraq were not only restricting free speech, but they were also spreading 'positive' messages in the Iraqi media to influence the public, as discussed in the following section.

Order 14 was followed by two others – Orders 65 and 66 – on March 20, 2003. These two orders regulated the work of the National Communications and Media Commission (NCMC). According to Order 65, the CPA stated that the NCMC should follow a regulation that provides 'the fullest exercise of freedom of expression as defined by International Convention, must encourage pluralism and diverse political debate and must empower rather than restrain independent and impartial commentary' (CPA/ORD/20 March 2004/65). The governments of the UK and the USA were directly involved in forming the NCMC. The British Foreign Service Office, in co-ordination with the British Media Development and Advisory Team, was responsible for the 'media and broadcast institutional framework at the NCMC', whereas the US government focused on providing 'technical advice on the telecommunications area' (Wikileaks 2005c).

Finally the CPA issued Order 100, its last decree, which stated that Order 14 remains in effect but the Iraqi prime minister, instead of the CPA civil administrator, has the authority to enforce it (CPA/ORD/28 June 2004/100). In other words, the CPA decree is still valid in Iraq even though the occupation has officially ended.

On June 13, 2003, the CPA selected the IGC's 25 members. In March 2004 the CPA issued an interim constitution known as the Transitional Administrative Law (TAL), which guaranteed freedom of speech and religious expression. The TAL also stipulated that the national assembly election should be held by January 31, 2005. The IGC later formed an interim government which was announced in June 2004, two days before the end of the US-led occupation, according to the UN Security Council Resolution 1546. The reason why the CPA did not hold free elections in the country to choose an interim government was mainly its fear that unfavourable Iraqi figures would emerge. Instead, Tony Blair's special envoy for Iraq attributed the cancellation of the election to the nature of Iraq's culture, which was ' "too weak" for democracy' (Mahajan 2003).

On the same assumption, IMN was managed by the same media regulations that had existed during Saddam Hussein's rule because the Iraqi culture was not yet ready for an independent media. Orayb A Najjar confirms that the new media law in Iraq is more 'restrictive' than the regulations found in some neighbouring Arab countries like Kuwait (2009, p. 46). In a study conducted by Article 19 on hate speech in 14 countries, it found out that many governments accused certain media outlets of spreading hate and inciting violence as a pretext to silence the opposition (D'Souza and Boyle 1992, p. 20). In other words, the US administration used the slogan of democracy and free media as a façade to convince the people that a new positive change had occurred, but in reality media freedom was relatively limited. Despite the clear statements that the CPA protected free speech and defended an independent Iraqi media, there were plenty of incidents on the ground that indicated the opposite (see Al-Rawi, 2011). After forming an Iraqi interim government, the overall management of the media became the responsibility of former Prime Minister Ayad Allawi.

The Iraqi interim government's media

When the CPA and IGC were dissolved, the Iraqi interim government was established to replace them. On June 28, 2004, the new political situation was presented as if Iraq had gained its sovereignty; however, the occupation of the country continued because the US coalition had the final say in whatever happened. The only change that occurred was the placing of an 'Iraqi face' over the occupation. The members of the new government were chosen by the IGC. The key figures were: the Iraqi President Ghazi Al-Yawir, a Sunni Arab who held a ceremonial position and had two deputies – Ibrahim Al-Ja'afari, a Shiite from the Dawa party, and Rowsch Shaways, a Kurd from the KDP. Barham Salih, a Kurd from the PUK, worked as Prime Minister Ayad Allawi's deputy for national security. As for the prime minister, he was a Shiite but with secular orientation. Allawi depended on some British think tanks and media organisations to monitor and assess the media scene. Among the organisations he relied on were the Adam Smith Institute[6] and the Media Development and Advisory Team, which worked closely with the Communications and Media Commission (CMC). One of the positive outcomes of Allawi's premiership was his anti-sectarian policy, but he could not work properly because he faced great pressures from inside and outside the government.

IMN was placed under the direct control of the prime minister. Instead of gaining independence from the US authorities, IMN became closely associated with the actions of the government and tended to express its policies even more than it did during the CPA's era, especially in terms of news content and programmes on public issues. In addition, it clearly became more pro-Shiite than before since most of the politicians in the government were Shiites (Cochrane 2006; Metcalf 2006).

As mentioned earlier, the main media regulatory council was the Iraqi National Communications and Media Commission (NCMC) headed by Siyamend Othman. Yet it was not independent from the authority of the prime minister. On November 23, 2004, Allawi forced four out of the NCMC's nine commissioners to resign (Wikileaks 2005c). This was a recurrent practice carried out by consecutive prime ministers, as Nouri Maliki 're-staffed' the NCMC's board members in 2009 based on his own preferences (Wikileaks 2009e). Noteworthy, NCMC changed its name to CMC during Maliki's first term.

Later, Allawi preferred to form a new media body, calling it the Higher Media Commission (HMC), to exert his full control over IMN and the Iraqi media, so he appointed his long-term friend and media advisor Ibrahim Al-Janabi as its head. The original idea of HMC came when Allawi and Al-Janabi tried, during the autumn of 2004, to persuade the government to make IMN an official mouthpiece of state policy by setting 'aside space in news coverage to make the position of the Iraqi government, which expresses the aspirations of most Iraqis, clear' (International Federation of Journalists 2004). According to Hiwa Osman, Allawi 'illegally appointed' IMN's 'Board of Governors' (Wikileaks 2006c) in order to serve his own interests. As Allawi failed in his efforts to make IMN his official media outlet, he resorted to establishing HMC. Ideally speaking, it was supposed to perform an advisory role by 'developing policy for the government that evaluates and assesses performance, that charts new directions, and that helps to identify opportunities' (Price 2007, p. 17). However, Al-Janabi started to impose very strict rules on media outlets with the announcement of the state of emergency. For instance, any kind of unnecessary criticism against the prime minister was not tolerated.

The 'red lines' or media restrictions were varied, including the mere broadcasting of a Friday speech sermon like that of Muqtada Sadr. When the latter criticised Allawi by calling him 'America's tail', Al-Janabi warned the media channels that to 'broadcast the sermon could be banned' (Pelham 2004). One of the first decisions taken by Allawi's government was to close down Al-Jazeera channel 'indefinitely'. In November 2004, the government even declared that any journalist found reporting for Al-Jazeera would be arrested. US journalist Dahr Jamail reported that his French friend, Sophie-Anne Lamouf, who had covered the events in Falluja city in 2005, was taken by Iraqi security forces from her hotel and was exiled (2007); a measure reminiscent of Saddam Hussein's regime.

On the other hand, supporters of Allawi claimed that the prime minister was liberal and called for a free media, citing one example. Sadr's newspaper *Al-Hawza*, which was closed down by the CPA, was allowed to start publishing again (Pelham 2004). However, what commentators overlooked was the fact that Allawi wanted to gain Sadr's movement's approval for his government because of Sadr's popular appeal. Nevertheless, Allawi's efforts were in vain after he approved the assault on Sadr's militia, the Mahdi Army.

As for the work of the CMC, it remained almost non-influential. It was originally formed to follow Western models like the US Federal Communications or the UK's Ofcom, and had an annual budget of 6 million dollars (Piper 2004). On July 27, 2004, CMC's Interim Broadcasting Code for media outlets in Iraq was passed by the Iraqi parliament. It was followed by an Interim Media Law that stressed that CPA Order 14 should be amended for further clarification. However, the amendment remained 'vague', according to an Article 19 report (2004, p. 25). The new law added a section on fair and impartial programming, stating: 'News reporting should be dispassionate and news judgments based on the need to give viewers and listeners an even-handed account of events' (CMC 2007, p. 14).

In relation to IMN, the CMC's regulation pointed out that Iraq's public broadcasting service should remain independent and must not 'advocate the positions or interests of any particular political, religious, commercial or other party. In doing so, the IMN must ensure the public is aware of different points of view in order to create informed public opinion' (CMC 2007, p. 14). Besides, clear efforts should be followed to make sure that 'programmes about religion or religious groups are accurate and fair. The belief and practice of religious groups must not be misrepresented. Programmes must not denigrate the religious beliefs of others' (ibid.). Finally, in its new law issued on November 22, 2009, the CMC insisted that media channels should refrain from broadcasting any material that encourages hate and violence or incites sectarianism (CMC 2009).

One of the CMC's duties is to monitor the issues covered in different Iraqi media channels. The first report it published was related to the monitoring of 15 Iraqi TV channels; it covered the period from July 22 to August 9, 2010. The CMC is concerned with observing that the TV channels abide by the rules of decency and the basic principles of journalism as stated in its different reports. The findings of the report mention that only five channels broke the media rules; there were 58 breaches committed by five channels (Al-Sharqiya, Al-Rafidain, Al-Babelyia, Afaq, and Iraqia). With regard to Iraqia TV, the report mentions that the channel repeatedly broadcast an interview with Nouri Maliki, three times within two days, in addition to the channel's continuous reminders of the interview's timing in the subtitle (CMC 2010a).

In its second monitoring report covering the period between August 10 and September 9, 2010, the kind of detailed violation has not been mentioned. It states that 15 TV channels were monitored and seven of them violated the CMC's rules, including: Al-Rafidain, Al-Babelyia, Al-Sharqiya, Al-Baghdadia, Baghdad, Afaq, and Al-Sumeria. Al-Baghdadia came ahead of the other channels with up to 162 violations, which were mostly concentrated on breaching manners and public decency (CMC 2010b).

The third monitoring report that was released covered the period of October 1–15, 2010 (CMC 2010c). It marked some progress in terms of the number of channels investigated, which was 22 TV channels and eight radio channels, and the time recorded for each channel – 12 hours a day including the 'golden time', which refers to the prime time and its repetition in the morning. The report mentions that the Iraqi channels covered are all licensed by the CMC except for four – Al-Rafidain, Al-Hadath, Al-Anbar, and Al-Ra'i – and it states that violations of the CMC's media rules were observed in eight TV channels and on two radio stations. Al-Ra'i TV topped the list with 13 violations, and other channels followed: Al-Babelyia (8), Al-Baghdadia (4), Al-Sharqiya and Baghdad (2), Al-Hadath and Al-Masar (1).

Other reports followed with a new format and title since CMC posted the new reports in the *Rassed* newsletter. The first volume of the newsletter covered the period from October 1 to November 30, 2010 (CMC 2010d), while the second volume covered the period from December 1, 2010, to May 31, 2011 (CMC 2010e).

It is important to mention here that most of the channels which allegedly breached CMC's regulations stand in opposition to Maliki's government. The channels that usually top the breaches are: Al-Babelyia, Baghdad, Al-Rafidain, Al-Sharqiya, and Al-Baghdadia. However, the credibility of the CMC's reports is greatly doubted, especially as the investigators' partisan affiliations seem to play a role in any judgements. For example, very few violations were recorded if they deal with insults or breaches against government opposition and its political figures. The main emphasis in these reports is on monitoring what is said against the government and its senior Shiite figures, especially Maliki and his Dawa Party. Other Shiite channels, such as Al-Etejah and Al-Ahad, publicly call for supporting Iranian-backed Shiite militias like the Iraqi Hezbollah and Asa'aib Ahlul Haq, which are regarded by the US government as terrorist organisations (for more details, see Appendix II). This observation was supported by several Iraqi journalists in 2009, who discussed the CMC's monitoring activity and said that this media body is only a 'tool of PM Maliki and his allies – and too partisan to effectively mediate press reporting; several have expressed concern that the CMC is monitoring media reporting at all' (Wikileaks 2009f). The US Ambassador to Iraq, Christopher Hill, asserted in 2009 that the CMC's 'role as an independent regulator is far from solidified in Iraq's evolving political climate' (ibid.).

According to Article 103 of the 2005 Iraqi Constitution, the CMC is a 'financially and administratively independent' body. However, the CMC could not live up to the expectations of Iraqis because of government pressure and interference (Al-Jezairy 2006, p. 11). In December 2004 the CMC drafted a Media Code for the forthcoming elections to be held in January 2005. The code dictated the rules that should be followed by all political groups, and especially by IMN, which should remain neutral.

In early January 2005, the CMC published almost all of its media regulations in different newspapers, especially those related to the conduct of journalists and media channels during the elections. The newspapers included the Saudi-sponsored *Asharq Al-Awsat* (Baghdad edition), *Al-Mada, Baghdad, Al-Nahdha, Al-Dustoor, Al-Takhi, Al-Adalah*, and *Al-Itihad* (National Media Center n.d., p. 29). Nevertheless, Allawi made ample use of the Iraqia channel. For instance, he was shown on TV giving a speech as a prime minister and behind him was the banner of his electoral slate. Also, he started a talk show in which he answered phone calls from distressed Iraqis complaining about security issues and public services (Usher 2005a).

When a meeting was held by Allawi's slate to discuss their political programme, the channel aired it live to the public (Usher 2005a). During the second elections held in December 2005, many government Shiite ministers affiliated with the ISCI and Dawa parties had their own share in the Iraqia channel, making some Iraqis complain of obvious bias (Usher 2005b). Iraqi journalist Saad Al Saraf, from Star TV Network, revealed that the CMC could not successfully monitor the issue of 'media bias', particularly during the election. 'Indeed, there seems to be a sort of "look the other way" approach to enforcing the commission's rules, such as the ban on "spreading sectarian, racial and religious sedition and strife" ' (Cochrane 2006). (See Chapter 5 for more details.)

On January 30, 2005, a general election in Iraq was held to appoint the Transitional National Assembly, whose responsibility included drafting a permanent constitution. The Shiite coalition United Iraqi Alliance (UIA) won most of the seats, and Ibrahim Al-Ja'afari from the Dawa Party was selected as the new prime minister. He assumed office in April 2005 and remained there until May 2006. Following the second general elections in December 2005, Ja'afari remained in office representing UIA due to the support he got from all of Sadr's members in the Assembly. However, Iraq witnessed intense sectarian violence during Ja'afari's rule due to his narrow vision, pro-Shiite policies, and the attack that occurred against the Shiite holy Shrine in Samaraa on February 22, 2006.

With regard to IMN control, a conflict of interests happened between Allawi's loyalists and the newly elected prime minister's staff. When Ja'afari came to power, he paid careful attention to restructuring IMN by 'hiring and firing editors, and directing editorial policy' (Levinson 2006). The new prime minister made several changes to the management of IMN, such as at Iraqia TV and *Al-Sabah* newspaper (Al-Jezairy 2006, p. 11). Habib Al-Sadr was appointed as director of the Iraqia channel and Mohammad Jassim Khudayer was appointed its deputy director. Khudayer was also the second man in the Shiite Daawa Movement, which entered the 2005 election with list number 553 (Wikileaks 2005i). Other journalists were either fired or pressured. Mohammed Abdul Jabbar, editor-in-chief of *Al-Sabah*, was exempted from his duties because he did not toe the line of the Dawa Party; for instance, he did not highlight Ja'afari's activities on the newspaper's front page. Sawsan Al-Jazrawi, a senior Iraqi journalist working for IMN, revealed that the new prime minister's supporters 'pressured us to show certain interviews and to rerun programs that served Ja'afari's interests' (Levinson 2006).

But the prime minister's control of IMN ceased in September 2005 when the Shiite ISCI's former leader, Abdul Aziz Al-Hakim, took over. However, Habib Al-Sadr remained as director because he was related by marriage to Al-Hakim's family (Wikileaks 2005b),[7] and he started highlighting the activities of his new superior (Levinson 2006). When Maliki came to power, Al-Sadr remained in his position because he was used to satisfy the people in power. Former directors of IMN described Al-Sadr as an opportunist because he made IMN's coverage of Maliki 'overwhelmingly favorable and in some cases, "flattering"' (Wikileaks 2006c). Ahmed Al-Rikabi pointed out that Al-Sadr was keen to survive because his job included many benefits like receiving 'paychecks from several prominent politicians' (ibid.).

Again, due to the sensitive nature of information released by Wikileaks cables, it is important to refer to them in some detail, especially as no other source revealed such confidential and highly relevant information. The worst blow to Iraqia TV was to have Habib Al-Sadr, with his overtly sectarian affiliations, as its general director. The Iraqi president's media advisor, Hiwa Osman, once revealed that Al-Sadr was the one who 'allowed Al-Iraqqiyya to become more and more sectarian, allowing, for example, Shi'a music[8] to be played during intercessory periods between major programs' (Wikileaks 2007d). Osman further pointed out that the channel was instrumental in dividing Sunnis and Shiites, especially when it aired 'the morning prayer... [which] included the verse, "may God curse the first, second and third", which is a reference to the Sunni caliphs' (Wikileaks 2006c).

Another Wikileaks cable referred to an important meeting held on May 4, 2006, between US Embassy officials, Hiwa Osman and two former directors of IMN, Ahmad Al-Rikabi and Jalal Al-Mashta, during which many facts were revealed that showed the biased way that Al-Sadr led IMN. Al-Rikabi and Al-Mashta, for example, disclosed that the Iraqia channel 'routinely cuts away from scheduled programming to air live Shia celebrations in Najaf', and the two 'complained that Al-Sadr had completely removed any public service aspect from Iraqiyya's programming, and was actively using the medium to promote Shia, rather than national, unity' (Wikileaks 2006c). The three media experts were not able to 'recall ever seeing a single Sunni, Christian or Kurdish program on the station' (ibid.).

A Wikileaks cable revealed that Asa'd Al-Rubaie, an Iraqi journalist who worked for Iraqia TV, confided to a US Embassy official in Baghdad that Al-Sadr was responsible for deceiving the public since he 'was changing facts in news reports because he is loyal to some religious leaders who are his relatives'. This account confirms the other accusations directed against Iraqia TV, as stated earlier. Al-Rubaie confirmed that the 'top leadership of Al-Iraqiyya belongs to religious parties, and most of the staff of Al-Iraqiyya's staff of 3000 is cooperating with Habib Al-Sadr's orders, because they are afraid of him' (Wikileaks 2007d).

According to a CMC report in 2007, IMN seriously needed 'internal pluralism', which could only be achieved by 'the inclusion of women and representatives of Iraq's various ethnic, religious and political groups – among members of its board and management and among its reporters and on-air personalities' (2007, p. 42). The CMC described IMN as a biased media body that was not reliable enough to represent Iraqis in an objective manner:

> We are not yet at the day when the IMN is credited for reporting that is truly balanced, when the IMN has independent and guaranteed revenue streams, and when it is thought effectively to hold the government accountable. It is currently not designed to resist direct and indirect political pressure.
>
> (2007, p. 42)

Unfortunately, other Iraqi media outlets became polarised and followed the mainstream by siding with either Sunnis or Shiites, mostly after the Samaraa bombing (Al-Marashi 2007, p. 100). Hence, they only increased the sectarian tension in the streets (Roug 2006). Even Solagh, the Interior Minister, urged Iraqi journalists to follow 'objective reporting' and refrain from 'exaggerations' to avoid enhancing hatred and division in the society (cited in Abedin 2006). In fact, many Iraqi channels were preoccupied with their own groups, and in the process any other groups were eliminated from their daily shows. But what characterised this era was the fact that these channels presented their own groups as victims. For instance, Baghdad TV, run by the Sunni Iraqi Islamic Party, focused on presenting the crimes committed against Sunnis by Shiite security bodies and Mahdi Army militias. According to its director, Ahmed Rushdi, Baghdad TV should be contrasted with the state-run Iraqia channel because the former had 'no sectarian bias', saying: 'We are always showing the facts as they are' (Roug 2006). In fact, this is a claim that is adhered to by almost all Iraqi channels.

In contrast, Shiite-oriented channels like Al-Fayhaa TV, ISCI's Al-Furat TV, and Iraqia TV concentrated on showing the suffering of Shiites under Saddam Hussein's regime and the destruction that occurred to the Holy Shiite Shrine in Samaraa. Al-Furat TV, which is affiliated with two other channels – Al-Nahrayn TV in Kut and Ghadir TV in Najaf (Metcalf 2006), which are funded by ISCI – announced that Shiites should 'stand up for their rights', indirectly suggesting killing Sunnis (Cochrane 2006).

However, no action was taken against or a warning given to the channel by the CMC.

In general, in the midst of this highly tense situation, very few Iraqi TV channels were able to maintain independence. Mohammad Shaboot, former editor-in-chief of the governmental *Al-Sabah* newspaper, said in this regard that Al-Furat TV and Baghdad TV were both fermenting the sectarian spirit in the society, stating that: 'No one has invested in a real, nationwide Iraqi channel for all Iraqis' (Roug 2006).

Other channels that periodically broadcast talk shows, which involve hosting Iraqi figures and receiving phone calls and emails from Iraqis living inside and outside the country, do, in fact, incite violence and sectarianism. Saadoun Al-Bayati, a media analyst, says that the effect of these talk shows is 'more risky than carrying arms' (Ghazi 2006). All these types of tensions only lead to more media polarisation and fewer liberties. According to Fred Vultee, during civil conflicts the press becomes more restricted than during interstate wars (2009).

Finally, the US influence over the Iraqi media was slowly beginning to diminish as its influence became unseen due to the efforts of the Pentagon's media contractors, as discussed in Chapter 3. However, within the confusion that occurred during Ja'afari's government, the US authorities preferred to sit still and watch, yet the support remained. A US cable sent to the Department of State from Baghdad in June 2005 revealed that the US Embassy and the US international development agency supported the Iraqia channel in different ways (Wikileaks 2005b). However, there are still many questions which need to be answered. For example, why did the US forces not close down sectarian media outlets that incited hatred between Sunnis and Shiites even though they were quick in shutting other media outlets that incited violence against their soldiers? Why did the US military not react to Ja'afari's sectarian policies? Why did the US military not actively intervene to stop the violence that erupted after the Samaraa event? Why did the US authorities not exert pressure on the prime minister to protect IMN and assist in turning it into a real public broadcasting service? In one incident in January 2006, Iraqi journalist Dr Ali Fadhil, working for Channel 4 and the *Guardian*, was arrested after it was discovered that he was investigating claims that tens of millions of Iraqi funds disappeared after being held by UK and US authorities in Iraq (Fadhil 2006; the *Guardian* 2006). Again, this incident sheds light on the kind of freedom and independence that the Iraqi media has.

In brief, IMN's pro-Shiite sectarian policy, whose seeds were planted by the Pentagon, played a role in agitating the public, and in particular the Sunnis, against the government. Programmes like 'Terrorism in the Grip of Justice' only fuelled hatred and enhanced grudges from both Sunnis and Shiites.

Nouri Maliki's media monopoly

In 2006, after pressure from the USA, the Dawa Party, and the Iraqi parliament, Ja'afari stepped down to be replaced by Nouri Maliki, another prominent Shiite leader from the Dawa party. Maliki assumed office on May 20, 2006, and is still holding this post.

All in all, what happened on the political front was directly reflected in the media scene. In October 2006, death squads raided the building of the Iraqi Al-Shaabiya TV channel in mid-town Baghdad and killed 11 of its staff, including its manager Abdul Raheem Al-Shimiri. No reports from the Iraqi police or security bodies were released to the public about these murders (Jamail 2007).

During Maliki's government, an Iraqi TV channel called Al-Zawraa caused great controversy. It was run by Mishaan Al-Jubouri, a former Iraqi MP. The channel started broadcasting in Iraq but stopped because of government pressure, especially after airing footage of Iraqis mourning their former president, Saddam Hussein, after his execution. The channel's manager escaped to Syria as he was accused of corruption and embezzlement (McDonough 2007). Al-Zawraa later managed to air its programmes through the Egyptian satellite Nilesat, and focused on showing the activities of the insurgent groups; it called on Iraqis to wage a *jihad* against the occupying US forces. When the channel began to criticise the Shiite government and some of its politicians for their co-operation with US forces and for the attacks against Sunni civilians, some accused it of being sectarian. Al-Marashi claims that the channel made 'derogatory' remarks about Iraqi Shiites because it described them as *Safawis* (2007, p. 115) – a reference to the Safavid Iranian Empire that occupied Iraq in the 16th century and tried to turn it into a Shiite state. However, the term was used after Iraq's occupation in 2003 to refer to Iraqi Shiite politicians and groups who came from Iran and called for protecting Iranian interests. As a result of it airing anti-coalition footage, the US government pressured the Egyptian Minister of Culture to close the station down; thus, the channel stopped broadcasting after a short while.

Meanwhile, the Kurds found a golden opportunity to practise their control over the northern parts of the country, especially in the cities of Mosul and Kirkuk. This kind of power was manifested in the media sector, too. For example, the Kurds who are interested in having a federal Iraq to annex the oil-rich city of Kirkuk into Kurdistan, tried to spread the concept of federalism in the Arab-dominated areas. Accordingly, Kurdish officials gave bribe money to some Arabic newspapers like *Wadi Ar-Rafidain*, *Al-Masar*, and *Bela Ittijah* (Al-Jezairy 2006, p. 12), which are published in Mosul to achieve this purpose. Most Iraqis do not trust Kurdish media outlets since they are suspicious of the Kurdish separatist motives behind federalism. As a result, the PUK and KDP started to use other media channels for disseminating their ideology. For instance, the newspaper *Al-Mada*, which is backed by the Iraqi Communist Party, started to publish messages favourable to the Kurds' cause after getting support from the two main Kurdish parties (Al-Jezairy 2006).

As clarified earlier, the sectarian spirit spread in the society, and media channels played a role in enhancing hatred and schism. Maliki, who was partly responsible for what happened, confessed that the situation was out of control since TV 'channels, mosques, journalism, and people in the streets are all inciting in a way that this present government cannot control' (*The Associated Press* 2006).

During Maliki's era, media freedom was not better than that during Ja'afari's time. The Iraqi Ministry of Interior started to play a bigger role in silencing media outlets deemed too critical of the government. In a meeting on January 29, 2007, between Maliki's advisor on media affairs, Yasseen Majid, and US Ambassador Khalilzad, Majid partially attributed the closure of TV stations and the intervention of the Iraqi Ministry of Interior in such closures to the head of the CMC, Siyamend Othman. Majid claimed that the CMC had a strong role to play as a media watchdog under CPA Order 65, but it was not ready to perform its duties in the right manner (Wikileaks 2007b). Several channels, such as Salahadin and Al-Sharqiya, were closed down for allegedly inciting sectarianism. Al-Sharqiya, which is regarded as the most popular channel in Iraq, showed a protest against the execution of Saddam Hussein on December 30, 2006. Afterwards, a news presenter on Al-Sharqiya TV was shown wearing black as a sign of mourning (Jamail 2007). After its closure the channel started broadcasting from Dubai, but it remained active in covering Iraq's news. However, attacks against Al-Sharqiya did not cease. In September 2008 the channel aired a disturbing programme called 'Torture in Iraqi Prisons' about the atrocities committed by Shiite security forces mainly against Sunni Arabs. Six days later, four employees from Al-Sharqiya were kidnapped and killed in Mosul city. The manager of Al-Sharqiya, Ali Wajih, accused the Iraqia channel of being behind the attack because the latter started a 'campaign of slander against the journalists working in Al-Sharqiya' after airing the aforementioned programme. Wajih stressed that the 'government's channel and those who stand behind it bear ethical and moral responsibility for the crime' (*Agence France Presse* 2008; Gambill 2009).

In another incident, Major General Qassim Atta, the spokesperson for the Iraq Army's Baghdad Operations, threatened on April 13, 2009, to close down the office of Al-Sharqiya TV for airing false news about his alleged orders that ex-detainees freed by the US Army would be arrested again. Al-Sharqiya TV had only quoted the newspaper *Al-Hayat*, which later published an apology for the false news. Later, Atta filed a lawsuit against *Al-Hayat* and Al-Sharqiya TV. But a media war ensued after the two media outlets received threatening phone calls allegedly from Atta himself. Al-Sharqiya challenged Atta by airing the same story, which called him a 'Baathist, and questioned his professional qualifications and tribal affiliation'. The channel later described Atta as the 'Liar of Baghdad' and 'accused him of "insulting Iraqis, stirring sedition, and promoting sectarian discrimination"' (Wikileaks 2009b). According to Kadhim Al-Rikabi, the program manager for the International Research & Exchanges Board (IREX)'s Supporting Independent Media in Iraq programme, the true reason behind Atta's violent reaction was 'King Abdullah of Saudi Arabia's refusal to meet privately with Prime Minister Al-Maliki during the March 2009 Arab League Summit in Doha' (ibid.).

Finally, there was a great deal of corruption, too. Aside from the money wasted on IMN, some participants in the 2007 UNESCO conference voiced their concern over the cost of training 10 media professionals outside Iraq, which amounted to 250,000 dollars (Wikileaks 2007a).

On the other hand, positive signs started to appear with IMN in mid-2008 with the escalating US pressure on Maliki to establish a reconciliation with Sunnis and his need to include all the different groups in his government. For instance, programmes describing issues related to Sunnis and other groups in the society were shown, unlike before. As a result, Maliki decided to stop airing the distinctive Shiite call of prayer on Iraqia TV in 2008 (Cambridge Arab Media Project 2010, p. 29). Amnesty International, however, reported in 2010 that about 30,000 detainees were held in Iraq under similar conditions to those of Saddam Hussein's rule; the majority of those prisoners were Sunni Arabs, mostly detained without trial (Amnesty International 2010, p. 5, p. 6, and p. 20).

The National Media Center and IMN

The second phase of the post-invasion media in Iraq occurred in 2008 with the relative decline of the sectarian rhetoric in the media and the increasingly authoritarian control of the prime minister over the Iraqi media. Shik Hun Kim predicted that the Iraqi media, whose previous authoritarian experience resembles that of the former communist countries in Eastern Europe, will witness a further regression into an authoritarian press instead of having a libertarian press system (Kim 2007; Kim and Hama-Saeed 2008, p. 592).

Maliki established the National Media Center (NMC) on March 19, 2007. The Iraqi prime minister signed Decree 54, making NMC an official media body that is directly linked to the chairman of the Council of Ministers (Iraq's cabinet). In May 2009 the Council of Ministers ratified the law in its 18th session, allowing the centre to expand and become more influential. Similar to Ayad Allawi's Higher Media Commission, the NMC is formed to plan and implement the media policy of the central government, the provinces and governorates and unify their rhetoric to communicate media messages to local and international media. It is also responsible for creating programmes and policies to cover national ceremonies, measuring public-opinion trends, representing Iraq at international conferences, following up on the activities of media bureaus linked to the government, monitoring local and international media messages, writing down news and press releases, and facilitating the work of journalists to cover government activities (Presidency Council 2009; National Media Center n.d.).

In other words, the NMC is a substitute for the infamous Ministry of Information during Saddam Hussein's rule. According to several observers, the NMC is controlled by Maliki's office, as its head, Ali Hadi Al-Musawi, is one of Maliki's media advisors and must report to him directly. In an interview on Al-Baghdadia TV on January 25, 2010, Al-Musawi claimed that the 'Iraqi government does not have or run any media channel', not even 'Iraqia TV that is like the BBC'. Al-Musawi's statement is theoretically correct because he is referring to the fact that Iraqia TV is a public broadcasting station, as it was first envisioned to be. However, practically speaking the channel is far from being independent from the Iraqi government or being run by the public. Zuhair Al-Jezairy, who is closely affiliated with the Iraqi government, says that the NMC supervises the work of the official media channels, including Iraqia TV and radio as well as the newspaper *Assabah* (Al-Jezairy 2010b, p. 102).

An Iraqi journalist who worked for Iraqia TV secretly disclosed to a US official that Maliki's media advisor Yasseen Majeed used to control 'operations in Al-Iraqiyya by making direct phone calls to news directors. He noted, for example, there was one time when the PM's office ordered news directors to stop broadcasting coverage of a political official it opposed' (Wikileaks 2007d). In fact, Majeed abused the power given to him by the prime minister to exert more control over IMN. According to Dhia Al-Nasiri, the director of Al-Arabiya channel in Baghdad in 2007, Majeed had a 'say regarding who is employed at Al-Iraqiyya and that the PM's office pressures Iraqiyya producers, who remain silent because they are supporting families' (ibid.).

In early 2007, Maliki fired IMN board members without getting the necessary approval from the Council of Representatives as stipulated by law. The prime minister appointed a new board in February with a Shiite majority. The newly formed board consisted of eight members: five Shiites (one of whom was secular), two Kurds, and one secular Sunni (Wikileaks 2007c). It is important to note that one of Maliki's aides tried in late 2005 to replace some of the IMN board members with those affiliated with the Dawa party, but the attempt failed (Wikileaks 2005h). This kind of conflict clearly shows that the powerful political parties in Iraq are trying to control the top positions at IMN to secure a free-of-charge media voice that supports their agenda and interests.

Most importantly, Maliki paid the headquarters of IMN in Baghdad a visit on September 28, 2009, just a few months before the 2010 election. This was regarded as one way of influencing the editorial policy of the Iraqia channel. He gave a speech to the staff in which he revealed several important points that contradicted Al-Musawi's previous claims about the independence of IMN. Maliki asserted that the Iraqi media throughout all its stages was controlled either by a party or a government official. The Iraqi citizen was forced to consume the news whether he liked it or not. 'But today, there is confidence in the Iraqi media that increases day by day whenever the media responds to the concerns of citizens' (Iraqia Channel 2009). He also mentioned that the freedom of the media has limits that stop with the top national interests, freedom of others and the professional responsibility of journalists. Maliki confirmed the following:

Iraqia satellite channel is, in fact, the satellite channel of the Iraqi government which carries some commitments. When we say the satellite channel of the Iraqi government, it means that it should support the Iraqi state with its problems, challenges, and achieve-ments. It should promote the good actions [taken by the govern-ment] and correct the other [bad] practices. When we say the satellite channel of the Iraqi government, it should never be, necessarily, against the policy of the state or should repeat irresponsibly the mis-takes [that occur]. Instead, the channel should point out the mistake in a responsible manner. Hence, the Iraqi channel is a difficult case to balance.

(Iraqia Channel 2009)

The statement cited above clearly shows that there is no IMN indepen-dence and that it is far different from the BBC, for example. However, Maliki turned to other senior managers at IMN and they agreed that IMN followed the examples of CNN and the BBC. In this regard, the Iraqi prime minister said: 'I asked some [experts] whether the BBC voices some views that oppose the state policy, and I was informed that it does not do so' (ibid.). It is not clear who those experts are or to which period he is referring to. Maliki also pointed out that other private satellite channels that voice the opinions of parties are free to say what they want because they represent particular parties. 'Sectarian channels are also free to speak because they talk about their sect or ethnic origins. But al-Iraqia is the mouthpiece of the government, and the [Iraqi] state has many sects, doctrines, races, and parties, so its responsibility is grave, serious, and difficult' (ibid.). Maliki expressed his gratitude and appre-ciation for the 'supportive stance' of IMN staff towards promoting the Iraqi government, which Maliki confirmed to be 'their responsibility'. He also wanted the staff to report on 'the positive achievements of the Iraqi government' (ibid.).

The Iraqi prime minister accused the Iraqia channel of lacking profes-sionalism and being biased. 'There were some practices that did not suit the government's channel when it [covered] some [events] or actions that are only fit for ordinary citizens' (ibid). He referred to the channel's one-sided coverage because some people raised 'questions on why does not the channel cover the activities of the other [parties], or particular group[s] or race[s]' (ibid.).

Specifically, Maliki was upset by the fact that the channel covered the activities of some political figures from other parties. He declared that there were accusations that the channel is being 'politicised or con-trolled by others. If it falls under such an accusation, its danger will be bigger on the Iraqi government' (ibid.). He also gave an example about the lack of professionalism. There was once a discrepancy between the official stance of the government towards a terrorist investigation and what the Iraqia channel showed on its subtitle.

In an unprecedented move, Maliki tried to dictate to IMN staff how to report and what to say. For example, he said that when some shortcomings in the Iraqi state are highlighted, some correspondents would say: 'This is the role of the national unity government, so where are the slogans that you used to talk about?' (ibid.). Maliki disappointingly states: 'This is not the right rhetoric that should be aired by Iraqia channel'. Then he accuses the correspondent of being an 'infiltrator into the channel whose aim is to ruin its work.... There is an [agenda] that is backed by some sides that want to harm [the government] through al-Iraqiya channel' (ibid.). Finally, he threatens such correspondents who point their finger towards the government by saying: 'By God's will, such examples who benefit from working at Iraqia channel to disseminate such ideas will not stay' (ibid.).

In another example of his editorial intervention, Maliki mentioned that 'when you make an interview, you usually bring two guests with opposing views. But Iraqia channel interviewed once two Egyptian experts who are on one side and they both have animosity against [us] and regard [the government] as criminals and killers' (ibid.). The Iraqi prime minister admitted that he 'immediately called the chairman of Iraqia channel and questioned him about his choice' (ibid.). As a result, the programme manager 'stopped airing the show while it was live on air' (ibid.). In a clear and direct manner, Maliki pointed out his real intention behind visiting the channel by saying that the Iraqia channel 'should not promote any party in the election. It is the equilibrium between professionalism and nationalism' (ibid.).

Despite all the criticism against the channel for siding with the Shiites against the Sunnis, Maliki praised Iraqia TV because it had 'a good stance during the sectarian tensions', but he asserted that the channel 'cannot side with one sect over the other' (ibid.). Maliki announced in May 2009 that Iraq was the best country in the Middle East in terms of press freedom, regardless of the fact that tens of defamation lawsuits were filed against journalists and all the media restrictions imposed by the Iraqi government on media outlets. He claimed that Iraq is 'proud not to punish journalists and not to impose restrictions on their work' (*Agence France Presse* 2009). Maliki was probably eyeing Article 38 of the 2005 Iraqi Constitution that guaranteed freedom of speech, but what he overlooked was the report issued by Freedom House that listed the ranking of countries in terms of freedom of the press. In 2009, Iraq's media was described as 'not free' and came at number 9 out of 19 countries in the Middle East and North Africa and at number 148 out of 195 countries around the world (Freedom House 2009).

Finally, Maliki expressed his hope that Iraqia will co-ordinate with other channels to make them follow its example. 'Thanks to God they are other "good" channels . . . that are also termed government channels because they are owned by parties that are represented in the government or parliament' (Iraqia Channel 2009). Maliki admits here that many channels that belong to political parties are no different from the Iraqia channel since they all support the government and its policies.

Maliki confessed once that many violations are committed against Iraqi journalists and justified them by saying: 'we [Iraqis] have inherited from the previous regime a certain kind of mentality, scheme, and way of thinking that need time to change' (Iraqia Channel 2009). The prime minister's justification is similar to the way that Saddam Hussein's Ba'ath regime used to justify government inaction and a lack of services since it used to cite the effects of the 'economic sanctions' and the 'imperialist conspiracies' against Iraq.

Less media freedom and more libel suits

Iraqi journalists remain in a state of fear despite the political change and the calls for democracy. Unlike the period that characterised Saddam Hussein's autocratic rule, when journalists knew the red lines (politics, religion, and some socio-cultural taboos), today those journalists are exercising stricter self-censorship to avoid falling into difficulties with the different political parties and armed militias that have different agendas and topics of which coverage is forbidden (Prusher 2003b). Also, new work practices have emerged, such as the custom for some journalists to accept small bribes from some officials to cover certain events or write favourably about them due to the low wages they get from their media institutions (IWPR 2009).

With the help of the US Embassy in Baghdad, IREX organised several round-table talks with Iraqi journalists, media NGOs, and academics. At the third meeting held on May 14, 2009, at Al-Monsoor Hotel in Baghdad, the group that were extremely critical of the Iraqi government media monopoly called themselves the 'February 30 Committee' because 'the chance of there being freedom of the press in Iraq is about the same as the existence of the date February 30' (Wikileaks 2009c). Among the topics discussed was the status of media freedom in the country. The attendees expressed their concern over the growing self-censorship practised by Iraqi journalists and pointed out 'the difficulty in exposing fraud and corruption within the government, as such claims, even if true, would likely lead to civil or criminal prosecution, confiscation of property and equipment and further censorship'. Ziyad Al-Ajili, JFO director, concluded that 'there is no such thing as freedom of press in Iraq; it does not exist' (ibid.).

During another closed round-table discussion held on the July 9, 2009, with US Baghdad Embassy staff, IREX, and a group of Iraqi media journalists and experts, the Iraqi journalists voiced their dissatisfaction with Maliki's media restrictions. The US report mentioned that the participants were 'universally critical of the government's manipulation of the press and condemned the use of public money – including some from USG [US government] sources – that fund politicians' and political parties' media outlets'. Further, the attendees felt that they ' "have no voice" to defend themselves against a crackdown on freedom of the press', stating that the Iraqi government's methods were 'both overt (direct threats, arrests and confiscation of equipment) and more subtle (an increase in lawsuits against individual journalists and media outlets)' (Wikileaks 2009d).

As stated earlier, Maliki wanted to exercise his authority over IMN, whose heads and staff vary in their allegiances, and over the CMC, by creating a more powerful media body. In reality, the NMC has only complicated the Iraqi media scene because it intensified the struggle for media control in the country.

Many Iraqi government officials become agitated and start a backlash against journalists when they are criticised in the media. The CMC's 2007 report revealed that 'journalists face the challenge of reporting on other parties critically.... Journalists who are too critical of other factions often have been subjected to blackmail and death threats, if not death itself' (2007, p. 5). The purpose of the continuing libel suits is to pressure journalists, force them to abandon criticising the officials, and make them practise self-censorship. For example, two journalists working on a newspaper in Wasit province were given a prison sentence by an Iraqi judge in April 2005 after criticising the provincial government and police for the lack of services and security (Finer 2005, A01).

The defamation charges were based on the Iraqi Penal Code of 1969, as stated above. In 2009, Ahmed Abdul Hussein, an Iraqi journalist working for the newspaper *Al-Sabah*, was threatened by senior ISCI leader Jalal Al-Deen Al-Sagheer during a Friday prayer speech for criticising his party members who were involved in killing eight bank guards and stealing 3.8 million dollars (*Middle East Online* 2009a). This action led tens of Iraqi journalists to protest the kind of media freedom they had in the new Iraq (*Middle East Online* 2009b). Hence, it is very normal that other journalists would not dare to criticise and would be gradually silenced.

Many libel suits were filed in the courts against Iraqi media outlets and journalists. For example, the Iraqi Minister of Trade filed two libel suits against the newspapers *Al-Mashriq* and *Al-Parlaman*, which accused him of corruption. Fortunately, the minister dropped the cases later. The daily newspaper *Al-Baynah Al-Jadeedah* received two complaints and its managers were taken to court for libel suits filed by the Oil Ministry and Al-Mansour Company (RSF 2009a). Also, Prime Minister Nouri Maliki filed a defamation suit against an Iraqi website called Kitabat, which is run from Germany because one of its writers, Ayad Zamili, accused the prime minister's chief of staff of favouritism in securing jobs for his relatives (RSF 2009b).

Furthermore, TV channel Al-Diyar was ordered to pay 10 million dinars for a defamation lawsuit filed on April 19, 2009, by the director of the Real Estate in the Ministry of Transportation. Ironically, the lawsuit was brought after the channel aired a programme in which a TV presenter read a piece of news from an Iraqi newspaper (JFO 2009).

Finally, Maliki filed a libel suit against British newspaper the *Guardian*, for publishing an article written by its Iraqi reporter about the authoritarian way that Maliki ran the country. An Iraqi court ordered the newspaper to pay 52,000 pounds as compensation for defaming the prime minister (Chulov and Borger 2009). Despite this the newspaper refused to disclose the identity of the Iraqi intelligence officer who revealed the information about Maliki's intervention in the national intelligence agency and his autocratic rule.

In another development, the government issued stricter media regulations than those seen after 2003. For instance, it decided to monitor all the publications imported into the country (*Middle East Online* 2009b) and to cross-check any publication issued inside the country before giving the publishing house the green light to print it (*Al-Hayat* 2009). As a reaction to the government censorship, some private printing houses in Iraq, especially in Sunni areas, started publishing books that were deemed 'dangerous' by the Iraqi authorities without getting the required approval from the Ministry of Culture. Most of these clandestine printing presses publish sensational books dealing with the resistance and the abuses of US and Iraqi forces in detention facilities (Al-Mukhtar 2009). The government also imposed new rules on the use of the Internet; it decided to deny access to any websites containing references to sectarianism, pornography, and terrorism (Salaheddin 2009).

It is important to note that the Iraqi government also added another media tool to its belt to reach more people, especially 'Iraqis living abroad; it launched its own YouTube channel, which is also sponsored by the NMC. At its inauguration Nouri Maliki mentioned that this channel is meant to be one of the means of communicating with the outside world (YouTube 2009a). According to the website, the channel was launched on February 9, 2008.[9] NMC head Ali Al-Musawi, in an interview on the Iraqia channel, said that the YouTube channel is founded not only to promote the achievements of the government but also to show the reality of life in Iraq in its different facets. It was meant to fill a gap 'since there is no active media outlet that can communicate the achievement of the Iraqi governments in terms of the economy, security, politics, and the formation of a democratic state'. He also asserted that the YouTube comments posted on the clips that contain some negative remarks or insults are deleted (YouTube 2009c). In other words, the Iraqi government wants a media channel that only reflects positive news rather than the negative, just like the way that its news editor produces news, as mentioned above.

Conclusion

After Maliki was re-elected as prime minister in 2011, several protests were organised in different parts of Iraq demanding an end to corruption and joblessness. Many Iraqi news outlets criticised the government and some political parties for their alleged role in the deterioration of living standards and the spread of lawlessness. As a result, several journalists were beaten in Basrah on March 4, 2011, and the office of the JFO, which is supported by the Institute of War and Peace Reporting, was destroyed by security forces in Baghdad. In the Kurdish city of Sulymaniah, Voice radio station together with Nalia Radio and Television were stormed by men wearing security uniforms and closed down for airing the protests that were held against the main political party (Barzanji 2011; Tawfeeq 2011). In other words, there is no improvement, if not a regression, in the way that Iraqi media outlets and journalists have been treated in the past few years.

Following the 2003 Iraq War, Iraq has become the worst country in the world for the safety of journalists since the Second World War, with an unprecedented number of journalists killed. The number even exceeds those murdered in the 20 years of the Vietnam War and the Algerian civil war. More than 230 media personnel have died, including journalists and their assistants; 93 per cent of them were men. Hundreds of other journalists have been forced to flee to neighbouring countries (RSF 2009b and RSF 2010). According to the Committee to Protect Journalists (CPJ), 136 journalists were killed as a direct result of their media work up to the end of 2008; 90 per cent of them were Iraqis (CPJ 2008). For six consecutive years, from 2003 to 2008 Iraq had the highest number of murdered journalists whose cases have yet to be resolved. Noteworthy, the number of murdered journalists from 2003 to early 2012 increased to 150 (CPJ 2012). From 2001 to 2011, 92 journalists have been killed, but the government is either 'unable or unwilling to prosecute the killers' (CPJ 2011). Also, Iraq is regarded as 'the world's biggest market for hostages. Over 93 media professionals were abducted' from 2003 to 2010, 'at least 42 of whom were later executed. Moreover, 14 are still missing' (RSF 2010). The Global Peace Index of 2010 mentioned that Iraq came in at number 143 and ranked as the worst country in the world in terms of the lack of security and peace (Institute for Economics and Peace 2010).

Aside from the governments of Saudi Arabia and Iran, Turkey provided its support for the Iraqi Turkomen's media, while other regional powers showed their mostly sectarian affiliations, such as the Wahabi/Salafi movements in Saudi Arabia, the Muslim Brothers in Egypt, the Shiite Hezbollah in Lebanon, and other Shiite groups in the rich Arab Gulf. All of these groups exerted their influence on the Iraqi media by different means, like pouring in money, empowering political parties, spreading ideology, and enticing selected Iraqi audiences by means of fear and reward. In the end, there was more disunity in the Iraqi society and consequently more polarisation in the media. Indeed, there are different channels affected by the intervention of foreign powers, the influence of internal disputes and political interests, and the effect of ethnic and sectarian differences. According to an Iraqi observer, politics undermined the media in Iraq and made it so divided that very few journalists can express their opinions without fear (Mohammed 2010). The CEO of the CMC, Burhan Shawi, reveals that 'there is no completely independent media in Iraq because all the channels are either related to political parties or to other sides' (*Al-Sabah Al-Jadeed* 2010). In other words, many negative aspects have been introduced into the new Iraqi media.

To sum up, the Iraqi media that emerged after the 2003 Iraq War are complex because they do not contain one main trend or feature. One can conclude that the media channels can be divided into three main types: (1) governmental/partisan, such as Iraqia TV, Al-Furat TV and Al-Mansour TV; (2) semi independent/commercial, such as Al-Baghdadia TV, Al-Rasheed TV, and Al-Sumeria TV; (3) regional channels that are supported by other countries/regional groups, such as Al-Sharqiya TV, Al-Rafidain TV, Ahul Al-Bayt TV, and Al Ahd TV (see Appendix II). During the 2007 UNESCO conference cited in Chapter 3, some participants pointed out that 'Iraq's media is divided by lines based on affiliation with political parties, religious groups, civil organizations, and others claiming to be independent media'. Among the 200 media personnel who attended the conference, 'only six or seven hands when [sic] up when participants were asked if they represented "independent" media' (Wikileaks 2007a).

With regard to regional channels, the current head of the Iraqi CMC, Burhan Shawi, stated that some Iraqi TV channels are supported by foreign intelligence agencies, naming Saudi Arabia, Iran, and Syria as potential supporters, but the 'CMC cannot do a thing toward such channels because there is no party law in Iraq that forces all the political sides to reveal their sources of funding' (*Al-Sabah Al-Jadeed* 2010).

In terms of the classification of Iraqi TV channels based on sectarian grounds, the US Ambassador to Iraq Zalmay Khalilzad once remarked that 'Sharqiya's coverage is generally considered to be independent', but he pointed out that 'some have complained that its news is "Sunni-Arab slanted"' (Wikileaks 2007b). Khalilzad's above comment on the views of some observers was echoed by Al-Marashi, who claimed that Al-Sharqiya is a 'Sunni channel'. Al-Marashi further says that the channel 'has its own agenda. It covers "Shiite news," but there is always a negative spin with any piece of news having to do with Maliki' (cited in Amos 2010, pp. 6–7). This same argument is voiced by an Iraqi journalist, Razzaq al Saidi, who accused Al-Baghdadia channel of the same thing: 'Dr. Awn Hussain al Khaskhlok, an Iraqi businessman who once worked for Saddam's intelligence agency, founded the [Al-Baghdadia] station and, despite his Shiite background, the station's editorial policy reflects a Sunni point of view' (cited in Amos 2010, p. 14). Another Iraqi journalist living in Basrah, Bachari, gave a justification behind Al-Sharqiya, Al-Baghdadia, and Al-Summeria channels' negative coverage of some US-sponsored projects, by attributing it to the assumption that they are 'owned by Sunni foreigners' (Wikileaks 2010a).

Unfortunately, this generalisation is rather superficial. For example, Al-Sharqiya and Al-Baghdadia channels' tendencies and programmes are both liberal and secular; they always show beautiful Iraqi ladies wearing Western clothes who present live talk shows, unlike the other religious channels that show heavily veiled anchorwomen and female presenters. Indeed, Al-Sharqiya channel, which is part of Azzaman Media Network, is covertly supported by Saudi intelligence (Pallister 2005), which has always backed Ayad Allawi – a secular Shiite figure (see, for example, Wikileaks 2006a) – since the time he was in the opposition front against Saddam Hussein's regime. In the 2005 and 2010 elections, the Saudi-funded Al-Arabiya channel overtly favoured Allawi by giving him more time and attention than all the other political candidates.[10]

In a secret US cable sent from Baghdad to the Department of State, Maliki and his close aid Ali Al-Adeeb were described as 'extremely critical of Ayad Allawi and Minister of Interior Jawad Al-Bolani's cross-sectarian coalitions, frequently conflating "secularism" with Ba'athist ideology or anti-Shi'a discrimination' (Wikileaks 2010c). This kind of association is not restricted to Maliki and aides but it extends to US officials, too. For example, a US official recommended in a US cable describing Al-Baghdadia channel that while the channel's 'reporting on Iraq has been factual – and critical of Saddam – the channel's Ba'athist, anti-coalition themes bear close monitoring and evaluation' (Wikileaks 2005e). The US official further clarified that the channel's 'message parallels old Ba'athist precepts, advocating Iraqi national unity and drawing speakers from all sects, ethnic groups, and religions. It is also largely secular' (ibid.). The contradiction in the statement above is that the channel is critical of Saddam Hussein and the Ba'ath party, but it remains a Ba'athist media outlet. In other words, Al-Baghdadia TV is viewed to be a Sunni Ba'athist channel because it primarily criticises the US and the Iraqi government. Likewise, it is true that Al-Sharqiya channel is critical of Maliki's government, but its stance is based on political reasons rather than sectarian ones as Allawi and Maliki are well-known rivals. Unfortunately, Al-Marashi's claim is similar to the way Maliki described Ayad Allawi's 2010 Iraqiya electoral slate of being a 'Sunni' slate (*BBC Arabic* 2010), though it contained Shiite and Christian candidates. In other words, any kind of criticism directed at Maliki's government or the US authorities is viewed by some politicians and media experts as a Sunni-sponsored Ba'athist voice. This is part of Maliki's rhetoric that he always employs when he is cornered to silence any opposition (see, for example, Arango 2011, A4). This is reminiscent of Saddam Hussein's technique of accusing his opponents of being 'foreign proxies' or 'Dawaa party members'.

It is important to note here that it is in the interest of the Saudi government to support a secular Iraq because having a fundamental Sunni government may anger the Shiite parties and make Iran more inclined to disturb the status quo. On the other hand, having a fundamental Shiite government makes the situation worse for Saudi Arabia in terms of its external and internal policies. For the former, Iran and the Shiites of the Gulf area will become stronger, exerting more pressure on the Arab governments to concede for reforms and rights for Shiites. Second, the Shiites in Saudi Arabia will feel more confident that they can make a change in their country since they can follow the example of their Iraqi Shiite neighbours. Hence, Al-Sharqiya channel supported secular figures like Ghazi Al-Yawir and Ayad Allawi, who had relations with Saudi Arabia during Saddam Hussein's rule. Also, the channel continuously attacked the idea of federalism because it's against Saudi Arabia's interests, especially the fear of a stronger Shiite presence in Iraq with the assistance of Iran.

All in all, there were clear media regulations which were known to everyone before the 2003 US invasion, yet in today's media environment one can hardly know where the red lines of expression are because of the various political and armed groups that control the situation. Noureddine Jebnoun puts it right when he says: 'Iraqi journalists lost in safety what they gained in freedom' (2009). By 2010 there were clear signs that the CMC had started to exert some power over a handful of Iraqi channels that were not supported by the major parties, like Al-Baghdadia TV. Also, new regulations were implemented that forced media outlets to be legally registered or have their licences revoked. In return, the CMC would offer access and protection to journalists. However, some worrying evidence emerged that linked the CMC to the previous Iraqi Ministry of Information. In some cases, journalists need to have official approval from three government bodies and an Iraqi army escort before reporting events in the country (McEvers 2010).

One hope might be that a strong CMC and IMN, which are both independent of the prime minister's authority, can be built by the direct assistance of an impartial government. If this is achieved, other Iraqi media outlets will respect the laws and refrain from inciting violence or hatred in the society.

5
TV and Iraqi Elections

Despite all the talk of bias and partisanship in the Iraqi media, there have been many accusations that are not based on sound and objective methods. Hence, it is important to carefully examine Iraqi media channels and determine their trends and ideologies by following solid social-science methodologies and not resorting to sweeping generalisations and unfounded impressions.

Why TV?

TV is regarded by some media scholars as 'an educator virtually without peer' (Iyengar and Kinder 1987, p. 2), as it shapes the way that people view the world and, in particular, the political issues around them (Kubey and Csíkszentmihályi 1990). TV is commonly endorsed by the general public in many countries as their most important source of news, and its news is considered to be the most trustworthy (Hartley 1995, p. 177). However, this does not mean that TV news presents more information on elections or other events in general, because newspapers can cover more details due to the nature of their publication. But TV coverage is believed to have an effect on viewers which is not only limited to 'changing everyday life', but also alters 'public perceptions of issues and problems' (Altheide 1976, p. 27). As part of the theory of cultivation, the public share values, attitudes, and even sentiments owing to the influence of TV, in what is called 'mainstreaming' (Huston et al. 1992, p. 35). In other words, TV is regarded as a cultural force that moulds public opinion and social practices. Ellis asserts that TV 'attempts definition, tries out explanations, creates narratives, talks over, makes intelligible, harness speculation, tries to make fit....' (2000, p. 79).

In the European Union, for example, 60 per cent of the citizens mentioned that TV news is their basic source of information on European issues and affairs (European Commission 1996–1999). It is argued that TV viewership in emerging democracies, such as Mexico, has a very large role to play, especially during election times (Lawson and McCann 2005). However, this does not mean that state-run TV channels have a direct influence on the people's political views or the way they see the world. In relation to the Arab world, there is very little research, if any, conducted on the role of TV in shaping political attitudes, since such kinds of audience research studies are usually rejected by typical Arab governments due to their sensitive nature that usually touches on the reality of the existing political systems.

In relation to Iraq, most Iraqis prefer to take their news from the TV, although the number of Iraqi newspapers and radio stations far exceeds that of TV channels. The US Department of State conducted a survey in October 2003 in which most Iraqis claimed that they watched TV more than listening to the radio or reading newspapers. Almost 93 per cent of those surveyed owned a TV set (CPA 2003, M-146-03). More than any other medium, TV is considered the main source of news for Iraqis, according to the Iraqi Communications and Media Commission (CMC 2005, p. 5).

In another survey conducted in 2005, 95 per cent of the respondents said that they owned a TV set rather than radio and telephone devices (USATODAY 2005). This ownership finding is not proof of viewing or the importance of TV in a political context. Furthermore, 68.1 per cent of Iraqis surveyed in November 2005 said that they relied on TV to know about the events in the country more than any other medium (Iraq Centre for Research and Strategic Studies 2005). Finally, the International Research & Exchanges Board (IREX) sponsored a poll survey in 2010 that revealed that most Iraqis get their news from TV channels, especially Iraqi satellite TV. On a daily basis an average of 16 million Iraqis watch TV, whereas around 7 million listen to the radio, another 7 million browse the Internet, and about 5 million Iraqis regularly read a newspaper. Here, the time spent on browsing the Internet is longer than that devoted to listening to the radio (IREX 2010, p. 9).

The main reason behind the popularity of TV is that its news is fast and provides an audiovisual coverage of events, making it very appealing to viewers (Butler 2002). In Iraq's case, TV covers almost all of the events taking place (International Media Support 2003), including programmes on the news coverage of newspapers. Besides, security risks prevent people from moving around to buy newspapers, so many prefer to return to their homes immediately after work and receive the news via the TV (Ghazi 2006).

After the 2003 occupation, the number of newspaper sales relatively declined because many from the educated middle class, who were the ones who read newspapers, began to leave the country after the escalation of violence (Al-Jezairy 2006, p. 20). Also, newspaper distribution was affected by the prevailing violence, which surely hindered the delivery of different publications to their readers.

Another factor that makes TV superior to newspapers is that not all Iraqis are literate, making TV a preferred outlet for many of them. According to UNESCO, the rate of illiteracy in Iraq skyrocketed after 2003, which was mainly due to the violence and the government's preoccupation with security rather than education. One in five Iraqis aged between 10 and 49 years old cannot read or write (UNESCO 2010).

Finally, serious content-analysis-based studies on the new Iraqi TV channels are very scarce. Ibrahim Al-Marashi, for instance, studied a handful of Iraqi TV stations, but his study lacks the depth of content analysis as he made some generalisations on the channels' trends and affiliations based on some statements or even words (Al-Marashi 2007). Another study was conducted by a researcher(s) associated with the Cambridge Arab Media Project. The Sunni Cairo-based Al-Rafidain TV and the Shiite Furat TV were examined by analysing two weekly religious shows aired by Al-Furat and one show broadcast by Al-Rafidain TV. However, the findings of the study, which claim that the two channels endeavour to be objective and balanced, are based on generalisations. There is neither a discussion of the methodology followed nor any details on how the researcher(s) reached the conclusions (Cambridge Arab Media Project 2010).

CMC and the elections

In early January 2005, the Iraqi Communications and Media Commission (CMC) published all its media regulations and codes that were designed by Western media professionals, especially those related to the conduct of journalists and media channels during the elections. The newspapers that published these regulations and codes included *Asharq Al-Awsat*, *Al-Mada*, *Baghdad*, *Al-Nahdha*, *Al-Dustoor*, *Al-Takhi*, *Al-Adalah*, and *Al-Itihad* (CMC 2005, p. 29). The websites of the CMC, the International Research & Exchanges Board (IREX), and the National Media Center (NMC) include most of these media regulations.

To organise the work of the media channels, CMC insists that any media outlet that violates the laws must be stopped by different ways, such as: 'sending a warning, requesting an apology to be published, issuing a fine, cancelling a media license or closing a media channel' (CMC 2005, p. 4).

In the appendix, the CMC published the 'Code for Media during Elections' on December 15, 2004. The same Code was posted on the CMC website by changing the date only in 2008 and 2009. This Code came into effect on July 27, 2004. However, there the draft had many shortcomings. For example, the Code is said to be applied to and 'is binding upon all Media transmitted, published, received or available in Iraq in connection with any election at the municipal, regional or state level during any and all Campaign Periods' (CMC 2005, p. 39). These regulations are to be followed by Iraqi media channels before the elections; however, many Iraqi satellite channels broadcast from abroad and target Iraqis inside the country, so it is not clear whether these channels should abide by the CMC's rules or not. There are other shortcomings. For example, the 'campaign period' was defined in Article 1 as 'the period that precedes the elections as determined by the Independent High Electoral Commission (IHEC)' (p. 38), giving IHEC the upper hand in deciding when the media channels can start their campaign. This usually results in some kind of confusion because some media channels might start their media campaign before the others since the CMC has no say in the country from which they are broadcast.

Furthermore, and in relation to the current study, Article 3 entitled 'Fair Reporting' states that: 'In covering any Political Entity or Coalition, or any of their candidates, no Media shall engage in intentional distortion, suppression, falsification, misrepresentation or censorship of information. All Media shall ensure due accuracy and fairness'.[1] Some regulations given to media channels are important here, such as: '(3–1) ensure that the information they report is balanced and unbiased; (3–2) treat all Political Entities and Coalitions, and their candidates, fairly and impartially, showing no favour or partiality toward, or prejudice against, any of them; and (3-3) make an effort to hear and represent all sides of the question, noting where one side of a controversy has refused to make itself available' (CMC 2005, pp. 39–40).

Despite the fact that most Iraqi media channels are partisan in nature, the Code insists that no media channel 'shall endorse any Political Entity or Coalition, or any of their candidates. In all such media, opinion shall be clearly distinguished from fact so as not to be confused with news coverage or current affairs programming'. This is too idealistic since no partisan Iraqi channel can be run in this manner.

Other Articles are also relevant. For instance, Article 7 prohibits any media channel from publishing opinion polls 72 hours prior to opening the voting stations (CMC 2005, p. 42). Article 8 states that the 'Media Silence Period' commences 48 hours before opening the polling stations until they are closed. The Code clearly states that 'there shall be no Media coverage of any political campaigns of any Political Entity or Coalition, or any of their candidates' (CMC 2005, p. 42). This is another difficult requirement since most Iraqi channels do not abide by this rule, as will be shown in Chapter 6.

In Article 9, the Code stipulates that every broadcast media channel must 'provide equitable access, equitable presentation, and equitable coverage of Political Entities and Coalitions, and any of their candidates, including with respect to newsworthy events and election activities in which they are involved'. The equitable access mentioned above is measured by the time allotted to each candidate or political party and the placement of the news item or report, having in mind the variations that occur among political entities because of their regional and political influence over the different segments in the society (CMC 2005, pp. 42–43). Also, equitable access suggests fairness in terms of emphasis: 'prime-time versus late night broadcasts, or front-page versus back-page publication'.

In the 'Guidelines of Equitable Access as Required by the Code for Media during Elections' (CMC 2005, pp. 45–46), the CMC emphasises that 'equitable access' does not mean that 'each Political Party must be allotted equal time' since 'larger Political Parties and Coalitions should be given greater exposure' and fair access should be 'proportionate to the significance of the Political Party, taking into consideration such factors as, for example, the number of candidates in such Political Party up for election, the territorial organisation and presence of such Political Party, Coalition or candidate, and its cultural, political and historical significance'. However, the factors mentioned here are rather problematic because there are no clear or defined 'territorial organisations' of the political parties in Iraq. For example, the city of Najaf includes different parties which compete for influence, such as Sadr's movement and the Islamic Supreme Council of Iraq (SCIRI) which later changed its name into the Islamic Supreme Council of Iraq (ISCI). Also, no one can exercise the right assessment to judge the cultural and historical significance of any party. As an example, the two parties Dawa and SCIRI are viewed by many Iraqi Sunnis, and even some Shiites, as agents to Iran, making their members traitor-like figures and therefore not trustworthy. The same allegation is applied to Sunni parties that are accused of being supported by some Arab countries. In other words, it is impossible to assess the fair access of news following the above loose criteria.

Other media issues that might occur during the election are mentioned. Government officials should be given the time to talk on different media channels; however, if they start advocating their political parties or coalition, the treatment should differ. More caution should be exercised in this case.

As for the role of the Iraqi Media Network (IMN) during elections, the Code makes it very clear that IMN should not support any party and refrain from siding with any group. According to Article 5 'Educating Voters: Special Obligations of the IMN to Educate the Public', IMN media outlets must inform the public about the activities and nature of the candidates and their parties' policies by 'providing practical information relevant to voting'; such information must reach all groups. Besides, free TV airtime must be given and technical resources must be employed by IMN to assist candidates in reaching out to the public, especially in relation to political debates and other forms of discussion.

There are strict media regulations stipulated in the 'Guidelines on Accuracy and Balance' (2007) published in Arabic and English to be followed by Iraqi journalists when covering election news. For example, in the 'General Steering' (n.d.) published on the CMC's website, news bias is clearly defined and clarified. Achieving accuracy and balance in the news means the avoidance of 'bad journalism' or 'propaganda', according to the document. A media channel will not be given a licence unless it signs a document that states the necessity to respect the rules of fairness, accuracy, and objectivity in reporting.

In the commission's 'Vocational Charter' (n.d.), the concepts of objectivity, accuracy, and honesty are described and emphasised in reporting. The document stresses that fair and balanced reporting must be achieved regardless of the political or religious background of a media organisation's owners. 'Opinion should be clearly distinguished from fact. News reporting should be dispassionate and news judgements and on the need to give viewers and listeners an even-handed account of events.' The document insisted that the ideal is to 'seek to present different and opposing views in a fair and balanced manner and in a way that is professional and far from being biased'.

Although it has not dealt with the Iraqi media, one of the few content-analysis studies conducted on the coverage of the 2005 Iraqi election was done by Garyantes and Murphy (2010), which compares Al-Jazeera.net (the English version) with CNN.com's coverage. The study concludes that there is an ideological slant in reporting the elections; for example, CNN framed the election by focusing on the positive side and highlighting the efforts to make Iraq follow a westernised democracy, whereas Al-Jazeera viewed the results of the election with doubt and questioned its legitimacy.

In general, Iraqi journalists benefit during the election season more than at any other time, as politicians start luring them with payments and rewards. Iraqi journalist Majed Al-Brekan mentions that most politicians start giving promises to the public, and they need media outlets to voice their statements. However, Al-Brekan advised that it is better for Iraqi journalists not to pay much attention to the 'typically unmet and wild promises and lies' uttered by politicians during election times (Wikileaks 2009g). In other words, keeping some distance from political power and staying impartial can surely add credibility to Iraqi journalists.

The 2005 and 2009 elections

One of the CMC's first publications was a bulky document entitled *Mass Media and the Election Campaign: National, Regional and Local Elections January 30, 2005*. This attempted to organise the Iraqi mass-media channels during the elections for the National Assembly that was responsible for drafting the new constitution. The aim of the CMC's report was to guarantee that Iraqi channels adhere to objective, impartial, and balanced reporting. In its general assessment of the manner in which some Iraqi news channels reported the 2005 elections, the report commends these channels for highlighting the 'national, historical and religious responsibility of Iraqis for voting' (CMC 2005, p. 1). The report indirectly refers to the continuous Shiite Marja'yah's (highest religious authority) calls to cast votes on Election Day, which is in contrast to the way that most Sunnis boycotted the elections in 2005. Among the report's other recommendations is the need to have a change in the 'political ownership of mass media channels', which is a reference to the control of political parties over the mass media. The CMC admits that some political parties have a group of international experts who speak on their behalf in the media as well as the financial ability to buy media loyalties for temporary periods (CMC 2005, p. 2). Also, the report mentions the necessity to reform IMN to make it a 'real public broadcasting means', which is a clear confession of the Iraqi government's influence over IMN.

Indeed, the report makes accusations against different media outlets without presenting the adopted methodology or referring to the use of the basic requirements of content analysis. The findings of the report are stated without knowing how the author(s) reached their conclusions. Furthermore, it seems that the report was politicised, as it was sponsored by the succeeding prime minister, Maliki, and was written to demean Allawi's monopoly of IMN. The report is only posted on the website of the NMC, a Maliki-run media body. The CMC investigated eight Iraqi satellite channels: Iraqia, Al-Sharqiya, Al-Fayhaa, Al-Furat, Kurdistan, Al-Hurria, and Al-Nahrain and Al-Diyar (CMC 2005, p. 19). In fact, Al-Diyar is an Iraqi channel run by Faisal Al-Yasseri's son, although the Saudi-owned Arab Radio and Television was instrumental in establishing it.

The media campaign started on December 16, 2004, which was 45 days before January 30, 2005 – Election Day. The recording, which was done during Iraqi TV's prime time (from 18:00 to 22:00), and lasted 15 days (January 15–30, 2005), was limited to the newscasts and some special programmes on elections and political commentary. The investigation included documenting the place and time given to the political parties and figures, the way they were presented, and the level of bias reflected in the report. There was also an evaluation of the time allotted to women in the election news. All of the TV channels provided ample space for political advertisements, especially during the last two weeks leading up to Election Day when the media campaign intensified (CMC 2005, p. 22).

In its conclusions, the report mentioned that the channels Iraqia and Al-Sharqiya were biased because they favoured Prime Minister Ayad Allawi in their reporting. However, there was no indication or reference to the methodology followed by the CMC to measure this kind of bias. The general tone of Iraqia TV in reporting the election was positive and the event was shown in an optimistic and positive manner. The channel followed the government political line without introducing any criticism; the election was pictured as a tool to combat terrorism. However, there was a clear bias towards Ayad Allawi. For example, in a newscast that lasted 30 minutes, the first 13 minutes were devoted to the activities of the prime minister.

The criteria for determining the value of news and its worthiness were focused on the government; for example, the official visits of the prime minister to hospitals and universities were mentioned before the more important developments in the security situation. But this emphasis on Allawi decreased during the last days of the campaign (CMC, 2005, p. 20). Kathleen Ridolfo of Radio Free Europe observed that Allawi 'whether by virtue of being prime minister or by intention has dominated the airwaves' (UNESCO 2008, p. 9). Due to the security threats, opinion pollsters were not allowed to come close to the polling stations. This has certainly empowered the Iraqi media channels to report accurately and fairly, and gave them another responsibility in 'backing up decisions on physical safety. The tone of the coverage as well as the facts reported played as much of a role in this' (UNESCO et al. 2008, p. 11).

Another problem that appeared was the use of religion and religious symbols by some political parties during their campaign. For example, the Iraqi Shiite Alliance used the picture of Grand Ayatollah Ali Sistani, the highest Shiite authority. Iraqia continuously aired the statement issued by Sistani that emphasised his support for all Iraqi parties; however, when one of Sistani's aides announced that the Ayatollah supported the Shiite Alliance, the Iraqia channel ignored the new statement and continued airing the previous one despite the fact that many Arab and international media channels broadcast it (CMC 2005, p. 21).

There was an indication that Al-Sharqiya TV favoured secular parties like that of the Sunni Ghazi Al-Yawir who headed Iraqiyun slate. But in mid-January, the channel focused on Allawi more than Al-Yawir throughout its news programmes and live interviews. This stance showed a turn in its editorial policy that first evolved around criticising the provisional government and its achievements. As an example, the channel devoted 21 minutes out of a 30-minute newscast to the prime minister. Also, the TV crews of Iraqia and Al-Sharqiya were given exclusive rights to accompany the prime minister whenever he had some festival or celebration to attend. However, this kind of favouritism decreased after Election Day (CMC 2005, pp. 22–23).

As for Al-Furat TV, it was clearly supportive of the Shiite United Iraqi Alliance (UIA) slate, devoting most of its programmes to airing interviews with representatives of SCIRI. In the beginning, UIA refused to air political advertisements on TV, preferring to meet people face-to-face and talk to them during the Friday prayers speeches. But later, they changed their minds and aired a few ads in Arabic on Iraqia TV and one in Persian on an Iranian channel broadcasting from Iran (CMC 2005, p. 27).

The same point applies to the Assyrian and Turkomen TV stations that were biased towards their ethnic groups. The Shiite Al-Fayhaa TV also aired biased programmes towards the UIA, who got a high percentage of the broadcast time (CMC 2005, p. 23). Bias was also shown on the Kurdish channels Al-Hurria, Kurdsat, and Kurdistan TV, which were clearly in favour of the Kurdish Coalition. The most balanced channel was Al-Nahrain, which is owned by Egyptian businessman Naguib Sawiris, who also owned Iraqna mobile network.

Unfortunately, there were no CMC reports published on the general election held on December 15, 2005, when Ibrahim Al-Ja'afari became the prime minister after Ayad Allawi. However, Al-Mir'at (Mirror) Center for Monitoring and Developing Media Performance conducted its own monitoring activity of the Iraqi media during the 2005 and 2010 general elections. It discovered some very interesting findings that show the way that IMN's coverage wavered with the people in power.

Al-Mir'at was established in August 2005 with the help of the US National Democratic Institute (NDI n.d.). During the 2005 general election, five local media non-governmental organisations (NGOs) aided Al-Mir'at, and they were all involved in the monitoring activity. These NGOs were: New Iraq Media Organisation in Dhi Qar; Bent Arafidain Organisation in Babil;[2] Kirkuk Institute for Human Rights Studies; Organisation of Social and Democratic Support; and Organisation of Ideal Youth. Al-Mir'at monitored 13 TV channels, 8 radio stations, and 22 newspapers from November 14 to December 16, 2005.

All in all, Al-Mir'at's report claims that quantitative and qualitative measures were followed in analysing media messages. Yet, the coding frame used was very basic since it contained just a few items to be filled by the coder, such as the news item sequence, duration, and name of candidate shown. As for the candidates' attributes, the coder assigns the positive-neutral-negative tone based on a five-point scale, yet no explanation was given about this measurement (Al-Mir'at 2005, p. 103 and p. 104).

In relation to the Iraqia channel, it aired programmes and news on Ayad Allawi's slate, National Iraqi List (NIL), but it sided against the former prime minister since only 10 per cent of its coverage was positive and the remaining 90 per cent was negative. The percentage of footage shown on NIL was 13. Since the ownership of IMN moved to the Shiite Dawa party, which was part of the UIA, we find that the percentage of UIA footage shown was 56 per cent, which was the highest amount when compared with the other parties. UIA got 54 per cent positive coverage, 43 per cent negative, and 3 per cent neutral. As for the Kurdiah Alliance, it received 22 per cent coverage with 23 per cent of footage. As the Patriotic Union of Kurdistan (PUK) and Kurdistan

Democratic Party (KDP) were on good terms with the UIA, Iraqia TV devoted 47 per cent of positive coverage to their slate, 23 per cent neutral, and 30 per cent negative (Al-Mir'at 2005, p. 91 and p. 96). Finally, Al-Ja'afari, who was the prime minister at that time, got the highest percentage of local radio coverage with 37 per cent (ibid., p. 99). A US official confirmed what was said above in a cable sent on December 5, 2005, saying: 'Prime Minister Ja'afari has made liberal, some would say excessive, use of al-Iraqiya to highlight the successes of his government' (Wikileaks 2005f).

Many vivid accounts of the 2005 media campaign can be found in some US cables leaked by Wikileaks. A group of Iraqi journalists interviewed by officials working for the US Embassy in Baghdad mentioned that there were many restrictions on media outlets. For example, only one polling station was open for journalists and many media personnel were 'detained and held for days…when they attempted to enter polling sites' (Wikileaks 2009a). US Ambassador to Iraq Zalmay Khalilzad described the media campaign in reports written on December 8 and 15, 2005, saying:

> Voting and electoral coverage ramped up again December 13 to cover voting by Iraqis in hospitals, detention facilities, military bases and overseas. Channels pulled out all the stops to drum up support and participation. Most newspapers stopped publishing December 12, so voters turned to television. Most channels devoted 50–75% of their airtime to the election. Themes included motivational and informative public service announcements, paid advertising for candidates and lists, and debates and talk shows, with the debate becoming more heated in the final stretch of the campaign.
>
> (Wikileaks 2005i)

It seems that many media channels violated the rules of IHEC. Khalilzad cited tens of cases, including one committed by the US-sponsored Al-Hurra channel. He also mentioned that all the media outlets 'except perhaps al-Fayha TV' violated the rule of the media silence day on December 14 (Wikileaks 2005i). In terms of objective coverage, the ambassador clarified that the channels Al-Sharqiya and Al-Fayhaa were more balanced than the other channels, whereas the 'KDP (Barzani), SCIRI (Hakim), and IIP (Tarik Al-Hashemi) outlets' showed 'the least regard for media ethics' (ibid.). On the other hand, Al-Sharqiya TV started airing statements made by several political figures who mostly denied false news aired by some channels like Al-Furat TV about possible slate-merging agreements. Khalilzad labelled Al-Sharqiya TV as the 'Voice Against al-Furat TV' (ibid). The ambassador further elaborated on Al-Sharqiya channel's coverage during the 2005 election, saying:

Sharqiya aired ads for all sects and affiliations. These ran the gamut from home videos for a small Sunni party in Mosul to Allawi's sophisticated spiel. Sharqiya – unlike Iraqiya – also carried ads critical of the coalition. Salih Al-Mutlaq's Iraqi Accord Front aired an ad showing US tanks and bullets and blood on a wall, with the comment: 'Iraqis did not suffer from the occupation, they suffered from its aftermath.' At the same time, Sharqiya aired security promotions which are usually only seen on Iraqiya.

(ibid.)

Furthermore, the competition and animosity among the political parties became rather personalised. For example, in an attempt to link Ayad Allawi with the former Ba'ath regime, 'anti-Ayad Allawi posters and flyers has [sic] appeared, comparing Allawi with Saddam Hussein.... One of these posters shows half of Saddam Hussein's face and half of Ayad Allawi's face and asks, "Who does this man remind you of?"' (Wikileaks 2005g).

Among the topics that attracted attention was a controversial programme called 'The Opposite Direction' and it was aired on Al-Jazeera on December 14, 2005. One of the Iraqi hosts argued that the US government had made a mistake by allowing religious leaders to rule Iraq. The Shiite Al-Furat TV made use of the show to gather supporters for UIA, claiming that Al-Jazeera's host had insulted Ayotallah Ali Sistani. As a result, many protests were organised in different parts of Iraq, and many Al-Furat TV viewers 'called to condemn' Al-Jazeera, regarding it as 'the mouthpiece of "Ba'athists and Salafists". One caller noted "Sistani needs to just give us the word and we'll put an end to these Jazeera reports". The presenter cautioned moderation, advising "you don't need a sign from Sistani, just go and vote for the right people and that will solve the problem"' (Wikileaks 2005i). Also, the state-run Iraqia TV and Al-Fayhaa channel both attacked Al-Jazeera for airing the programme.

On the other hand, the Sunni Baghdad TV, which is affiliated with the Iraqi Islamic Party (Accord slate – Tawafoq) concentrated its coverage on the importance of ending the Iranian intervention in the country as well as calling for the 'departure of occupation forces'. Baghdad TV was the only channel that the US Embassy in Baghdad monitored to air a news item from news agency AFP about the alleged discovery in Wassit governorate of a truck carrying false Iranian ballots. Also, the channel aired an advertisement which 'depicted a snake curling out of Iran to encircle Iraq' (Wikileaks 2005i).

There were many other campaigning methods that the Iraqi political parties used to win potential voters. The Shiite slate UIA carried the electoral number (555) with a candle image. UIA interpreted this number in a religious manner, implying that 'if you vote for the candle (555) list, God will be with you' (Wikileaks 2005i). UIA sent a text message to Iraqis with an Iraqna mobile phone, which stated: 'The pillars of Islam are 5, the family of Muhammad are 5, there are 5 prayers in a day, and the number of the Coalition is 555. Vote, O Shia, and win in this world and the next' (Wikileaks 2005g). On the other hand, the Sunni Accord slate showed a picture of famous Iraqi footballer Ahmed Radhi on their campaigning posters and billboards (ibid.).

It is important to note that the US government was involved in the 2005 general election. US international development agency USAID, for example, sponsored TV advertisements for the competing political parties that were aired on the Iraqia channel. It also funded a talk show entitled 'Elect for Iraq' on the same channel; it was aired three times a week to encourage Iraqis to vote and express their views on the election (Wikileaks 2005g).

In relation to the 2009 provincial elections that were held on January 31, the local Iraqi NGO, Tammuz, monitored the main TV stations and newspapers and concluded that many violations did occur. For example, Iraqia TV heavily covered the activities of Prime Minister Nouri Maliki by showing his visits to the governorates and meetings with tribal leaders, intellectuals, and journalists. In most cases the prime minister's coverage was aired live and the same footage was shown more than once. On the other hand, the president of Iraq, MPs, and other prominent official figures did not receive the same kind of coverage (Al-Jezairy 2010a, p. 18).

Iraqia TV also focused on showing the activities of other Shiite figures, like Abdul Aziz Al-Hakim who visited one of the polling stations on Election Day. The channel aired the jubilation that accompanied Al-Hakim's visit and 'the sectarian chants' that were uttered (Al-Jezairy 2010a, p. 18). Finally, the channel aired a special elections programme on January 21, 2009, to which a group of political figures were invited; however, there was an 'implicit attack' against the Sunni Iraqi Islamic Party (ibid., p. 19).

Other TV channels that violated the media election law included Al-Sharqiya, Al-Diyar, Biladi, and Al-Hurria. For example, Al-Sharqiya

TV showed an advertisement directed against Mu'in Al-Khadhumi, the head of Baghdad governorate's council, stating: 'Don't elect the thieves'. On the other hand, Al-Diyar TV showed a programme entitled 'Among the People', which propagated for Al-Khadhumi by showing positive signs of improvements in the streets of Baghdad and its markets (Al-Jezairy 2010a, p. 20). Finally, most of the channels breached the CMC's rule of media silence one day prior to Election Day.

The 2010 general election

The March 7, 2010, election was meant to elect a Council of Representatives or parliament. In its 2005 electoral law, which was amended in 2009, IHEC stipulated that 325 seats were allocated for the Council of Representatives – eight seats for Christians, Yazidis, and other minorities, and seven compensatory seats for the winning slates. In Iraq there are 18 governorates that each have 310 seats; each governorate has a certain number of seats allocated to it based on its population (IHEC n.d.).

In the 2010 elections, the Iraqiya slate won the most seats, 91, with its 2,851,823 votes. The slate is headed by former Prime Minister Ayad Allawi, who is regarded as a secular Shiite. Iraqiya slate has a Sunni majority. The second slate is the State of Law led by the present Prime Minister Nouri Maliki. It won 89 seats with 2,797,624 votes and has a Shiite majority. The third winner was the Iraqi National Alliance (INA), which is headed by the leader of the Islamic Supreme Council of Iraq, Ammar Al-Hakim. It scored 70 seats, most of which were secured by the Sadr movement that got 39 seats. INA has a Shiite majority, too. As for the fourth winner, this place was taken by the Kurdish Alliance with 43 seats. It is led by Masud Barazani and Jalal Talabani. As for the remaining winners, they were as follows: Gorran (8 seats); Iraqi Accord Front (6 seats); Unity Alliance of Iraq (4 seats); Kurdistan Islamic Union (3 seats); Islamic Group of Kurdistan (3 seats) (*The Associated Press* 2010a; *The New York Times* 2010). To make further alliances, some slates were merged to win a majority in the Council of Representatives. Most importantly, the State of Law and the INA slates got together in June 2010 to form a Shiite majority with 159 seats.

Once again, the US cables released by Wikileaks gave important details on the media campaign and the political parties running in the 2010 elections. The reports mentioned the details of political candidates' posters being torn or defaced, while some candidates were pressured, such as the case of some Turkomen politicians who were harassed in Kirkuk by Kurdish PUK members (Wikileaks 2010b and 2010e). Also, representatives of some political slates gave presents, blankets, and even cash to potential voters. The Iraqi NGO Tammuz observed similar irregularities during the media campaign. In one of its reports it mentions that some 'neutral channels' backed political figures at the expense of other slates, which was evident from the programmes that were aired, while some political candidates intentionally added the names of Shiite references to suggest that they were backed by religious leaders (Tammuz 2010, p. 2 and p. 3). One leaked US cable described the division among the competing parties as follows:

> Sectarian themes are evident in some campaign materials, and mud-slinging against rival candidates is notable. One ad features a cartoonish image of PM Maliki with photos of scenes of death, violence, and poverty under the caption, 'Five years of theft, destruction and sectarianism (Do you want another five years?' Along with the usual array of campaign propaganda, there has been a marked increase in satirical posters and cartoons appearing in some areas of Baghdad – mainly near universities – as well as on Internet sites and in newspapers. One doctored campaign photo shows a miniature ISCI leader Ammar al-Hakim dressed in infant clothes sitting on the lap of Iranian Supreme Leader Ali Khamenei.
>
> (Wikileaks 2010d)

Anti-Ba'athist advertisements were very popular at the time in southern Iraq, which is a predominantly Shiite area, and Allawi's slate, which was associated with Sunnis, became unpopular there. Despite the CMC's regulations on the importance of following balanced reporting and avoiding the incitement of violence and schism, many Shiite media outlets got involved in disseminating and airing materials that were anti-Ba'athist or anti-Allawi to unite the public and convince them to vote for their slates. One of the reports mentioned the following:

> Some campaign materials continue to display sectarian messages, particularly in the south where anti-Ba'athist sentiment is running high. One poster for former PM Ibrahim al-Ja'afari states, under his photo, 'There is no place for the Ba'ath in Iraq.' More disturbing has been the airing of gruesome television ads showing historical footage of Ba'ath Party loyalists killing Shi'a Iraqis. Both al-Furat TV, controlled by ISCI, and the al-Afaq station, affiliated with Maliki's Da'wa Party, have aired this footage. One ad on al-Afaq displayed the beheadings of Shi'a while a news headline underneath reminded viewers that

Sunni MP Saleh al-Mutlaq had been banned from the elections due to his Ba'athist connections.

(Wikileaks 2010b)

With regard to the CMC's monitoring activity, it published a very brief report on the media channels covering the 2010 general election. The monitoring period started with the beginning of the media campaign on February 12, 2010, and ended on March 5, 2010. The CMC covered 19 newspapers and 12 TV channels. It noted that five Iraqi channels breached its rule of avoiding airing advertisements before the official start of the campaign; they were Iraqia, Baghdad, Biladi, Al-Babelyia, and Salahadin channels (CMC 2010f). Also, the CMC did not monitor the channels during the media silence day, taking for granted that the channels would abide by its rules.

The total number of violations registered by the CMC during its monitoring period was 101 by ten different channels. The numbers of violations are organised as follows: Al-Sharqiya (33); Al-Furat (19); Iraqia (16); Al-Babelyia (12); Al-Hurra-Iraq (8); Biladi (6); Ifaq (2); Al-Hurria (1); and Al-Baghdadia (1) (CMC 2010f). Unlike its previous reports, the CMC did not cite any details or discussions on the kind of violations committed by each channel, so the readers are left to wonder about the justification of the breaches. In general, the report mentioned that the percentage of the channels' coverage which entailed incitement to violence or hatred was as follows: Al-Rafidain (42.6 per cent); Al-Sharqiya (38.3 per cent); Al-Babelyia (6.4 per cent); Biladi (4.3 per cent); Al-Baghdadia (3.2 per cent); Al-Furat (2.1 per cent); Baghdad (2.1 per cent); Ifaq (1.1 per cent) (ibid.).

Furthermore, Al-Mir'at Organisation monitored the 2010 general election and covered the period from November 15, 2009, to March 6, 2010. Its coders, who followed the same methods employed during the monitoring of the 2005 election, analysed the programmes aired on 21 TV stations, which included some pan-Arabic channels like Al-Arabiya and Al-Jazeera. Other media outlets were monitored, including 11 daily newspapers, 10 local newspapers, 9 radio stations, and 3 websites. In terms of TV coverage, Al-Mir'at focused on the news bulletins aired at 18:00, 19:00, 20:00, and 21:00, in addition to monitoring other programmes on the election.

With regard to Iraqia TV's coverage of the 2010 election, the report concluded that the station was biased towards Nouri Maliki's State of Law slate. For example, the channel 'allocated 28% of its time to the State of law Alliance, followed by other entities (small lists) by 19%, then the INA by 18%, then the Iraqi National Movement (Iraqiya) 15% and Kurdistan Alliance 8%, then the Al-Tawafuq 7%, and finally Iraqi Unity Alliance by 5%' (Al-Mir'at 2010, p. 7). In terms of negative reporting, Iraqia focused some of its programmes, which were repeated 14 times, on anti-Allawi coverage (0.4 per cent, which amounts to 1040 seconds). Among the charges against Iraqiya slate was that some of its members 'protect the criminals' and 'incite division' (ibid., p. 7). In its final recommendations on the election, Al-Mir'at advised IMN to be 'balanced' in covering the candidates and their slates (ibid., p. 28).

As for ISCI's Al-Furat TV, most of its coverage (96.5 per cent) was devoted to the election, especially towards UIA, which received 88.3 per cent mostly positive coverage; programmes and news bulletins that discussed UIA were repeated 634 times and amounted to 98,580 seconds of coverage. The negative coverage concentrated on Allawi's Iraqiya slate and the violence in the country was attributed to its members, who were accused of being 'terrorists' who work against the constitution; references to Al-Iraqiya were repeated 21 times, constituting 1598 seconds. Maliki's State of Law slate came second for negative reporting as references to this political entity were repeated five times (Al-Mir'at 2010, p. 8).

On the other hand, Baghdad TV devoted most of its coverage to the Tawafuq slate (Accord) with 65 per cent, while other lists were as follows: 14 per cent for other smaller blocs, 8 per cent for the Kurdish Alliance, 5 per cent for Al-Iraqiya, 4 per cent for Maliki's State of Law, 3 per cent for UIA, and 1 per cent for the Alliance for Iraq's Unity (Al-Mir'at 2010, p. 12). Most of the positive coverage was directed at the Accord slate, while 568 seconds were devoted to negative coverage of Maliki's bloc with programmes repeated eight times. The channel implied a negative tone by using terms like 'political deals', 'exploitation', 'agent', 'suspending' when referring to Maliki. 'The criticism reached its peak when the channel accused the guards of the head of the State of law list, Nuri Al-Maliki, by [sic] robbing the banks' (ibid.).

In relation to other Iraqi channels, the Saudi-sponsored Al-Sharqiya TV backed Allawi's slate with 44 per cent coverage that was mostly positive. This was followed by 20 per cent for other blocs, 13 per cent for UIA, 8 per cent for the Kurdish Alliance, 8 per cent for Maliki's State of Law, and 3 per cent for the Sunni Accord Front. Most of the negative coverage by the channel was directed against Maliki's slate (Al-Mir'at 2010, p. 13).

As for Nouri Maliki's Ifaq channel, it devoted most of its coverage to its sponsor, while Allawi's slate got most of the negative coverage with programmes repeated 97 times, amounting to 5356 seconds. There were personal attacks against some of Al-Iraqiya's slate members, like Tariq Al-Hashimi who was accused of disobeying the law, forging 'political deals', and 'hamper[ing the] Iraqi elections' (Al-Mir'at 2010, p. 9). Other channels, such as Al-Mousiliah, Al-Baghdadia, and Al-Rafidain favoured Allawi's slate, whereas Maliki's State of Law bloc got most of the negative coverage (ibid., pp. 10 and 11). On the other hand, the TV station of the Dawa Party – Iraq Branch, Al-Masar, favoured the Shiite bloc UIA. As for the negative coverage, it was exclusively focused on Allawi's slate, whose members were accused of being 'Baathists' and 'enemies of the people', with programmes repeated 18 times, constituting 790 seconds (ibid., p. 9).

On the other hand, just like during the 2005 general election, the US government got involved in promoting candidates in the 2010 elections. For example, the National Democratic Institute (NDI) monitored the election process, while the International Republican Institute (IRI) helped in placing, in one week, 1397 posters and billboards that called for Iraqis to vote. Other local Iraqi NGOs that were supported by IRI were expected to put 5 million 'voting instruction leaflets in a coordinated "door stop" campaign over the February 27–28 weekend' (Wikileaks 2010d).

Finally, International Media Support (IMS) reported during the 2010 elections that independent Iraqi media outlets that endeavour to maintain neutrality cannot survive because they will not have interested advertisers. IMS referred to daily newspaper *Al-Manara*, which shifted to weekly publication because of the hardship of finding the necessary funds. IMS estimated that newspaper sales skyrocketed before the elections because 'Iraqis have sought to familiarise themselves with the different electoral candidates' (International Media Support 2010), and newspapers more than any other medium can provide a great deal of information.

The Dutch director of the Independent Media Centre in Kurdistan, Judit Neurink, trained Iraqi journalists and media employees in Iraqi Kurdistan on the methods of objective and fair reporting. After observing some media channels, Neurink confessed that during the election time, 'most newspapers and all TV stations in Iraq turn into "propaganda" mechanisms for the political parties, making it virtually impossible for citizens to find any information about the issues that affect them'. She regretted the fact that there was an obvious 'return to old habits' as most journalists sided with their preferred political parties. Neurink stated that Iraqi TV channels can be classified into three types:

'independent, semi-independent and partisan' (American University of Iraq 2010); however, she did not identify which channels fell into which grouping.

In brief, the media monitoring of the 2005 and 2010 election coverage by Al-Mir'at Organisation and the CMC showed that there were great breaches committed by most of the Iraqi channels. The tendency of each channel clearly depends on its owner or sponsor; as a result, negative coverage becomes rather personalised, which reflects the animosity among the politicians themselves.

Unfortunately, most of the previous studies on the election employed basic coding frames with no clear guidelines about the method for assigning the different attributes; hence, more solid scientific methods need to be applied to accurately determine the tone of the coverage instead of giving the coders complete freedom to assign the candidates' attributes, which ultimately leads to subjective findings. In the following chapter I will present an analysis of the evening newscasts of four Iraqi satellite TV channels – Iraqia, Al-Furat, Al-Hurria, and Baghdad – for the 14 days that preceded the Iraqi general election on March 7, 2010. This chapter seeks to examine the application and presence of the principles of good journalism practice in these newscasts based on a content-analysis methodology, and to see whether some channels framed the news of the election campaign in a certain direction.

6
Iraqi TV Coverage of the 2010 General Election

This chapter presents the analysis of the evening newscasts of four Iraqi TV channels that are mostly partisan in nature. Except for the government-run Iraqia TV, the three other channels are run, supported, and funded by political parties, so they are 'partisan'. For the sake of brevity, I have not included many parametrical and non-parametrical tests and I have avoided lengthy discussions on the study's theoretical background and the channels' coverage.[1]

As a reminder, Al-Furat TV is supported by the Shiite party Islamic Supreme Council of Iraq, Baghdad TV is run by the Sunni Iraqi Islamic Party, and Al-Hurria TV is backed by the Kurdish Patriotic Union of Kurdistan (PUK). The 14 days leading up to the March 7, 2010 election were the focus of this study. There were 6172 candidates running in the general election, with 325 parliamentary seats up for grabs. The candidates represented 306 political slates, which formed 14 coalitions or alliances. In total, 56 evening newscasts, making up 857 separate news stories, were analysed, which amounts to 121,431 seconds of programme running time.

Programme-level analysis

In the first stage of analysis, the 'programme level', the data collected can give us an understanding of the way that political parties/candidates and issues were represented or under-represented. Indeed, this aspect of the analysis provides a clear insight into the four TV channels' application of the principles of good journalism, such as balance and impartiality.

The Sunni Baghdad channel aired most news stories, with 234 in total. The Shiite channel Al-Furat aired 221 stories, closely followed by the

Kurdish channel Al-Hurria and the state-run Iraqia channel, which each had 201 stories. Indeed, the four channels were close to each other in the number of news stories that they aired. However, Baghdad channel was more concerned with covering news and reports on the elections, though the very same channel had refrained from airing news related to the election for a whole day.

In terms of time allotment (see Figure 6.1), differences were found between the four channels. The biggest differences occurred between Al-Hurria and Baghdad. In fact, Al-Hurria aired fewer stories because it was not the only media tool used by its owner, Jalal Talabani, who is head of the PUK and the president of Iraq. The PUK's main target audience is Kurdish speakers, so it seemed that Al-Hurria paid less attention to producing Arabic news and reports on the election than did the other channels. This was also evident in the type of news format that was used most. Unlike Al-Hurria channel, Baghdad TV was the only Sunni channel whose sponsors were represented in the government, and it was definitely the sole TV medium used by Ayad Samarai and his slate.

In terms of the topics covered, Iraqia channel covered all the topics except for 'federalism' and 'supporting electoral slate'. As part of its mandate is not to side with any party, the channel showed no direct preference for any political bloc. However, there were indications that the channel was slightly subjective towards the prime minister. Furthermore, the channel placed the most emphasis on airing stories

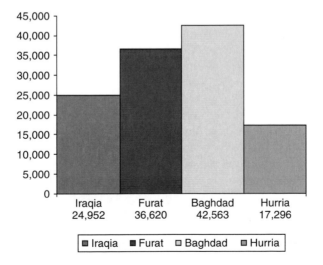

Figure 6.1 Time allotted to news stories in seconds

related to 'IHEC' (number of stories and time allotment) and 'other' (time allotment), as Iraqia TV closely followed the Iraqi government's policy to cover IHEC's activities and urge Iraqis to vote in the election. The Kurdish Al-Hurria TV showed the least keenness in promoting its Kurdish sponsors in terms of the number of stories, airtime, and news formats. Also, the channel was close to Iraqia TV in many aspects, particularly the amount of coverage on 'IHEC' and 'other' topics. This is mainly due to the fact that both channels are closely affiliated with the Iraqi government. The only topic that Al-Hurria TV showed more interest in airing was 'federalism', although Baghdad TV aired an equal number of stories on this. This is understandable because Al-Hurria is owned by a Kurdish party that strongly advocates federalism.

On the other hand, Al-Furat TV's coverage showed a typical partisan channel that was trying to promote its sponsor. There was a clear one-sided view of the events and topics covered as the opponent parties or slates either did not appear on the channel or they were criticised. The channel showed the greatest degree of emphasis on airing the topics of 'political difference', 'democracy', 'election fraud', and 'security/terrorism' (only in terms of time allotment).

As for Baghdad TV, it was not very different from Al-Furat channel since both set for themselves the priority of promoting their parties, and they exclusively focused on covering the activities of their candidates. Both were concerned with covering the performance of the government headed by the prime minister, who was one of their strongest political opponents. Baghdad TV was ahead of the other channels in the attention it gave to the topics of 'security/terrorism' (in terms of the number of stories), 'public services', 'corruption/violation', 'national unity/political dialogue', 'federalism', 'supporting electoral slate', and 'other' (in terms of time allotment).

In relation to the news formats, I mostly followed Hartley (1988) and Grabe and Bucy's (2009) classifications. The coding frame was divided into eight formats: newsreader (Talking Head); voice-over; voice-over-sound-on-tape (VO/SOT); recorded interview; live interview; package; film report (reporter unseen); in-studio interview.

Most of the stories ($n = 224$) centred on voice-over, which was either accompanied by a still image or footage. This is mainly due to the fact that the voice-over involves less effort and time than the other formats but is regarded as more important than the newsreader style since the visuals that accompany the news in the voice-over format make the news more interesting and have an impact on audience recall of information (Edwardson et al. 1992). Al-Hurria TV had the most stories using this format, which partly explains the channel's tendency to lay less emphasis on its news production, as explained above. The second greatest number of stories used VO/SOT, with 183 stories. This time, Al-Furat TV was first for using this news format, with 76 stories. The third-highest-scoring story format was film report (reporter unseen). Baghdad TV had the most stories of this type, with 86 stories (which was also the greatest number of stories in any format). Rather than having a technical reason for using this format, it seems that the channel's policy was to avoid showing its reporters for fear of them being kidnapped, assassinated, or harmed following the major attack on its station.

At the other end of the scale, the lowest-ranking story format was in-studio interview, with only six stories. It seems that the Iraqia channel tackled in this study did not prefer this type of format. Furthermore, the second-lowest number of stories involved a newsreader (Talking Head) with only 24 stories, which is known to be the least interesting news format.

Based on the discussion above, we can conclude that the main news formats that require more time, effort, and money are: film report (reporter unseen), package, live interview, and VO/SOT. Hence, the channels that presented news items with more 'visual weight' can be classified according to the total number of stories shown following the codes specified above:

1. Baghdad (211 stories)
2. Al-Furat (171 stories)
3. Iraqia (129 stories)
4. Al-Hurria (115 stories)

The results shown above on the channels' news formats indicate that Baghdad TV was far more concerned about the impact of its news on the audience and was more active than the other channels in promoting its candidates, suggesting one kind of bias towards its own party members. On the other hand, Al-Hurria TV devoted the smallest amount of time and effort in promoting its candidates and showed the least kind of interest in influencing the audience.

In brief, and based on the number of stories, time allotment, and type of news formats used, we can conclude this discussion by saying that Baghdad TV came ahead in its effort to cover the election and promote its political sponsor, followed by the Al-Furat channel. Iraqia channel came third in its emphasis on covering the election, but not on promoting candidates, while Al-Hurria TV was the last channel in promoting its political bloc and the least interested in covering the election.

Story-level analysis

The second stage in the content analysis of newscasts was centred on the stories themselves. Using a separate coding frame, the research analysed the stories by highlighting their prominence: time allotment, number of stories, and format type. Although there was usually a close correlation between the number of stories and time allotment, there were some variations due to the nature of the stories presented.

In addition, the analysis examined the presence/absence of: (1) narrative references to political candidates; (2) featured film/image of the candidates; (3) featured interview with the candidates. This area sheds light on the emphasis laid by the channel to either promote its political candidates or pay some attention to other candidates from different parties eager to speak about their political programmes. It is important to point out the narrative reference to candidates to see the number of references that give an indication of emphasis. Indeed, introducing still images or footage to accompany the narrative reference denotes more attention shown by the channel. Finally, interviews have more effect on the viewers than the other format types because of the effort, time, and effect they have (Grabe and Bucy 2009, p. 200; Detenber et al. 1998; King and Morehouse 2004, p. 304). Also, viewers see the candidates as more significant when they are presented on TV. If they are repeatedly shown on screen, the candidates tend to become more important, too (McCombs and Shaw 1972). Certainly, conducting interviews with political candidates is indicative of the attention and emphasis given by the channel to the politician because they entail a personalised encounter with the candidate giving him/her the chance to voice the political programme and thereby become closer to the viewer. Less importance and influence is found in the moving film shown, but the latter has more recall effect on the viewers than the still images (Gunter 1979) or the narrative reference to the candidate.

Finally, the story-level coding frame allowed the researcher to examine whether or not some channels introduced the horse-race issue into their newscasts to promote some parties at the expense of others.

Channels' narrative references to candidates

This section will discuss the stories that featured narrative references to political candidates. We can see from Table 6.1 and Figure 6.2 that Baghdad TV scored the largest number of stories (164) and the greatest time allotted (31,470 seconds) with its narrative references to candidates

Table 6.1 Number of stories by the four channels featuring narrative references to political candidates

	Iraqia TV	Al-Furat TV	Baghdad TV	Al-Hurria TV	Chi-square	Asymp. Sig.
Maliki	1^a	1^a	1^a	2^a	0.78	$p < 0.855$
Allawi	4^a	0^b	0^b	6^a	12.30	$^*p < 0.006$
Hakim	0^a	120^b	1^a	2^a	386.20	$^{**}p < 0.000$
Sadr	0^a	5^b	0^a	0^a	14.46	$^{***}p < 0.002$
Talabani	1^a	0^a	0^a	43^b	110.33	$^{****}p < 0.000$
Samarai	1^a	0^a	164^b	1^a	529.52	$^{*****}p < 0.000$
Others	0^a	0^a	5^b	2^a (Baghdad)	8.58	$^{******}p < 0.035$

Note: Scores that share the same superscript are not significantly different at the $p < 0.05$ level. In a few cases, the channel that does not share a significant difference with another is written between brackets though the superscript is different.

$^*p < 0.006$ (Allawi: There is significant difference among the four channels in the way this slate was covered).

$^{**}p < 0.000$ (Hakim: There is significant difference among the four channels in the way this slate was covered).

$^{***}p < 0.002$ (Sadr: There is significant difference among the four channels in the way this slate was covered).

$^{****}p < 0.000$ (Talabani: There is significant difference among the four channels in the way this slate was covered).

$^{*****}p < 0.000$ (Samarai: There is significant difference among the four channels in the way this slate was covered).

$^{******}p < 0.000$ (Other: There is significant difference among the four channels in the way this slate was covered).

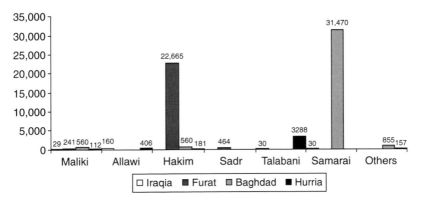

Figure 6.2 Time allotted (in seconds) by the four channels to narrative references to political candidates

representing the Iraqi Accord Front (IAF), the slate that sponsors the channel. These stories constituted 69.7 per cent of the total number of stories aired by the channel. Just five stories (running time of 855 seconds) were devoted to other parties/groups that were either unknown by the public or ineffective in the society.

The Al-Furat channel came second in rank in terms of the number of stories and time allotted to its party's candidates. The channel aired 120 stories (22,665 seconds) on the party's candidates. The stories made up 54.2 per cent of their total number analysed throughout the period of study. Furthermore, the channel also aired five stories that spanned more than 464 seconds of narrative references to Sadr's movement/candidate. This is understandable because Hakim and Sadr formed from the beginning the Iraqi National Alliance (INA), so the two Shiite groups stood together against other competing political blocs.

Al-Hurria TV aired 43 stories (3288 seconds) on the Kurdish Alliance (KA), which constituted 21.3 per cent of the total number of stories aired by the channel. The channel devoted six stories (406 seconds) to Allawi's bloc, two stories to Maliki's slate (112 seconds), and two others for Hakim's alliance (118 seconds). There were four references to Allawi's Iraqiya slate (406 seconds) because some of its candidates were subjected to the De-Ba'athification process to exclude them from running in the election. In fact, this move created a great deal of controversy about the credibility of the government and its Accountability and Justice Commission, which was led by Ali Al-Lami (who was also a candidate running in the election).

Finally, Iraqia TV did not allot more emphasis to one political group over another. Four stories (160 seconds) were devoted to Allawi's bloc. However, the dominant issue relating to this political group was the law suits filed against some of its candidates. In presenting the different political blocs, the channel established itself as the most balanced and objective of the four channels.

In brief, Baghdad TV stressed the importance of its IAF candidates more than the other channels by airing more stories (and therefore time) referring to them. Al-Furat came next, followed by Al-Hurria TV.

Film reports/images of candidates

In this section, the discussion is centred on the stories that featured film reports or still images of candidates sponsoring the channels. Here, Baghdad TV once more finished in first place with the largest number of stories and greatest time allotted to it. The 160 stories (31,130 seconds)

Table 6.2 Number of stories by the four channels featuring film/image of political candidates

	Iraqia TV	Al-Furat TV	Baghdad TV	Al-Hurria TV	Chi-square	Asymp. Sig.
Maliki	1[a]	0[a]	1[a]	1[a]	1.07	$p < 0.785$
Allawi	2[a]	0[a]	1[a]	1[a]	5.75	$p < 0.125$
Hakim	0[a]	114[b]	1[a]	2[a]	363.12	*$p < 0.000$
Sadr	0[a]	4[b]	0[a]	0[a]	11.55	**$p < 0.009$
Talabani	1[a]	0[a]	0[a]	33[b]	106.81	***$p < 0.000$
Samarai	1[a]	0[a]	160[b]	1[a]	513.36	****$p < 0.000$
Others	0[a]	0[a]	3[a]	2[a]	5.03	$p < 0.170$

Note: Scores that share the same superscript are not significantly different at the $p < 0.05$ level.

*$p < 0.000$ (Hakim: There is significant difference among the four channels in the way this slate was covered).

**$p < 0.000$ (Sadr: There is significant difference among the four channels in the way this slate was covered).

***$p < 0.000$ (Talabani: There is significant difference among the four channels in the way this slate was covered).

****$p < 0.000$ (Samarai: There is significant difference among the four channels in the way this slate was covered).

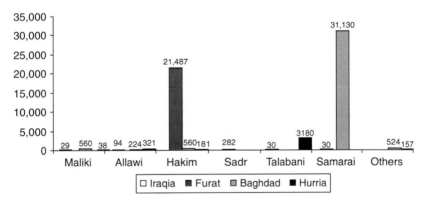

Figure 6.3 Time allotted (in seconds) by the four channels to film/image of political candidates

constituted 68.08 per cent of the total number of stories aired by the channel for 14 days. Again, Al-Furat TV came second with 114 stories (21,487 seconds), which comprised 51.5 per cent of the total number of stories. Finally, Al-Hurria channel was last with 33 stories (3180 seconds), which formed 16.4 per cent of the total number of stories (see Table 6.2 and Figure 6.3).

In general, the number of stories and time allotments that featured a film or still image of candidates from other blocs were less than the number of stories and time allotted to featuring narrative references from the same category. As cited earlier, presenting a film or still image on the channel has more impact on the viewers than just making a narrative reference; hence, the channels discussed here, except for Iraqia TV, wanted to stress the importance of their own candidates by paying less or no emphasis to candidates from other parties.

Interviews with candidates

The last part in this section deals with investigating the number of stories and time allotted to interviews with political candidates. Once more, Baghdad TV scored the largest number of stories and time allotment among the other channels (see Table 6.3 and Figure 6.4). There were 126 stories (25,775 seconds) making up 53.6 per cent of the total number of stories aired on its IAF candidates. The Al-Furat channel came second and aired 42 stories (8850 seconds), which made up 19 per cent of the total number of stories broadcast. Al-Hurria TV came third with only 16 stories (2140 seconds), which made up 7.9 per cent of the stories aired.

It is worth noting that the number of stories and time allotted to featuring interviews with candidates from other political blocs were less than the number of stories and time devoted to featuring narrative

Table 6.3   Number of stories featuring interviews with political candidates

	Iraqia TV	Al-Furat TV	Baghdad TV	Al-Hurria TV	Chi-square	Asymp. Sig.
Maliki	0^a	0^a	0^a	0^a	0.00	$p < 1.000$
Allawi	0^a	0^a	0^a	0^a	0.00	$p < 1.000$
Hakim	0^a	42^b	0^a	1^a	122.18	$^*p < 0.000$
Sadr	0^a	0^a	0^a	0^a	0.00	$p < 1.000$
Talabani	0^a	0^a	0^a	16^b	53.15	$^{**}p < 0.000$
Samarai	0^a	0^a	126^b	0^a	392.83	$^{***}p < 0.000$
Others	0^a	0^a	2^a	2^a	3.94	$p < 0.268$

Note: Scores that share the same superscript are not significantly different at the $p < 0.05$ level.
$^*p < 0.000$ (Hakim: There is significant difference among the four channels in the way this slate was covered).
$^{**}p < 0.000$ (Talabani: There is significant difference among the four channels in the way this slate was covered).
$^{***}p < 0.000$ (Samarai: There is significant difference among the four channels in the way this slate was covered).

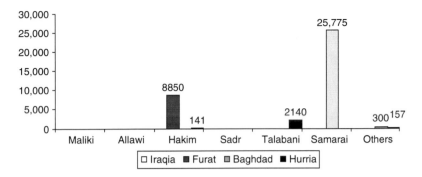

Figure 6.4 Time allotted (in seconds) by the four channels to interviews with political candidates

references and films or images of candidates from the same category. As mentioned earlier, conducting interviews with candidates is seen as a very effective tool to influence the viewers (King and Morehouse 2004). Al-Furat TV, for example, never showed a story that contained an interview with a candidate from other blocs, not even from Sadr's movement. Al-Hurria TV only aired an interview with a representative of Hakim's INA and two interviews with representatives from other smaller parties, lasting only 298 seconds in total. Finally, Baghdad channel aired two interviews (300 seconds) with candidates from other parties that seemed to be weak in influence.

In terms of 'other parties', it seems that the channels Al-Hurria and Baghdad were more relaxed in airing interviews with candidates in this category. On the other hand, Al-Hurria showed one short interview lasting 141 seconds with Hakim's bloc. This might have been due to the channel's awareness that future alliances must be established with other parties for the Kurds to get some political gains when parliament is established. The events following the general election support this explanation, since the KA made an alliance with INA and Maliki's State of Law slate, which then formed a majority in the Iraqi parliament.

Horse-race issue

Before every election, poll surveys appear to give indications on the popularity of the political candidates running in the elections. Some of these polls tend to be erroneous as they are used for promotional purposes. For example, an official at the US Embassy in Baghdad commented on the increasing number of poll surveys conducted by different media outlets just before the 2005 election in Iraq. The official warned about possible partisan bias in such surveys, saying: 'Iraqi media outlets are increasingly citing "polls" to report on trends or to boost their own party's standings. Methods and reliability are impossible to gauge, as evidenced by widely divergent results, although independent outlets are seen as more likely to present credible results than party organs. Some polls have apparently touched a nerve and provoked threats against editors' (Wikileaks 2005f).

The coding frame used in this study revealed whether or not the channels presented the horse-race issue in their coverage of the 2010 general election. First, it is important to note that there were few stories aired by the Baghdad and Al-Furat channels in which the anchorperson or reporter mentioned that the channels' political sponsor got more popular approval by the people than the other slates but without presenting any figures or pieces of evidence. With a total of six stories, only two channels referred to poll surveys dealing with the public's voting preferences and the expected sequence of political parties running in the elections. Out of 221 stories aired by Al-Furat during the period of study, five stories referred to a horse-race issue (see Table 6.4). All the stories aired claim that INA was ahead of the other political blocs in the polls. Twice, Maliki's slate was said to come second, whereas Allawi's bloc was twice reported to come third.

Interestingly, Baghdad TV aired one story that contained references to two poll surveys, both of which do not mention IAF. The report stressed that the polls were false because they were biased and politicised.

Table 6.4   Number of stories featuring horse-race issue and the parties' sequence on Al-Furat and Baghdad channels

Candidates' slates	Al-Furat TV Number of stories and sequence	Baghdad TV Number of stories and sequence
Maliki	2 (sequence 2)	1 (sequence 2) 1 (sequence 3)
Allawi	2 (sequence 3)	2 (sequence 1)
Hakim	5 (sequence 1)	1 (sequence 2) 1 (sequence 3)
Sadr	0	0
Talabani	0	0
Samarai	0	0
Others	2 (sequence 4)	0

Ironically, Allawi's slate was shown to be ahead of the other blocs in the two polls, which was truly what happened in the election. Maliki and Hakim's slates alternated between second and third position in the polls, which also proved to be true later. In brief, the Iraqi channels tackled in this study did not seem to pay much attention to horse-race issues except for Al-Furat TV, although it aired very few relevant stories.

In general, the four channels aired topics with different degrees of attention by using various format types, number of stories, and time allotments. These vital aspects shed light on the way that each channel viewed the importance of the topics it covered. The preferred or dominant story format used in covering each topic was selected by choosing the largest number of stories and the most time allotted to each topic in every channel. This method was followed to reach sound results on the amount of emphasis laid by each channel on the different issues tackled. In general, Baghdad TV placed more emphasis on covering the election and the different topics investigated in this study. Al-Furat TV came second, followed by Iraqia. On the other hand, Al-Hurria TV showed the least amount of interest in covering the election and the different topics.

In terms of the stories featuring narrative references to political candidates, film/image of the candidates, and interviews with the candidates, Baghdad TV was once more far ahead of the other channels. It was followed by Al-Furat TV and then Al-Hurria, while Iraqia TV was not directly involved in the promotion of political candidates. As expected, the channels tackled in this study showed obvious bias towards their own respective sponsors; they simply negated the existence of other political factions and preferred to air favourable views of the parties that supported them.

The above findings give us a clear indication about the (non-) application of the principles of good journalism, especially neutrality and impartiality. TV channels must be more aware and cautious in covering topics and candidates because they all signed a pledge to remain objective and balanced in their coverage of the election. Yet, the findings show that the four channels were only concerned about presenting their own agenda and conveying favourable ideas about their candidates/sponsors rather than pursuing the truth or criticising their own parties. This was expected because the Iraqi media after 2003 did not witness a real radical and positive change that would enable them to transcend old media practices and partisan allegiances.

What was not expected was the low number of stories featuring horse-race issues. It seemed that the channels preferred to present the candidates' programmes more than predict what might happen on Election Day. However, Al-Furat TV was more interested in airing horse-race issues than the other channels.

Sub-story-level analysis

The last level of content analysis in this study was the investigation of the four TV channels' tendencies in covering the topics and candidates. Tendency here refers to the way each topic or candidate was presented, be it in a neutral, positive, or negative manner. To reach sound results on this aspect of the study, the author classified the most common words or expressions that normally accompany any reference to the topics or candidates based on reading, personal experience, and the outcomes of the pilot study. Hence, the author counted these neutral, positive, or negative words to determine the way that the four channels depicted the topics or candidates.

Whether related to topic or candidate, one can investigate balance on TV news when the numerical sum of positive and negative references is computed, forming a scale of which the point in the middle becomes the neutral point.

Before starting the discussion on the channels' coverage of topics and candidates, it is important to point out some limitations observed in conducting this level of analysis. First, most of the channels tried to avoid any direct reference to other political blocs, especially if it carried negative connotations. For example, Iraqia TV started its February 24 newscast with an editorial speech that made an indirect reference to former Iraqi Prime Minister Ayad Allawi's previous public statement that mentioned the reappearance of unidentified corpses in Baghdad's morgue. Allawi, who was the strongest opponent to Maliki's slate, made a statement that coincided with the election campaign, but it was meant to suggest that the security situation had worsened and reached a level similar to what Iraqis had witnessed during the civil war era, especially in 2006. The story lasted 63 seconds with a newsreader only and was followed later by another story that lasted 190 seconds and tackled the same issue. Iraqia TV accused the people behind making up and disseminating such a claim to be from the Ba'ath party – a term that has very negative connotations for many Iraqis. However, I could not assign any negative attributes to Allawi and his followers because there was no direct reference to the candidate.

Furthermore, Hakim's Al-Furat TV followed the same procedure in its coverage of the Iraqi Prime Minister Nouri Maliki's abuse of power in promoting his slate during the election campaign. For example, one story mentioned the decision to employ 20,000 former Iraqi officers as political propaganda, but no reference was made to Maliki, who was the one who took that decision. Also, there were several reports on a slate whose candidates conspired to buy people's votes by either giving them cash, offering presents, or promising them land and jobs. In all the reports aired, Maliki's slate was not mentioned but only implied – stories aired on the February 28 (sequence 10), March 1 (sequence 12), March 2 (sequence 19), March 3 (sequence 9), March 4 (sequence 16), and March 7 (sequence 11). It is important to note here that all the stories aired by Al-Furat TV in which Maliki was indirectly mentioned were packages denoting the importance given by the channel to such reports.

Topic-level analysis

The first part of this discussion focuses on the discussion of the neutral/positive/negative attributes of each topic. Each topic's attributes are calculated and compared with other channels.

Political differences

With the first topic, as with all the rest, neutral tone refers to reporting the topic without siding with or against it. Positive attributes refer to the efforts, hopes, and aspirations for overcoming any differences among the political parties. On the other hand, the negative tone entails division, discord, and disagreement between the parties.

The neutral and positive references to 'political differences' were somehow similar as there were few discrepancies; however, there were greater differences with negative references to this topic. Al-Furat TV came first with 222 references, followed by Baghdad TV with 129. It seems that Iraqia and Al-Hurria TV did not want to highlight the political differences like the other two channels despite the gloomy reality on the ground. This is partly due to the fact that Iraqia TV is run by the government, whereas Al-Hurria is closely linked to it. This, however, does not mean that the two channels were subjective in their coverage of this topic since the highest number of references centred on the negative attributes.

Security/terrorism

In relation to the topic of 'security/terrorism', the neutral attributes denote reporting the facts on the ground without deletions or additions. In addition, there should be no unwarranted praise of the government's effort to establish security or unsubstantiated criticism against other parties or officials. As for the positive tone, it refers to the flattering and/or pointless applause given to the security forces or the government in restoring peace and order. This could surely be seen as one way of giving credit to the government in terms of its alleged success in achieving remarkable security gains.

Finally, negative attributes entail that there is an unnecessary or overstated amount of criticism against the government, security forces, or the army. It could be related to some unproven or unconfirmed accusations or claims that are meant to discredit the government and its ability to protect the Iraqi people. Indeed, Iraqia TV showed imbalance and subjectivity in reporting this topic. Unlike the reality on the ground, the greatest number of references to security/terrorism was on the positive attributes, followed by the neutral references. As for the negative references made by this channel, they constituted about 9.5 per cent of the total number of references to this topic.

A similar feature was found in the coverage of the channels Al-Furat and Al-Hurria, which mostly mentioned positive references to this topic. This is probably due to the fact that Iraqi security forces are mostly made up of members from Hakim's military Badr Brigade and Talabani's Kurdish Peshmerga. On the other hand, the Sunni Baghdad TV mostly referred to security/terrorism in a negative manner, with about 55.6 per cent of the total number of references to this topic, which marked a major gap in differences in relation to the other channels. This is probably related to the fact that Iraqi Sunnis are under-represented in the security forces and are the most persecuted segment in the society in terms of subjection to random arrests, interrogation, and detention.

Democracy

As for the topic of democracy, it is a relatively new concept in Iraq since it was not really practised during Saddam Hussein's rule. The US administration tried to disseminate it to the public though it was rarely applied by all of the parties concerned. However, democracy is always linked to the new Iraq, along with freedom of speech and the ethnic and religious diversity in the composition of the government. In this study, the negative attributes of democracy are related to the lack of it or its abuse by some political parties.

As for the positive tone, it denotes praise of the new democracy that Iraq allegedly enjoys. The positive references to this topic can give us a good indication of the nature of the four channels. Iraqia TV came first with the most positive references, followed by Al-Furat and Al-Hurria.

Baghdad TV came last with the least positive references. The fact that Iraqia TV never made any negative reference to this topic and that 92.1 per cent of its total number of references were centred on its positive features suggests that Iraqia TV presented a one-sided view of reality. This is because the channel ignored the presence of the negative aspects of this topic that are seen abundantly in everyday life in Iraq.

Public services

The topic of 'public services' is of great concern to many Iraqis due to their great shortages. About seven years after the US-led coalition invaded the country in 2003, Iraq regressed and became one of the worst countries in the region in terms of education, health care, and the rapid spread of illiteracy. Public services include the provision of water and sewage services, electricity, education, and childcare. It also involves assisting Iraqis working in other sectors, like agriculture and industry. In terms of the negative feature, it refers to the lack of or intentional negligence by the government to provide public services to the people. On the other hand, positive attributes mean that there is some kind of applause for the government or a political party for their efforts to provide these services.

Baghdad TV was the most critical channel although it aired the largest number of positive references on this topic, too. It was followed by Al-Furat TV and then Al-Hurria channel, although the two channels focused on presenting the positive references more than the negative ones. On the other hand, Iraqia TV did not seem to be interested in reporting on this topic, despite the fact that Iraqis were preoccupied by it. Except for Baghdad TV, the other three channels did not cover this topic objectively as the facts publicly known gave us a completely different picture.

Corruption/violation

The fourth topic is 'corruption/violation'. Indeed, Iraq is still regarded as one of the most corrupt countries in the world (Transparency International 2010). Here, the positive attributes related to this topic refer to successful efforts to combat or counter corruption in the country. In other words, there is some kind of praise for the government or the political parties concerned in stopping corruption. As for the negative features, they are related to the critical and harsh views that depict corruption with some kind of emotionalism. Baghdad TV came first once more with its negative references to corruption, followed again by Al-Furat TV and then Al-Hurria channel. Interestingly, the same sequence was found in the positive references to this topic with a greater gap separating Baghdad TV from the others. This was not expected; however, Baghdad TV's focus was not on praising the government but rather on airing how its IAF candidates would restore transparency and combat corruption if they got elected. On the other hand, Iraqia TV did not give this topic enough attention and mainly concentrated on reporting it in a neutral manner. Again, this aspect of Iraqia TV's coverage proved that it was not balanced in the way that it reported on corruption.

National unity/political dialogue

'National unity/political dialogue' was an important topic because Iraq went though a civil war following the 2006 bombing of the Samaraa Shiite shrine. After 2008, Iraqi TV channels generally tried to avoid any kind of direct confrontation and criticism of ethnic or religious groups in the country to calm down the already tense situation; the channels were adhering to the Communications and Media Commission's (CMC's) media regulations. The negative references to national unity/political dialogue denote the failure to establish a dialogue between conflicting parties. On the other hand, the positive attributes are related to showing the successful fruits of political dialogue and/or praising the national unity enjoyed by Iraqis in general and the political parties in particular. There is a concentration on the positive references to this topic. One might expect that Iraqia TV would come first as it always presented positive news on the progress in the country; however, Baghdad TV was ahead. This was probably done to avoid any kind of accusations that the Sunni IAF slate had narrow sectarian orientations. In the end, more Iraqis might be convinced to vote for IAF candidates. The same argument could be applied to Al-Furat and Al-Hurria, which also concentrated on positive references.

Election fraud

The seventh topic is 'election fraud'. During the election campaign, many observers specifically shown by Al-Furat TV noted that election fraud might take place because of several factors, including Maliki's alleged monopoly of IHEC and the suspicions that accompanied the political allegiances of its members. This was understandable because there were plenty of corrupt officials in Iraq and many doubts were voiced during the 2005 general election. Positive references to election fraud denote that there were successful efforts to counter or stop it. As for the negative attributes, they mainly referred to the alleged presence of fraud or an attempt to forge the election results. Interestingly, one would have expected Baghdad TV to air more negative references that the other channels, but it was Al-Furat TV that did so. The latter's large number of negative references were all focused on the way that Maliki's slate monopolised the state's powers for political propaganda. Though Maliki was rarely mentioned, the reports aired on the Al-Furat channel were very critical, carrying suggestions that Maliki's bloc would win in devious ways. As expected, Iraqia and Al-Hurria mostly focused on the positive side of election fraud, by presenting a mostly transparent electoral process.

Federalism

Another topic is 'federalism', which is a thorny subject because it entails a separatist tendency that is rejected by most Iraqi Arabs. There was a modest number of references to this topic in comparison with the number of references to other topics. Surprisingly, Baghdad TV aired the number of positive references to this topic though one would expect the Kurdish Al-Hurria channel to do so. However, the only negative references to federalism were aired by Baghdad TV. In fact, the negative references were used by some candidates as a powerful promotional tool to convince potential voters that they would fight against any attempt to divide Iraq.

Supporting electoral slate

Probably the most relevant topic to our study is 'supporting electoral slate' because it shows the amount of attention and the dominant tone used in covering this topic. The negative references denote some kind of criticism against the slate that sponsors the channel, whereas the positive features mean some kind of praise for or compliment to the same political slate. As expected, Iraqia TV refrained from supporting any slate; however, there was an indication that it supported Maliki. First, there were some negative references aired on Maliki's competitor, Allawi, and his candidate slates. In fact, Iraqia TV never criticised any other slate. Also, Maliki was shown almost daily using package, voice-over or VO/SOT, either to inaugurate a new construction project and other public-service facilities – see Iraqia TV, March 2, sequence 14, package, 204 seconds and Iraqia TV, March 3, sequence 18, package, 189 seconds – or to follow up on security matters. Almost always he was praised for his achievements, especially on security matters such as inking the Iraq–US agreement to withdraw US forces by the end of 2011. Certainly, airing such footage has a priming effect on the viewers. As a reminder, priming denotes that media channels have a later influence on the viewers that is related to an earlier exposure to news (Bryant and Zilmann 2002, p. 97). In other words, many TV viewers might be convinced to vote for Maliki after repeatedly seeing him in such positive scenes.

Other Iraqi politicians, like the president and his two deputies, were given neither the time nor the frequency to appear in this manner though they also performed similar activities. To give a few examples, Maliki was shown on the February 22 urging Iraqis to vote (26 seconds) in which 'voice-over' was used; however, no other Iraqi politician was given this opportunity. Then, on the March 6, 2010, which was the media silence day, Iraqia TV aired two stories (voice-over) to urge Iraqis to vote. The first story (sequence 5) showed Maliki for 69 seconds, whereas the second story (sequence 6) presented Samarai, who talked for only 37 seconds.

Baghdad TV came first with the largest number of stories and the most time allotted to 'supporting electoral slate'. This surely corresponded with the positive references to 'supporting the electoral slate'. Al-Furat TV came second with a slight gap separating the two channels. Finally, Al-Hurria TV came third with the lowest number of positive references. On the other hand, there were only a few negative references echoing some kind of criticism against representatives of the political blocs that sponsor the channels. Normally, the stories would mention the 'false' accusations to be followed by an intensely fierce defence.

IHEC

The tenth topic is centred on the Iraqi High Electoral Commission (IHEC). Most of the references concentrated on the neutral side, especially those from Iraqia TV. This was expected because this channel is the official one that is responsible for conveying information about the election process to all Iraqis in a timely manner. But what was not expected was the way that Al-Furat TV depicted IHEC. There were many accusations of fraud and suggestions that IHEC's decisions were biased and politicised. Al-Furat TV publicly voiced its frustration against IHEC and even refrained from making any reference to it for two consecutive days (March 1 and 2, 2010).

Other

Finally, the last issue is centred on 'other' topics. As mentioned before, most of the 'other' topics were related to urging Iraqis to vote in the election. Iraqia TV in particular advocated airing most of these calls because it was in the government's interest to have a high turnout.

As for Al-Furat TV, it scored the greatest number of positive references; almost all the calls for participation in the election came from Shiite religious leaders, which was an indirect way of political promotion by insinuating that INA was supported by those leaders. Baghdad TV followed the same technique used by Al-Furat but to a lesser extent, since Sunnis, unlike Shiites, do not have a unified religious leadership to follow.

In brief, the different attributes given to the topics tackled in this study suggest that each TV channel presented its own version of reality; the one that it found most suitable for its audience. To have a deeper look at the differences among the channels in covering the different topics, Kruskal–Wallis' tests were computed on the neutral, positive, and negative attributes of each topic across the four TV channels. The results revealed that few topics showed significant differences among the four channels. The greatest degree of statistically significant differences was generally centred on the topics' negative attributes (six topics) to be followed by the positive references (five topics) and finally the neutral ones (four topics). The topics of 'public services' and 'IHEC' in particular showed significant differences along three different attributes, whereas the topics of 'election fraud' (neutral and negative) and 'corruption/violation' (positive and negative) showed significant differences along two attributes.

Candidates' attributes

The second major results output of this level of coding is the understanding of the candidates' scores along three scales: neutral, positive, and negative. Based on the calculation of the neural/positive/negative words, adjectives, and expressions, I evaluated the tone associated with the candidates' presentation. As mentioned previously, Iraqia TV refrained from covering the activities of political candidates; however, there was a slight concentration on Allawi and his slate. Five negative references were made compared with three neutral ones. Iraqi President Talabani and the parliament speaker, Samarai, both received one neutral reference. Although Maliki was mentioned on a daily basis on this channel, and mostly in a positive way, he was always presented as the prime minister.

As for Al-Furat TV, the concentration of references was naturally on Hakim's slate, with 124 positive attributes. This was expected; however, the ten negative references to Maliki's slate were not expected from this channel. These negative references were made largely because Maliki decided to withdraw from the Shiite alliance that was formed in 2005 to present himself as a unifier of Iraqis, whether they be Sunni or Shiite. Hence, Maliki tried his best to include Sunni figures in his slate, such as the senior members of the Awakening Council of Anbar. Indeed, this move angered Hakim and his bloc, who then seemed to take an antagonistic attitude towards Maliki and his slate. Other references made by Al-Furat TV included nine positive ones on Sadr and his bloc because the two groups had formed an alliance, as mentioned earlier. Finally, there were a few other neutral references made (eight for Hakim and six for Sadr).

The third channel investigated was Baghdad TV. There were few negative references to political blocs, with 20 concentrated on others who were either unknown or unnamed. As for the positive attributes, we find that the largest number of positive references among the four channels was 639 for Samarai's bloc and eight for other slates. In fact, Baghdad TV scored the largest number of stories, greatest time allotment, and the largest number of references to its IAF candidates. Finally, there were seven neutral references to Samarai's bloc.

The last channel investigated was Al-Hurria TV. In terms of the positive references, there were 38 on Talabani's slate, seven for Allawi's bloc, and four for Hakim's slate. As mentioned earlier, the Kurds did not focus on Talabani and his slate because they were investing in other Kurdish-language channels. As for the positive references to other blocs, it seems that the channel had in mind the idea of future alliances with other slates without which the Kurds could not form a majority in parliament. There were few negative references, too. The greatest number of such references was centred on Talanabi's slate (ten), Maliki's slate (six), and Allawi's bloc (three). Finally, neutral attributes were given to Talabani (12), while Sadr and Samarai got one reference each.

Magnitude of inter-channel differences

To examine the details of the differences in covering the candidates among the four channels and between pair-wise channels, further Kruskal–Wallis and Mann–Whitney Tests were computed (see Tables 6.5, 6.6, and 6.7). In terms of the neutral attributes, there was only one significant difference in the coverage of Talabani and his slate, which was due to Al-Hurria TV's large number of neutral references to its sponsor. As expected, the greatest degree of significant differences was centred on the positive terms and, in particular, the slates of Allawi, Hakim, Samarai, and Talabani.

Table 6.5 Kruskal–Wallis and Mann–Whitney tests: ranking of candidates' neutral attributes

	Iraqia TV Number of references	Al-Furat TV Number of references	Baghdad TV Number of references	Al-Hurria TV Number of references	Chi-square	Asymp. Sig.
Maliki	0^a	0^a	1^a	0^a	2.66	$p < 0.447$
Allawi	3^a	0^a	0^a	0^a	3.26	$p < 0.353$
Hakim	0^a	8^a	1^a	0^a	3.41	$p < 0.333$
Sadr	0^a	6^b	0^a	1^a	5.82	$p < 0.121$
Talabani	1^a	0^a	0^a	12^b	18.83	$^*p < 0.000$
Samarai	1^a	0^a	7^a	1^a	1.07	$p < 0.786$
Others	0^a	0^a	0^a	0^a	0.00	$p < 1.000$

Note: Scores that share the same superscript are not significantly different at the $p < 0.05$ level.
$^*p < 0.000$ (Talabani: There are significant differences in covering this candidate/slate among the channels).

Table 6.6 Kruskal–Wallis and Mann–Whitney tests: ranking of candidates' positive attributes

	Iraqia TV Number of references	Al-Furat TV Number of references	Baghdad TV Number of references	Al-Hurria TV Number of references	Chi-square	Asymp. Sig.
Maliki	0^a	0^a	0^a	0^a	0.00	$p < 1.000$
Allawi	0^a	0^a	0^a	7^a	6.54	$^*p < 0.088$
Hakim	0^a	124^b	0^a	4^a	63.36	$^{**}p < 0.000$
Sadr	0^a	9^b	0^a	0^a	5.76	$p < 0.124$
Talabani	0^a	0^a	0^a	38^b	19.70	$^{***}p < 0.000$
Samarai	0^a	0^a	639^b	0^a	326.67	$^{****}p < 0.000$
Others	0^a	0^a	8^a	0^a	2.66	$p < 0.447$

Note: Scores that share the same superscript are not significantly different at the $p < 0.05$ level.
$^{**}p < 0.088$ (Allawi: There are significant differences in covering this candidate/slate among the channels).
$^{**}p < 0.000$ (Hakim: There are significant differences in covering this candidate/slate among the channels).
$^{***}p < 0.000$ (Talabani: There are significant differences in covering this candidate/slate among the channels).
$^{****}p < 0.000$ ((Samarai: There are significant differences in covering this candidate/slate among the channels).

Table 6.7 Kruskal–Wallis and Mann–Whitney tests: ranking of candidates' negative attributes

	Iraqia TV Number of references	Al-Furat TV Number of references	Baghdad TV Number of references	Al-Hurria TV Number of references	Chi-square	Asymp. Sig.
Maliki	0[a]	10[a]	0[a]	6[a]	3.98	$p < 0.264$
Allawi	5[a]	0[a]	0[a]	3[a]	4.11	$p < 0.250$
Hakim	0[a]	0[a]	0[a]	0[a]	0.00	$p < 1.000$
Sadr	0[a]	0[a]	0[a]	0[a]	0.00	$p < 1.000$
Talabani	0[a]	0[a]	0[a]	10[a]	3.26	$p < 0.353$
Samarai	0[a]	0[a]	0[a]	0[a]	0.00	$p < 1.000$
Others	0[a]	0[a]	25[a]	0[a]	5.33	$p < 0.149$

Note: Scores that share the same superscript are not significantly different at the $p < 0.05$ level.

As for the rest of candidates, there were no differences in the way that they were covered by the four channels. However, the greatest degree of significant difference was found in Samarai's slate due to the large number of positive references made by Baghdad TV to its sponsor. Hakim's slate came second, and Talabani's slate came third, while Allawi was last. It is worth noting that there were no significant differences among the four channels in the negative references to the different candidates. This was probably due to the channels' tendency to avoid criticism of other candidates in order to abide by the CMC's regulations, as stated above.

In relation to the pair-wise comparisons of channels, the greatest degree of agreement in terms of the neutral attributes was between Iraqia and Baghdad, with all of the seven candidates/slates having no significant differences. This was not expected as the two channels are very different in nature.

As for the lowest degree of agreement, it was between Al-Furat and Al-Hurria, with only five candidates/slates that had no significant difference. In relation to the positive attributes, the channels did not have unique or excessive disagreements or agreements. For example, Iraqia and Baghdad on the one hand, and Iraqia and Al-Hurria channels on the other, had six candidates/slates each with no significant differences, whereas Al-Furat and Baghdad on the one hand, and Al-Furat and Al-Hurria on the other, had four candidates/slates each with no significant difference. Finally, all of the four channels had no significant differences in terms of covering the negative attributes of candidates/slates corresponding with the Kruskal–Wallis test, cited above.

Other production techniques

A further important aspect of this level of analysis was the investigation of the production techniques used by the four TV channels in their efforts to influence the viewers by making them pay more attention to the candidate(s) shown. The first section in this type of examination is the presence/absence of political contenders in the news stories. This is a very important indication of whether the channels are balanced enough to present two conflicting or opposing views within the same story. With all the talk of the new media freedom in Iraq and the claims that Iraqi channels are objective and balanced in their coverage, we find the exact opposite in the results cited below. Iraqia TV, for instance, showed only four candidates, without introducing any contenders. Also, Al-Furat TV aired a total of 126 stories without contenders, whereas Baghdad TV aired 157 stories and Al-Hurria TV had 39, with each channel showing two interviews with political contenders from small political parties. Indeed, the tiny amount of attention given to contenders reveals that these channels have ignored other political candidates by regarding them as almost non-existent. Indeed, this aspect of the channels' coverage shows clear imbalance and subjectivity.

On the other hand, we find that these channels aired many stories showing interviews with political affiliates who almost always praised and expressed their allegiance to the concerned parties. As expected, the greatest number of interviews with political affiliates was aired by Baghdad TV, with more than 153 interviews. The last item coded in this section mentioned 'five affiliates or more' because the news story might have contained interviews with more than five affiliates, which actually occurred in very few cases. In the second rank came Al-Furat TV with more than 132 interviews, and then Al-Hurria TV with 45. Finally, Iraqia TV aired five interviews with political affiliates from different parties.

Candidates' spatial relationship

A further aspect related to production technique was the candidate's spatial relationship with others. I followed Patterson and McClure (1976) and Murphy (1998) who classified the spatial relationship of the candidate with others into five categories: candidate shown alone, touching distance to audience, speaking distance, public distance, further or unable to determine (1998, pp. 35–36). Just like the discussion on the 'visual weight', there is a strong link between the way the candidate is shown on screen and the effect on the viewer. For example, there is more influence on the viewer if the candidate is shown within touching or speaking distance of the audience. With this study I added 'candidate shown with others', which carries similar weight to the previous two techniques since the candidate is not always shown speaking to the audience. On the other hand, public distance is assigned when the candidate appears on a stage that is above the level of the audience. This technique is less intimate and has a lesser influence on the viewer because the candidate is made to look isolated from the people around them. The same argument is applied to a candidate 'shown alone'.

In Table 6.8 we find that the greatest number of stories showing one to three candidates within 'speaking distance', 'touching distance' and 'shown with others' was aired by Baghdad TV. As stated above, these production techniques have been identified as having specific influences on viewers. Al-Furat TV came first with the number of stories showing the first candidate in public distance in relation to others. In fact, this

Table 6.8   Candidates' spatial relationship

		Iraqia	Al-Furat	Baghdad	Al-Hurria
Candidates 1	1. Shown alone	4	43	107	21
	2. Shown with others	1	31	45	19
	3. Touching distance to audience	0	10	21	0
	4. Speaking distance	0	2	22	0
	5. Public distance	0	65	36	5
	6. Further or unable to determine	0	0	0	0
Candidates 2	1. Shown alone	1	12	30	5
	2. Shown with others	1	0	7	2
	3. Touching distance to audience	0	0	3	0
	4. Speaking distance	0	0	4	0
	5. Public distance	0	1	14	0
	6. Further or unable to determine	0	0	0	0
Candidates 3	1. Shown alone	0	5	17	4
	2. Shown with others	0	0	4	1
	3. Touching distance to audience	0	0	2	0
	4. Speaking distance	0	0	1	0
	5. Public distance	0	0	6	0
	6. Further or unable to determine	0	0	0	0

technique was forced upon the channel because there were always large numbers of people showing up at public gatherings that were organised by Hakim's slate during the election campaign. Finally, Baghdad TV came first in the number of stories that showed candidates alone, followed by Al-Furat TV and then Al-Hurria channel. In brief, Baghdad TV showed more emphasis on its candidates than the other channels, which was clear by the way that it presented them.

Finally, a Kruskal–Wallis test was computed to understand the significant differences among the four channels. The results showed that the channels had significant differences in relation to all the positions of the first and second candidates' spatial relationship with others except for 'further or unable to determine'. As for the third candidate, the significant differences were only centred on 'shown alone', 'shown with others', and 'public distance'.

Camera angles

The final phase of analysis in this coding frame was related to the camera angles used when a candidate(s) is shown. Kepplinger (1982, 1983) investigated how some camera angles used in filming candidates can influence TV viewers' impressions of those candidates. The results of that study showed that the positive effect of the camera angle is achieved when the camera is held at eye level. This is probably due to the viewer's feeling of being equal with and close to the candidate. As for a bottom-angle shot, this has a negative impact on the viewer but it is meant to show power and authority. In addition, Graber examined how camera angles can influence the manner in which the audience comprehend the message; for example, 'audiences are likely to pay more attention to close-ups and identified elements' (2001, p. 197). Grabe and Bucy confirm that:

> when candidates are portrayed in close-up shots that promote emotional involvement and establish social proximity between televised subjects and viewers.... By minimizing the psychological distance between viewing audiences and actors on the political stage, television prompts viewers to regard candidates in personal terms, fostering familiarity and trust.
>
> (2009, p. 153)

In other words, there is more 'visual weight' with the camera's close-up and eye-level positions, increasing the importance of the candidate.

Table 6.9 Camera angles

		Iraqia	Al-Furat	Baghdad	Al-Hurria
Candidates 1	1. Eye level	5	117	153	41
	2. Full top view	0	1	1	0
	3. Bottom view	0	0	3	0
	4. Close-up	0	98	130	27
Candidates 2	1. Eye level	2	13	44	7
	2. Full top view	0	0	0	0
	3. Bottom view	0	0	2	0
	4. Close-up	1	13	34	5
Candidates 3	1. Eye level	0	5	25	5
	2. Full top view	0	0	0	0
	3. Bottom view	0	0	1	0
	4. Close-up	0	5	21	4

As expected, we find in Table 6.9 that Baghdad TV placed more emphasis on its IAF candidates by showing them more than the other channels did in close-up and eye-level angles. This was not only confined to the first candidates but also to the second and third candidates when available. In the second rank came Al-Furat TV, which was followed by Al-Hurria channel.

To sum up, Baghdad TV was more fervent than the other channels in its emphasis on the importance of its candidates at all the production levels. The channel scored more stories and used more 'favourable' techniques than the others in terms of the number of political affiliates interviewed, its candidates' spatial relationship with others, and camera angles (eye-level view and close-up). Based on the same criteria, Al-Furat TV came second in relation to the attention given to its candidates, while Al-Hurria came third. As for Iraqia TV, the main emphasis was on the topics aired rather than political candidates.

Conclusion

Based on the data reported above, we can conclude that all the TV channels examined in this study showed some kind of imbalance and subjectivity in their coverage of either the topics or the candidates. Balance is measured by counting the negative and positive references to topics/candidates, and what we observed was that all of the channels, except in a few cases, tended to align either with the positive or the negative side. To answer two of the research questions in this study – How did these channels present different issues in the election campaign? And which issues were made prominent? – we need to discuss whether the channels discussed above presented the election news in a certain direction. In their study, Garyantes and Murphy (2010) compared Al-Jazeera.net (English version) with CNN.com's coverage of the 2005 Iraqi election. The study concluded that CNN framed the election news by mainly presenting positive news, whereas Al-Jazeera pictured the election with some kind of negativity by projecting doubt about the election results. Yet, this study is limited to the English-language websites. Research on the election coverage of Al-Jazeera.net and CNN.com in the Arabic language was not conducted, despite the fact that the candidates are mostly Arabs and their political statements are almost always communicated in Arabic. Also, conducting an empirical TV study on Al-Jazeera and CNN's coverage of the Iraqi election would probably have yielded a great deal of information about framing and news values.

In this study, Iraqia TV presented the election news in a certain direction that mostly showed the positive side and completely ignored negative events or issues. Except for the topic of 'political differences', which was mildly shown in a negative manner, the channel presented the topics of 'security/terrorism', 'democracy', 'national unity/political dialogue', and 'other' in a positive way by highlighting the achievements of the Iraqi government. In some cases the channel ignored or downplayed the importance of certain issues that irked Iraqis, such as 'public services' and 'election fraud', which mostly had a neutral tone, and 'federalism'. Based on what is discussed above, Iraqia TV was not balanced in its coverage of the election because it intended to follow the Iraqi government's policy of showing the bright side and ignoring the reality on the ground. Hence, the channel deviated from its mandate to remain independent from the state's policy.

Also, Iraqia TV emphasised the issue of participating in the elections and downsized the topic of 'security/terrorism' to project an ideal image to the audience. All the other channels aired news stories that encouraged Iraqis to vote. Although there are no Iraqi audience studies that can be referred to, the 2010 general election witnessed a high turnout despite the security concerns. Media outlets must have had a role in this high turnout, especially in the Sunni areas, as Iraqis mainly get their news from the TV. IHEC mentioned that 11,526,412 Iraqis voted in 2010 out of 18,892,000 registered voters.

The second channel discussed was Al-Furat TV. It differed from Iraqia TV in presenting some topics, especially 'political differences', 'corruption/violation', and 'election fraud', which had extremely negative tones to discredit Maliki's government. What was implied and directly stated in 'supporting electoral slates' was that the channel set its candidates above the others in terms of their alleged sincerity and faithfulness to building Iraq and serving its people. As Al-Furat TV belongs to Hakim's slate, which had a large representation in the government, it was not surprising to find that the topics of 'security/terrorism', 'democracy', 'public services', 'national unity/political dialogue', and 'other', which mainly called on Iraqis to vote in the election, were presented in a positive manner. Also, Al-Furat TV highlighted the topics of 'election fraud' and 'corruption/violation' to discredit Maliki's government and convince more voters to vote for Hakim's slate rather than Maliki's group. A US cable written at the beginning of 2010 revealed that INA based its media campaign on 'the principles of a unified, sovereign Iraq that draws authority from the constitution, and is run by a strong federal government in conjunction with empowered local administrations and governments'. Yet the issue of De-Ba'athification became one of the most important topics that INA played upon (Wikileaks 2010g). The 2010 election results showed that Maliki failed to win the majority; instead, Allawi's Iraqiya slate won 91 seats in parliament. Different TV channels must have contributed to Maliki's loss since he was attacked by many opponent sides.

Baghdad TV, on the other hand, was the only channel that presented the news in a way that significantly differed from the rest of the channels. This was mainly due to the nature of the channel's Sunni sponsors, who seemed to feel that they needed to overstate the shortcomings of Maliki's government and stress that its candidates would be better alternatives. Certainly, the production techniques used, such as the candidates' spatial relationship with others and the camera angles, overemphasised the importance of IAF's candidates. The channel presented the topics of 'political differences', 'security/terrorism', 'public services', 'election fraud', and 'other' in an extremely negative tone. Surprisingly, the topics of 'federalism', 'corruption/violation', and 'democracy' were presented in a positive way, although the channel was expected to project dominant negative attributes to them. However, the channel's intention was to stress that its candidates would be the right choice for Iraqi voters in order to establish a democratic state in which corruption and calls for federalism would be strongly dealt with. The main themes of IAF's media campaign were stressing 'the importance of improving security and the provision of public services', according to Osama Al-Tikriti (Wikileaks 2010f).

In fact, the Iraqi Islamic Party entered the 2010 election in a bad shape, especially after losing Tariq Al-Hashimi, Rafi' Al-Eissawi, and Salih Al-Mutlaq's National Dialogue Council (who joined Allawi's Al-Iraqiya's slate instead); hence, the IAF toiled 'to position itself as the most coherent, dependable, and non-Ba'athist option for Sunni voters' (Wikileaks 2010f). Contrary to Baghdad TV's desire, Samarai's slate suffered a great blow during the 2010 elections. In the December 2005 election the Iraqi Islamic Party, which was affiliated within the IAF, had 44 seats in parliament, yet it ended up with just six seats in the 2010 election.

This was mainly due to the lack of trust among Sunnis towards the Iraqi Islamic Party's false promises for change. In the end, IAF mainly appealed to a small number of 'Sunni Islamists, who look with suspicion at more secular parties' (Wikileaks 2010f). Hence, Baghdad TV's efforts to promote its slate and polish the image of its candidates by its continuous coverage and exaggerated emphasis were in vain.

Finally, Al-Hurria TV, due to the nature of its sponsor, presented the news in a way that showed its close link to the Iraqi government. Similar to Iraqi TV, Al-Hurria channel showed the topics of 'security/terrorism', 'democracy', 'public services', 'national unity/political dialogue', 'election fraud', 'federalism', and 'other' in a positive way. Only the topics of 'political differences' and 'corruption/violation' were presented in a slightly negative way. In other words, Al-Hurria TV was on the extremely positive side, while Baghdad TV had the opposite negative position. The main themes of the PUK's media campaign were 'the delivery of services, responsiveness to citizens, and transparency' (Wikileaks 2010bb).

Similar to Baghdad TV, Al-Hurria failed to win voters in central and southern Iraq since the Kurdish bloc won most of their seats in Kurdistan. A US cable described how a senior member of the PUK, Friad Rwanduzi, worked on finding a voice for the Kurds in Baghdad to 'advocate for Kurdish rights', which will ultimately lead to achieving the Kurds' 'need for stability and prosperity' in Kurdistan (Wikileaks 2010bb). Contrary to the official Kurdish expectations, the Kurds suffered great election losses in Baghdad, where millions or hundreds of thousands of them were believed to reside. In a statement that testifies to the presence of Kurds in Baghdad and reflects the kind of ethnic division that characterises modern-day Iraq, Muhammed Amin Daloyee, head of the KDP's Baghdad branch, once stated: 'If you say half of Baghdad are Kurds yet you don't get their votes in the elections, we should then say they are all traitors' (Saadi and Ahmed 2011). It seems that Al-Hurria TV did not have much influence on those Kurds.

In brief, all of the four channels presented the news story topics in directions that generally reflected the policies of the channels' sponsors. The analysis cited above reflects the partisan nature of these channels and the mostly one-sided outlook by which they viewed the issues and candidates investigated in this study. All of the channels, except for Iraqia TV, gave generous attention to their political candidates, whether in their verbal narratives, still images, films, production techniques, spatial relationships with the audience, and use of camera angles.

Conclusion

The US political design to shape Iraq as a democracy had catastrophic consequences on the country's political and social levels, which will remain apparent for decades to come. The new ethno-sectarian Iraqi media, an extension of this new political reality, has played a major role in enhancing the divisions in Iraqi society. In their book *Erasing Iraq* (2010), Otterman, Hil, and Wilson refer to the change that occurred in Iraqi society after the occupation as a 'sociocide' caused by forced displacement and targeted violence. This is, unfortunately, part of the USA's pragmatic policy, which also entails a misreading of Iraq's history and society and a miscalculation of the potential damage of sectarianism. Although the sectarian violence in the country has dramatically decreased in recent years, and the Iraqi media rhetoric has positively improved, there is still a physical and social rift – the city of Baghdad and other strategic regions have become divided into Sunni and Shiite neighbourhoods that are mostly separated by concrete walls. Socially, intermarriages between Sunnis and Shiites have become a rare event. Indeed, the wounds inflicted during the sectarian tension need a great deal of time to heal, but first Iraqi media outlets must address Iraqis as a whole and seek independence from their sponsors before a positive change can occur.

If a comparison is made between the Iraqi media before the war and that after it, it is apparent that Iraqis have gained a pluralistic media but not much freedom because journalists are still practising self-censorship. Iraqi Media Network (IMN), especially the Iraqia TV channel, has been a tool used by consecutive prime ministers and high-ranking officials like Al-Hakim, who ruled the country after 2003. IMN has never attempted to alienate itself from the government nor has it criticised its policies or some of the violations committed by the US-led forces. This shows that the plan to establish independent media, such as a public broadcasting station, was only wishful thinking on the part of the US government, which itself worked on undermining IMN's independence. Accordingly, IMN staff were looked upon by many Iraqis as agents for the US and Iraqi governments. This fact probably justifies why IMN employees suffered the greatest number of casualties among all the other media outlets operating in Iraq. Hence, the US and some European governments that ardently support the Iraqi government must play a greater role in making sure that Iraq does not descend into the past and restore its infamous authoritarian press. Also, international human rights and media organisations will surely play a positive role here.

Iraqi media practitioners are fully aware of the rules of impartial and objective reporting and the regulations surrounding the coverage of elections. Almost all Iraqi TV channels assume they are objectively and accurately reporting the truth by following a Western model of objectivity. They basically agree on two things: reality should be covered objectively and violations of this norm are wrong. This study has addressed this issue to see whether Iraqi TV channels endeavoured to meet the principles of objectivity, impartiality, balance, and fairness in covering the 2010 general election. Despite the fact that journalists in Iraq today have relative freedom to publish their views, they generally tend to refrain from conducting serious investigative reporting and direct confrontation with the government. Indeed, they avoid criticising official policies, especially during election times. This is, in fact, reminiscent of the conditions for journalists in Europe before the 1980s, when journalists used to follow the *sacerdotal* editorial approach that greatly depended on the media policy of the ruling party (Semetko et al. 1991). As most Arab countries are still taking their first steps towards democracy and power-sharing systems, we can predict that in the coming decade(s), the state of journalism in the Arab world will be similar to what is currently found in Europe, where journalists generally follow the *pragmatic* editorial approach. Although the pace of change is rather slow, the popular revolutions that swept the Arab world, starting with Tunisia in late 2010, are true testimonies that better political accountability, transparency, democracies, and above all media freedoms will materialise sooner than expected.

The principles of good journalism, like objectivity and impartiality, are the main elements that this study is concerned with. I traced the (non)-application of these principles throughout my research. In relation to objectivity, it is usually associated with newsroom practices in which journalists produce news. Generally, it refers to 'giving a full and accurate account of events being reported which reflects as closely as possible the true facts of a matter. Thus, the facts of the matter can be independently verified and shown to be true' (Gunter 1997, p. 9). The verification of facts can be done by referring to the events taking place, figures, and statistics released or accepted by neutral bodies. Also, objective reporting means that journalists must maintain balance and fairness by devoting equal time to the different sides (Everette and Merrill 1996).

As for impartiality, Westerståhl (1983) states that journalists must keep their distance when they report the news and must avoid taking sides in any issue. Though it is a difficult task, journalists are expected to perform their job in the most professional manner to ensure that the public are both informed and educated correctly.

Furthermore, news values play an important role in directing journalists towards the selection of stories and later reporting these stories in the proper order. The 'intrinsic' news values associated with newsworthiness are: impact; timeliness; prominence; proximity; audience; oddity; celebrity; conflict; sensational; and magnitude (Ryan and O'Donnell 2001, pp. 49–52; Harrison 2006, p. 137). These are the basic elements that journalists are expected to look for. Unfortunately, some reporters avoid following the principles of good journalism, which normally leads to biased reporting.

In this context, bias is usually linked to the following traits: an unbalanced selection of presentation; partiality; attitude that hinders fair or balanced reporting; one-sidedness; sensational and personal preferences to one side; favouritism that deforms the facts; and irrational assessment (Sloan and Mackay 2007, p. 6). In his analysis of the news output of the BBC and his observation of the way its journalists worked, Schlesinger stressed that there were indications that the coverage of the conflict in Northern Ireland was biased despite the fact that the BBC journalists tried to be objective (1987, p. 12). One of the benefits of this study is that it gives an indication about the need to have external observers who can detect shortcomings and wrong journalistic practices without being directly involved in the work of the news organisation.

The results of the programme level of analysis showed that the four channels covered the election in a one-sided and partial way because they only presented their own viewpoints while excluding other opposing voices. Based on the number of stories, time allotment, and type of news formats, I concluded that Baghdad TV came in first place for covering the election and promoting its political sponsor, followed by Al-Furat channel. Iraqia TV came in third place, while Al-Hurria TV came last because it showed the least amount of interest in promoting its party and covering the election. This is mainly due to the fact that the Kurdish party that sponsors the channel had other media outlets broadcasting in the Kurdish language that targeted Kurds rather than Arabs. These findings are expected because the channels investigated in this study are mostly partisan and their aim is to promote their sponsors. Also, the state-run Iraqia TV differed from other official channels in the Arab world in the sense that it did not directly promote the ruling party during the general election. However, there were indications that Iraqia favoured Maliki's party.

In terms of the issues/topics covered, Iraqia channel covered all the topics except for 'federalism' and 'supporting electoral slate'. This channel highlighted the topic of 'IHEC' in the number of stories and time allotment and 'other' in the time allotment. As for the Kurdish Al-Hurria TV, it paid the least kind of attention to promoting its sponsors in connection to the number of stories, airtime, and news formats. In fact, this channel was similar to Iraqia TV in covering some topics, such as 'IHEC' and 'other', since both are closely affiliated to the Iraqi government. Al-Hurria TV focused on the topic of 'federalism' more than the other channels because Kurds advocated this kind of political system more than all the other ethnic groups in Iraq.

On the other hand, Al-Furat TV placed more emphasis on covering the topics of 'political difference', 'democracy', 'election fraud', and 'security/terrorism'. As for Baghdad TV, it came first in the emphasis it showed for covering the topics of 'security/terrorism' (in terms of the number of stories), 'public services', 'corruption/violation', 'national unity/political dialogue', 'federalism', 'supporting electoral slate', and 'other' (in terms of time allotment).

Turning to the story level, the results showed that the four channels did not abide by the principles of good journalism. At this level of analysis, the preferred or dominant story format used in covering each topic was selected by choosing the largest number of stories and the most time allotted to each topic. I concluded that Baghdad TV paid the most attention to the coverage of the election and its preferred topics, while Al-Furat TV came second. It was followed by Iraqia channel, whereas Al-Hurria TV came fourth for its emphasis on the election and the topics it covered.

Finally, the candidate/topic level of analysis also showed bias and imbalance exercised by the four channels. Here, balance is calculated by counting the positive and negative references to the candidates and topics. Except in a few cases, all of the four channels either covered the candidates/topics in positive or negative ways depending on the channels' background and ideology. In relation to the candidates' coverage, there was little criticism, which is somehow similar to other studies on the election in the Arab world. We find in these studies that there is a clear avoidance of criticising politicians and their parties, probably to keep away from troubles (see AWGMM's various reports 2009a, 2009b, 2009c, 2010a, 2010b, 2010c, and 2011).

In relation to the stories featuring narrative references to political candidates, film/image of the candidates, and interview with the candidates, Baghdad TV came first, followed by Al-Furat channel, and then Al-Hurria TV. On the other hand, the Iraqia channel did not directly promote any candidate though it indirectly favoured Maliki. The results above showed that these channels were subjective and partial in their coverage. Equal air time was not given to other parties even if they were not opposing the channels' sponsors. Indeed, these channels were only pre-occupied with projecting their own agenda by following the 'party logic' instead of the 'media logic'.

Presentation of the election on Iraqi TV

I concluded that all of the channels investigated in this study presented the general election in a manner that suited their own sponsor's background and political belief. Mazzoleni (1987) asserted that journalists and news organisations shape news values and the news stories presented to the audience. Of course, the aim of news selection is to influence the audience to take 'favourable' decisions, especially on Election Day.

Evidence for potential bias

Based on the analysis of the data collected, Iraqia TV presented many story topics in a mostly positive way and ignored the negative side. For example, this channel presented the story topics of 'democracy', 'national unity/political dialogue', and 'other' positively by emphasising the Iraqi government's accomplishments. On the other hand, Iraqia TV ignored other story topics that were important for Iraqis, like 'public services' and 'election fraud', because it wanted to show the bright side of the reality; it also downsized the importance of 'federalism', a topic that creates a great deal of controversy among Iraqis. Also, the channel highlighted the topic of election participation more than the others, while it neglected the issue of security/terrorism. This is part of the state-run TV station's agenda to urge Iraqis to vote to make the electoral process succeed and to show that Iraq is a secure and safe country due to the 'sincere' efforts of the government and its prime minister.

Despite the fact that there are no published audience-based studies on the Iraqi audience perception of the election and the issues that accompanied this event, it was known that the 2010 general election had a considerably high turnout. This was partly due to the disappointment that Iraqis felt towards the crippled political process and possibly because of the influence of TV, which is the favourite media outlet in Iraq.

In terms of Al-Furat TV, this channel emphasised the issues of 'election fraud', 'corruption/violation', and 'political differences' and presented them in a negative manner to present Maliki and his followers as corrupt people who cannot unite Iraqis. In this way, the channel was aiming to persuade potential voters to vote for other slates. The channel presented the story topic of 'supporting electoral slates' in an extreme favourable way by showing the 'achievements' of its candidates and highlighting their 'integrity'. Other story topics were covered in a positive manner, like 'security/terrorism', 'democracy', 'public services', 'national unity/political dialogue', and 'other'; Hakim's party played an instrumental role in the Iraqi government as many of its figures occupied important posts, so it was important to highlight some of their achievements. Hakim's party, which runs Al-Furat TV, won 70 parliamentary seats out of 325, yet most of these seats were won by the Sadr movement (39). In other words, Al-Furat TV did not seem to have influenced as many people as the channel had initially expected to.

Baghdad TV stood on the opposite side to the other channels mainly because it is run by a Sunni party whose members seek more power and influence in the government. Iraqi Accord Front's candidates were shown as the best choice for Iraqi voters; this was clearly manifested in the news formats and production techniques used, such as the candidates' spatial relationship with others and the camera angles. Baghdad TV covered the story topics of 'political differences', 'security/terrorism', 'public services', 'election fraud', and 'other' in a highly negative manner. Interestingly, more election coverage and emphasis on candidates do not always mean that the channel's sponsor is going to have more voters. Despite the tireless efforts of Baghdad TV to promote its candidates, Samarai's party lost in the 2010 elections by securing just six parliament seats.

Finally, Al-Hurria TV was similar to the Iraqia channel in the way news stories were presented. The channel showed the topics of 'security/terrorism', 'democracy', 'public services', 'national unity/political dialogue', 'election fraud', 'federalism', and 'other' in a positive manner. On the other hand, the story topics of 'political differences' and 'corruption/violation' were somehow presented negatively. Al-Hurria TV did not seem to achieve its aims by convincing Arabs or other Kurds who speak Arabic to vote for the Kurdish Alliance; the main Kurdish parties won only seven parliament seats in the provinces that are not geographically linked to Iraqi Kurdistan. In total, the Kurdish Alliance won 43 seats.

Throughout the presentation of topics, we can see that the channels investigated here followed the advocacy model and echoed the views of their sponsors. Though the media coverage is different, Donsbach reached similar conclusions about the coverage of the German Bundestag Election of 1994. The author found that the news presented the political process by analysing 18 German media channels that mostly supported certain political parties (1997).

When journalists endorse the ideology of some parties without any kind of questioning, they become 'agenda senders' instead of 'agenda setters' (Semetko and Canel 1997). Indeed, the ideology held by journalists plays a major role in news selection since they are driven to 'select some aspects of a perceived reality and make them more salient in a communicating text, in such a way as to promote a particular problem definition, causal interpretation, moral evaluation, and/or treatment recommendation' (Entman 1993, p. 52). In other words, the Iraqi journalists working for the different channels investigated in this study generally reflect the ideology of the parties that sponsor their TV channels. This probably explains why most of these journalists are selected according to their ethnic or sectarian backgrounds so there is minimal chance of conflict with the channels' editorial policies.

It is important to note that Iraq's media is not unique; other countries that have emerged from authoritarian rule still suffer due to the prevalent culture. For example, after the collapse of communism in Eastern Europe, journalism did not witness a radical and positive change. This fact was related to the political reality as the fall of communism did not resolve all the previous hardship and difficulties; instead, new problems emerged, such as government corruption (Jakubowicz and Sukosd 2008, p. 34). Though there are differences in the degree of change that occurred, most of Eastern Europe, including the former Soviet Union countries, is still suffering from a media that is 'highly politicised, particularly in the case of broadcasting, and with limited independence from the political elite' (Jakubowicz 2001, p. 59). Unfortunately, the negative impact of some old political and social policies affected journalism practice, which was mostly based on 'partisan advocacy rather than objectivity' (Aumente et al. 1999, p. 81). For example, Romanian journalists trained by Western experts to become more balanced and fair in their reporting still believe that their task is to voice their opinions in addition to the facts (Jakubowicz and Sukosd 2008, pp. 196–197). Georgiadis (2004) offers a description of post-communist Romanian media that is interestingly typical of the post-2003 media in Iraq:

> The media has diversified greatly... in post-Communist Romania. Election choices, international structures and nongovernmental agencies will continue to influence and change the political and media culture while a weak economy and authoritarian mentality in the government and legal system offer challenges to a developing free press and young democracy in Romania.
>
> (p. viii)

In Poland, where the press was previously polarised and centralised by the government (Kowalski 1988), Polish journalists still believe that it is 'their duty to take sides in the many divisions within Polish society and promote the cause they support' (Jakubowicz and Sukosd 2008, pp. 196–197).

In post-communist Russia, journalists are still struggling to voice their views without the fear of censorship and the influence of the past. Voltmer mentions that there are positive journalistic outcomes of the advent of the new political system, yet there is still a 'high degree of subjective evaluations indicating the persistence of the historical legacy of Russian journalism' (2000, p. 469). Ironically, Russian journalists who try to follow the Western standards of objectivity and balance in reporting are sometimes labelled as 'robots' by fellow journalists (ibid., p. 478). Oates (2006) confirms that the concepts of media freedom and objectivity are not 'central to Russian watching habits' (p. 20). Such as the case of Iraq, Oates observed that the 'problem of lack of objectivity or balance do not keep Russians from reading, viewing and listening to the mass media' (2006, p. 31).

Similar to post-communist countries but to a varying degree, the Western concept of objectivity in Latin America remains blurred. Waisbord (2000) investigated the kind of watchdog journalism that is practised in South America, where a culture of investigative journalism was prevalent in the mainstream media in the 1980s and 1990s. The author explores how, in particular, the concept of objectivity was affected by the kind of advocacy journalism that is somehow prevalent in many parts of Latin America, saying:

> Despite the long-standing influence of the U.S. press, neither objectivity nor 'journalism as science' acquired the status of *uber*principles in South American journalism. The view that news reporting implies a double process of assembling facts and separating facts from opinions never attained a dominant position. Consequently, the distinction between facts and opinion has been murkier than in U.S. journalism. Conventions of news reporting remained ambiguously defined.
>
> (Waisbord 2000, p. 121)

The liberalisation period in Latin America that followed the Second World War did not bring with it the expected adoption of the Anglo-American concept of objectivity. Instead, the 'tradition of journalism of opinion maintained its influence' (p. 121) and journalists looked at this concept with scepticism due to its unrealistic goal (p. 124). Since most news organisations were 'politically committed' (p. 125), following this journalistic principle was only wishful thinking. Similar to Iraq's case, the author stresses the difficulties faced by journalists who emerge from an era of dictatorship to a political system that calls for democracy and freedom. In their efforts to conduct investigative reporting, Latin American journalists face numerous challenges, such as: internal obstacles in the newsroom, the fact that 'editorial boards and publishers are timid', the 'verbal and physical threats' against journalists, and the 'absence of legal mechanism to have access to official records' (p. 244). Though the situation in Iraq is more intense, there are many similarities between the two political and media systems. In relation to this study, the Iraqi TV channels discussed here were rather reserved in showing the negative attributes of other candidates/slates because they either feared retribution, libel suits, or the breaking of possible political alliances in the near future, especially during the formation of the parliament. This situation is similar to what Europe went through in the decades that preceded the 1980s. Semetko et al. (1991) described it as a *sacerdotal* editorial approach that heavily relied on conservative official policies or the 'party logic'.

To improve the Iraqi media, IMN, with its affiliate media outlets like Iraqia TV, must become truly impartial and independent from the government; IMN has been aligned with the ruling entity since its establishment in 2003. Also, a stronger and more transparent role for the Iraqi Communications and Media Commission (CMC) is urgently needed. The CMC, which regularly monitors all the media outlets, has been a defender of the government and its prime minister instead of questioning everyone. Sadly, it blindly follows Maliki's orders in closing down TV stations just because they opposed his policies. Indeed, the CMC must be a separate entity that answers to no one but the Iraqi parliament and the public. Also, the Iraqi Media Center, which is run by Maliki's media advisor, must either be truly independent from the prime minister's grip or be dissolved because it is functioning as a propaganda tool for Maliki. Finally, pluralistic media outlets are surely needed in Iraq, but they must not be allowed to regard other sects or ethnic minorities as foreign to Iraq's mosaic of religious and ethnic groups. This will ensure that media channels will not be responsible for politically, socially, or culturally dividing the country.

Despite the new political change and the new talk on spreading and applying democracy, Iraqi journalists are generally reluctant to point out the shortcomings of their government or armed militias with whom they might share an ideological belief. Yet with the emergence of popular revolutions in the Arab world and in Iraq in particular, the near future might witness more freedoms and better media channels that can freely point out shortcomings and hold the government and its officials accountable for what they do.

Appendix I
Na'im 'Abd Muhalhal's Article

Al-Nasiriya, July 21, 2001

America, an obsession called Osama Bin Ladin

Osama Bin Ladin says that he took from the desert its silence and its anger at the same time. He has learned how to harm America and has been able to do it, for he gave a bad reputation to the Pentagon as being weakened in more than one spot in the world. In order to follow one step taken by Bin Ladin America has put to work all its apparatus, its computers and its satellites just as the governor cowboy of Texas has done. Bin Ladin's name has been posted on all the internet sites and an amount of 5 million dollars has been awarded to anyone who could give any information that would lead to the arrest of this lanky, lightly bearded man. In this man's heart you'll find an insistence, a strange determination that he will reach one day the tunnels of the White House and will bomb it with everything that is in it.

We all know that every age has its revolutionary phenomenon. In Mexico there was Zapata. In Bolivia there was Che Guevara, during the seventies came out Marcos and the Red Brigades in Italy, the Baader Meinhof Gang in Germany and there was Leila Khaled the Palestinian woman and others. They all appeared in violence and disappeared quietly. During the nineties Bin Ladin came out in the open having been completely overtaken in his mind by the robbery happening to his country and its treasurers. For him it was the beginning of the revolution. For this endeavour he mobilized everything that he had of money, of investments and Sudan was his first stop. Bin Ladin ended up in Afghanistan where his revolutionary drive pushed this stubborn revolutionary to plan very carefully, and in a very detailed manner, his stand to push back the boastful American onslaught and to change the American legend into a bubble of soap.

Because Bin Ladin knows what causes pain to America, he played America's game, just as an oppressed man entertains itself with the thing oppressing him. He countered with the language of dynamite and explosives in the city of Khobar and destroyed two US embassies in Nairobi and Dar al Salaam. America says, admitting just like a bird in the midst of a tornado, that Bin Ladin is behind the bombing of its destroyer in Aden. The fearful series of events continues for

America and the terror within America gets to the point that the Governor of Texas increases the amount of the award, just as the stubbornness of the other man and his challenge increases. This challenge makes it such that one of his grandchildren comes from Jeddah travelling on the official Saudi Arabia airlines and celebrates with him the marriage of one of the daughters of his companions.

Bin Ladin has become a puzzle and a proof also, of the inability of the American federalism and the C.I.A. to uncover the man and uncover his nest. The most advanced organizations of the world cannot find the man and continues to go in cycles in illusion and presuppositions. They still hope that he could come out from his nest one day, they hope that he would come out from his hiding hole and one day they will point at him their missiles and he will join Guevara, Hassan Abu Salama, Kamal Nasser, Kanafani and others. The man responds with a thin smile and replies to the correspondent from Al Jazeera that he will continue to be the obsession and worry of America and the Jews, and that even that night he will practice and work on an exercise called 'How Do You Bomb the White House'. And because they know that he can get there, they have started to go through their nightmares on their beds and the leaders have had to wear their bulletproof vests. Meanwhile America has started to pressure the Taliban movement so that it would hand them Bin Ladin, while he continues to smile and still thinks seriously, with the seriousness of the Bedouin of the desert about the way he will try to bomb the Pentagon after he destroys the White House . . .

The phenomenon of Bin Ladin is a healthy phenomenon in the Arab spirit. It is a decision and a determination that the stolen Arab self has come to realize after it got bored with promises of its rulers: After it disgusted itself from their abomination and their corruption, the man had to carry the book of God and the Kalashnikov and write on some off white paper 'If you are unable to drive off the Marines from the Kaaba, I will do so.' It seems that they will be going away because the revolutionary Bin Ladin is insisting very convincingly that he will strike America on the arm that is already hurting. That the man will not be swayed by the plant leaves of Whitman nor by the 'Adventures of Indiana Jones' and will curse the memory of Frank Sinatra every time he hears his songs.

This new awareness of the image that Bin Ladin has become gives shape to the resting areas and stops for every Arab revolutionary. It is the subject of our admiration here in Iraq because it shares with us in a unified manner our resisting stand, and just as he fixes his gaze on the Al Aqsa we greet him. We hail his tears as they see the planes of the Western world taking revenge against his heroic operations by bombing the cities of Iraq . . . .

To Bin Ladin I say that revolution, the wings of a dove and the bullet are all but one and the same thing in the heart of a believer.

Source: (September 12, 2002 US Congressional Record – Senate S8525 and S8526).

Na'im Abd Muhalhal's editorial article in Al-Nasiriya Newspaper, July 21, 2001

emil:babil@uruklink.net www.iraq2000.com/babil
الخميس 9 رمضان 1423هـ 14 تشرين الثاني 2002 م، السنة الثانية عشرة، العدد (3504)، 32 صفحة
DAILY-PUBLISHED WITH AUTHORAZATION OF PEOPLE-Thursday 14 November -2002،No:3504

أسامة بن لادن، زعيم تنظيم القاعدة

هذا اليوم في التاريخ

14 تشرين الثاني

- 1953 /ـ ليبيا تنضم الى جامعة الدول العربية.
- 1954 /ـ عزل اللواء محمد نجيب من منصبه كرئيس للجمهورية في مصر.
- 1979 /ـ الرئيس الاميركي جيمي كارتر يعلن تجميد الودائع الايرانية في المصارف الاميركية.

الرئيس القائد يرأس اجتماعا مشتركا لمجلس قيادة الثورة وقيادة قطر العراق للحزب

رأس السيد الرئيس القائد المجاهد صدام حسين حفظه الله اجتماعا مشتركا لمجلس قيادة الثورة وقيادة قطر العراق لحزب البعث العربي الاشتراكي حضره السادة رئيس المجلس الوطني ورئيس ديوان الرئاسة ووزيرو الاعلام والخارجية. وناقش الاجتماع قرار مجلس الامن للرقم 1441 ... ووجه السيد وزير الخارجية بأن يبعث برسالة للسيد كان عنان الامين العام للامم المتحدة تتضمن موقف العراق ازاء القرار المذكور.

نص الرسالة ص2

العلم الفلسطيني يرفرف فوق الدبابات الصهيونية التي اخذت مواقعها في المدينة القديمة في نابلس.

كندا تأخذ على محمل الجد تهديدات بن لادن

مونتريال 13/ 11/ (الساعة 2113).

خمسة ملايين دولار لمن يساهم في القاء القبض على شبكة ارهابية

واشنطن 13/ 11/ (الساعة 2956).

تنظيم يدعو الى اجتماع مجلس الوزراء الى ايصاء بوش عرفات

القاهرة 13/ 11/ (الساعة 1535).

لراب الاعتداءات في العرب وفلسطين والوايات المتحدة

نيويورك 13/ 11/ (الساعة 1859).

بلين... تأهبا رسالة من بن لادن على محمل الجد

واشنطن 13/ 11/ (الساعة 1708).

جنازة زيمن وفسحة مسعورين بتمسسوا الورزا نسل 2006

بكين 13/ 11/ (الساعة 1008).

الاعضاء الجدد في الاتحاد الاوربي لن يتمسسوا الورزا نسل 2006

بروكسل 13/ 11/ (الساعة 1422).

الكونغرس يؤيد اتفاق مع البيت الابيض بشأن أنفذ وزارة للامن الداخلي

واشنطن 13/ 11/ (الساعة 1542).

اغتيال رجل قرب البيت الابيض أكد أنه يعمل منفجرات

واشنطن 13/ 11/ (الساعة 1655).

2500 طالب يتظاهرون مجددا ضد الحكم بالاعدام على الأزهاري

طهران 13/ 11/ (الساعة 1225).

قص صاروخي من مروحيات صهيونية تجاه اهداف في غزة

غزة /(الساعة 0011).

مقتل طفل واصابة أمه في قصف مدفعي صهيوني برفح

مذبحة عسكرية صهيونية واسعة في نابلس

نابلس /الضفة الغربية/ (الساعة 0409).

اغتيال شخصين في جنوبي الجزائر على ايدي اسلاميين

الجزائر 13/ 11/ (الساعة 1154).

لا طالب يقسمون في كابول في اليوم الثالث

كابول 13/ 11/ (الساعة 1414).

الكيان الصهيوني يرد على عملية ميئز ويسيطر على نابلس وضواحيها

القدس 13/ 11/ (الساعة 1006).

وماذا بعد يا مجلس الامن ؟!

روما 13/ 11/ (الساعة 2233).

الطلبة الافغان يتظاهرون عبر احد خطوط الشرطة في كابول.. وقد استخدمت الشرطة الرصاص وخراطيش المياه لتفريق المتظاهرين.

سائدة وطلبة ايرانيون يتظاهرون في جامعة امير كابير ضد عقوبة الاعدام التي وجهتها احدى المحاكم المتشددة ضد البروفيسور البارز هاشم اغاجاري 2002/11/13

د. عبد الرزاق محمد الدليمي

Uday Saddam's Babil Newspaper and the List of Honor, 14 November 2002

﴿لائحة الشرف﴾

هذه قائمة من الرجال الرجال نشرها لتطلع عليها ابناء شعبنا العظيم

Uday Saddam's Babil Newspaper and the List of Honor, 14 November 2002

Appendix II
Inventory of Iraqi Satellite Channels

This is a list of the current, and some old, Iraqi satellite channels that appeared after the US invasion of Iraq in 2003. I compiled the list as I have personally viewed which is constantly changing these channels, mainly on Nilesat. Though most of them are partisan in nature, almost all of them claim that they address all Iraqi groups and ethnicities and present neutral, objective, and credible news and non-sectarian programmes. Also, many channels are digitally streaming online. This list does not include terrestrial TV stations, of which I believe there are more than there are satellite channels. According to Arab Advisors Group (AAG), more than half of the terrestrial channels in the Arab world are based in Iraq, Palestine, and Egypt, and they are generally controlled by the respective governments (AAG 2011).

Except for a few political advertisements in Arabic, Kurdish channels air their news and programmes in the Kurdish language. The only exception is probably Kurdistan TV, which sometimes shows a news subtitle in Arabic. Most of the channels listed below tend to write the Kurdish language in Latin instead of Arabic, as one way of asserting their national identity and cultural independence from the Arabs. These channels include: Kanal 4, Gelî Kurdistan, Zagros, Jamawar Kurdistan, Hawler (Sama Mosul or United Media), Korek, Kurdistan, NRT, Kurd 1, Kurdsat, ROJ, Kurdistan Parliament Channel (KPC), Kurd MMC, and ViN.

1. **Aghanina (Our Songs):** This channel airs from Jordan and is owned by Sameer Rassam. It started airing its Arabic and Iraqi programmes, which consist only of songs, in November 2007. The main revenues that the channel gets are from the text messages sent by viewers (Wikileaks 2008c).
2. **Al-Anbar TV:** This is based in the Anbar governorate and is supported by Anbar Government Council. Its programmes focus on the political developments in the country, and it highlights the cultural and economic events and concerns of this Sunni governorate.
3. **Al-Ahad TV:** This channel is pro-Shiite and follows the Sadr movement, which is represented by the Shiite Ayatollah, Kadhim Al-Hairi. It is against the practices of the former government of Saddam Hussein and is anti-occupational, too. It shows, for instance, the news of the pro-Iranian Asa'aib Ahlul Haq, the Mahdi Army splinter group that later kidnapped and executed several British employees working for a telecommunications company. The channel is mentioned on several Shiite websites and blogs, stressing that Muqtada Sadr does not sponsor it. It airs from Lebanon, and it shows

many Iranian-produced series on Islam that are dubbed into Arabic. It is not clear who supports it, but the Lebanese Shiite Hezbollah could be one source of funding for the channel. In general, it can be regarded as the most extreme Iraqi Shiite channel; for example, on its evening newscast on September 12, 2010, the anchorman mentioned the earthquake and floods that occurred in Pakistan stating that they could be God's wrath and curse for the wrong deeds committed by the Taliban and Pakistani militant groups. The anchorman was referring to the attacks conducted by the Salafis against Shiite Muslims in Pakistan. The channel's slogans are: 'One pledge . . . one homeland' and 'Commitment and Vow'. The channel's website was not functional as last visited in April 2012. http://www.alahadtv.com/.

4. **Ahul Bayt TV**: This Shiite channel airs its programmes in English, Arabic, and Urdu. It is based in London and run by the Shiite cleric Mahdi Al-Mudarissi, who lives in Karbala, Iraq. Its slogan is 'The Holy Household for Every Household', which refers to the Household of the Prophet Mohammed. Some of the presenters are Shiites from Iraq, Yemen, and other Arab countries. The channel gets other financial support from well-off Shiites living in the Arab Gulf, Europe, and North America. http://www.ahlulbayt.tv/

5. **Al-Babelyia TV**: This channel was first based in Cairo and then moved to Jordan, where it started broadcasting in early 2007. The channel's website mentions that it is independent from any political party or foreign government, and its programmes are neutral because it is loyal to Iraq alone. However, it is clearly supported by Al-Mutlaq an Iraqi Sunni MP, because it periodically shows his speeches. Besides, it is run and owned by Mutlak's brother, Sadiq. According to its website, the channel's aim is to 'address the human being by advocating a civil and balanced rhetoric. It is a channel for all Iraqis and its policy is to point out the positive aspects and criticise the negative ones no matter who has committed mistakes. Our weapon is dialogue'. Sadiq claims that the aim of the channel is to 'unify the ranks of all Iraqis and to reject heinous sectarianism' (Wikileaks 2008c). The channel's website is no longer functioning (http://www.albabelyia.com/), but when the channel changed its name into Al-Babelyia News, a new website was launched (http://www.albabelyia.tv/).

6. **Al-Diyar TV**: This channel is based in Baghdad and is run by Omar Al-Yassiri, son of the famous Iraqi cinema director and media expert Faisal Al-Yassiri. It started operating in March 2007 and it tries to remain independent and balanced. The channel has become popular by producing programmes that concern the general public. The most distinguished figure shown is Falah Azzawi, who always criticises the lack of public services and sides with ordinary Iraqis in his famous show 'Amongst the People' (Parker and Salman 2010). It is partly funded by the Saudi media company ART (Arab Radio and Television). The channel's slogan is an 'Arab satellite channel with an Iraqi flavour'. http://www.aldiyarsat.net/

7. **Al Etejah TV**: The programmes of this channel are mostly related to Iraq's news, and they generally show pro-government attitudes with a Shiite orientation. It is not clear who supports this channel, but it airs from Lebanon and occasionally refers to the news of the pro-Iranian Hezbollah Brigades, which are allegedly close to the Lebanese Hezbollah. In one of the Communications

and Media Commission's (CMC) reports, the channel was described as 'professional as it follows the media regulations' despite the fact that it airs some of the activities of Shiite armed militias, such as 'League of the Righteous', the 'Promised Day Brigades', and 'Hezbollah's Units in Iraq' (CMC 2010c, p. 35). The CMC report does not criticise the channel as it clearly sides with Nouri Maliki's Shiite-run government, which is aligned with Sadr movement http://www.aletejahtv.org/.

8. **Al-Fayhaa TV:** This channel first started broadcasting on July 25, 2004. It was originally located in Dubai but moved to Sulymaniah in northern Iraq after the expiry of its licence in the UAE. It became a controversial channel from the beginning because of its pro-Shiite programmes. When the UAE diplomat Naji Al-Naimi was kidnapped in Baghdad in 2006, the kidnappers demanded that the UAE government stop this channel's transmission. Zuhair Al-Jezairy assigned Al-Fayhaa to be one of the Shiite Iraqi National Alliance channels (Al-Jezairy 2010, p. 15). Also, a US cable described the channel as 'privately financed, Shia, secular' (Wikileaks 2005i). The channel mainly focuses on the plight of the Shiites during Saddam Hussein's rule and always brings up the issue of Iraqi detainees held by Saudi Arabia in Rafah Camp since the 1991 Gulf War. It usually airs programmes and shows that focus on the shortcomings of Arab leaders. Its slogan is 'freedom of opinion and the responsibility of the stance'. http://www.alfayhaa.tv/.

9. **Al-Furat Satellite TV:** This was established by the Shiite Islamic Supreme Council of Iraq (ISCI). It first started broadcasting from Iran during Saddam Hussein's rule as a propaganda tool against the former regime in Iraq. After the US-led invasion, it moved its main office to Iraq. On its website, it is described as an 'edifice of truthful and committed media'. Its slogan is a 'channel of balance and originality' which is concerned with the 'athletic, political, and social religious cultural and economic affairs of the Iraqi people'. The channel states that it addresses 'the Iraqi people with all their ethnic and religious groups and sects as well as the Arab and Muslim people'. See Chapter 4 for more information on this channel. http://www.alforattv. net/.

10. **Al-Ghadeer TV:** This is a Shiite channel run by ISCI's armed militia, the Badr Organisation, which is currently led by Hadi Al-Amiri. Most of its programmes are Shiite-oriented sermons and seminars. Its website mentions that it was the first Iraqi TV station to broadcast terrestrially after the fall of Saddam Hussein's regime. Four years later it began broadcasting via satellite. It also states that it is an 'Iraqi, Arabic, and Islamic channel that aims at spreading the noble principles and values and consolidating the concept of unity among Muslims. It also attempts to encourage dialogue, clemency, and communication among cultures.' http://www.alghadeertv.com/.

11. **Al-Hadhara TV:** This is a relatively new apolitical channel that airs on Nilesat. From its name (which means 'civilisation'), it aims to broadcast programmes that highlight the historical, cultural, and artistic achievements of Iraq. In other words, it tries to give hope for Iraqis who need to take pride in their history and culture.

12. **Al-Hadath TV:** This channel is based in Cairo and is run by Abdullattif Humaim, the head of the Iraqi Group of Intellectuals and Scientists. It started broadcasting on October 28, 2009. On its website, the channel's manager

Mohammed A Humaim claims that the channel has a 'committed national, Arabic, and Islamic orientation ... , and it does not belong to any side except what it believes to be a moderate trend that is closer to reality and farther from extremism'. http://www.alhadathtv.com/.

13. **Al-Hurria TV**: This Kurdish channel is led by the Patriotic Union of Kurdistan, which is headed by the Iraqi President Jalal Talabani. It was first established as a terrestrial channel and started broadcasting on April 17, 2003. On December 1, 2005, it was upgraded to a satellite channel and only started regular broadcasting on February 1, 2006, for 24 hours a day. Its programmes, which are pro-government, are broadcast in Arabic. According to its website, the channel advocates a balanced, logical, and reasonable rhetoric. It seeks to present objective news before breaking news 'amidst the sectarian media Iraq suffered from'. The aim of the channel is to 'disseminate the concepts of liberty, democracy, and lenience'. Its motto is 'Boldness, Reliability, and Tolerance'. www.alhurriatv.com/.

14. **Al-Iraq Economic TV**: This is a channel that is based in Jordan. Its programmes are exclusively devoted to business news in an attempt to open up opportunities for investors to work in Iraq. It clearly receives support from the Iraqi government, especially in terms of receiving money in return for the government advertisements that the channel airs.

15. **Al-Lafeta TV and Al-Arabi TV**: This channel, which is also called the 'Saddam Hussein Satellite Channel', started broadcasting for a few days during the most recent Eid holiday to commemorate the execution of Saddam Hussein. It aired footage of Iraq's former president and popular songs, but the channel agitated many people in Iraq. It called for resisting the US occupation of Iraq and organising a revolution to change the political system. Its website stated that its aim is to protect the rights of the Arabs and Muslims around the world. The channel was allegedly managed by an Algerian citizen and used to broadcast from an undisclosed location to protect its staff. Due to tremendous pressures from the Iraqi government, it stopped transmission, but it claimed that it would resume broadcasting after fixing some technical issues. www.allafeta-tv.net/.

16. **Al-Mansour TV**: This channel is based in Lebanon and is very critical of the Iraqi government; and it has a clear Ba'athist nostalgia for the former government of Saddam Hussein. For example, its subtitle news mentions Saddam International Airport instead of the post-2003 name Baghdad International Airport. It is managed by the former Iraqi Ambassador to Jordan, Sabah Yaseen. The channel stopped transmission on Nilesat, presumably due to pressures from the US and Iraqi governments on Egypt. It is not clear who supports this channel, but it follows the rhetoric of an Iraqi Ba'athist website that has the same name (http://www.almansore.com/index.php). It is worth mentioning that 'Al-Mansour', which means victorious in Arabic, was one of Saddam Hussein's epithets. The channel's website contained the slogan 'Hand in hand, we expel the occupier' and 'Al-Mansour TV: The Voice of Truth', but the website remained under construction for a very long time and disappeared later on (http://www.almansourtv.net/).

17. **Al-Masar TV & Al-Masar One TV**: These two channels are supported by the Shiite Dawa Party-Iraq Branch that is led by Abdul Karim Al-'Anizi. They are managed by Ayssa Al-Furaiji, who advocates the idea of 'responsible

Shiite media'. Their slogan is 'The Message of Committed Arab Media'. The programmes are religious with a moderate Shiite rhetoric. The TV channel Al-Masar One was launched to complement the programmes aired on Al-Masar TV. http://www.almasar.tv/.

18. **Al-Mashriq TV:** This channel is supported by the Sunni Sheikh Ghandi Al-Kastinzani, who is part of the Sufi Kastinzaniah order; Ghandi owns a newspaper with a similar name. The channel was based in Amman, Jordan, but it only aired for few months since the station could not secure enough profit to continue.

19. **Al-Mousellya TV:** It was established in 2006 and was entirely funded by the US forces, who are given 30 minutes a day to air favourable US messages. The channel airs from Mosul city and is managed and run by Ghazi Faisal. Its programmes are mainly related to the events happening in Mosul, which has a Sunni majority. In a US cable, the former governor of Mosul, Atheel Al-Nujaifi, once expressed his dissatisfaction with the channel because it edited one of his press conferences. It remains one of the most popular channels in Mosul and its 21:00 newscast is the 'most watched in the province' (Wikileaks 2009j). Also, the channel had a serious conflict with the Iraqi Media Network (IMN) because they both share a plot of land, prompting some Iraqia journalists to be overtly critical of Al-Mousellya staff. For example, a news story on the Iraqia channel aired on December 23, 2009, stated that the employees of Al-Mousellya channel are working as 'American mercenaries' (ibid.). The channel's slogan is 'Iraqi in Origin; its source is Mosul'. http://www.almowselya.com/.

20. **Al-Mutahida TV (United Media TV):** This channel mostly airs entertainment programmes and songs and is supported by the United Media Network, which is also affiliated with the Kurdish channel Hawler.

21. **Al-Naeem (Greetings to Sadr, the martyred):** This is a new Shiite channel that is clearly supported by the Sadr movement. It glorifies Muqtada Sadr's father, who was assassinated during Saddam Hussein's regime.

22. **Al Qethara TV:** This is called the 'channel of Iraqi Tunes' and is devoted to Iraqi music and art taken from the different regions of Iraq. It airs from Jordan, like Aghanina TV. http://www.alqiethara.tv/.

23. **Al-Rafidain TV:** This channel is based in Egypt and is supported by the Sunni Muslim Scholars Association (MSA), headed by Harith Al-Dhari. It was launched on April 10, 2006. It had an office in Baghdad, but recently it has been closed down because, according to the channel, of the different attacks it suffered. Since the MSA is closely aligned to the Muslim Brothers movement, there is a possible source of funding for the channel that comes from the Egyptian Muslim Brothers. The channel focuses on the plight of Sunnis in Iraq and is very critical of the Shiite-dominated Iraqi government and its policies. According to its website, the channel's aim is to 'call for the departure of the occupier' and emphasises 'Iraqis' and Iraq's unity' and 'despises the occupation and its cultural and political leftovers'. In a unique survey conducted by the staff of the US Embassy in Baghdad between February 24 and March 8, 2008, on Al-Rafidain TV, the results showed that the channel uses a rhetoric that is focused on 'venerating the "resistance" and disparaging the U.S. "occupation" and the Iraqi Government' (Wikileaks 2008a). The Embassy requested closing down the

channel for 'inciting violence' against coalition forces, and asked for the intervention of the Egyptian government to do so. The US cable classified the topics of interest into eight categories: 'anti-Coalition; anti-Iraqi Government; reportage of Coalition materiel being damaged or destroyed including soldiers' deaths; anti-Iran; anti-sectarianism; neutral; [MSA] statements; and pro-terrorism'. The survey, which covered 2415 items (programmes, bulletins, and shows), indicated that there was a clear bias against the US and Iraqi governments. It stated the following: 'Items with anti-Coalition message, explicit or implied: 719(29.8%); items with anti-Iraqi Government message: 80(3.3%); items stating damage to Coalition: 126(5.2%); items with anti-Iran message: 66(2.7%); items with anti-sectarian message: 41(1.7%); neutral items: 1328(55%); items dealing with MSA not falling into another category: 55(2.3%)' (Wikileaks 2008a). The channel's slogan is 'Because we are a civilization'. http://www.alrafidain.tv/.

24. **Al-Rasheed TV:** This is, allegedly, an independent TV channel. On its website it states that the channel follows an approach characterised by 'variety and balance'. It does not 'pass judgments but presents events as they are'. The channel's slogan is to be 'devoid of any sectarian and ethnic influences'. Mostly it airs Arabic series and documentaries, and the most famous programme that it broadcasts is 'Comedy Star', which presents Iraqis competing to become comedians. http://www.alrasheedmedia.com/.

25. **Al-Salam TV:** The channel is based in Khadimiah in Baghdad and is supported by the moderate Shiite cleric Hussein Ismael Al-Sadr. According to the channel's website, it follows a 'moderate political and religious rhetoric' and it 'produces different programmes focusing on children, politics, religious, cultural, and social issues'. The channel is regarded as the most moderate Shiite TV channel due to the policy followed by its founder. Its slogan is 'Our message is peace' and *salam* means peace in Arabic, too. http://www.tvalsalam.tv/.

26. **Al-Shams TV:** This is a new Iraqi channel on Nilesat, but it has not actually started transmission yet. It is not clear who supports the channel as there is no official website available. Its general director is Maki Awad, the famous Iraqi actor.

27. **Al-Sharqiya TV:** This is one of the most popular Iraqi TV channels. Based on Saudi funding, the channel started broadcasting from Iraq in 2004, then moved to Dubai after having security problems with the Iraqi government. It is regarded by many as the most popular TV channel, mainly due to its reality TV shows and other series, that harshly criticise Iraqi officials and the current situation, such as 'Night Wolves', 'Love and War', 'An Owned Chair', and 'Who Will Win the Oil?' (Hussein and Ashton 2009). The channel is known to favour Ayad Allawi (Wikileaks 2006a) and is described as a Ba'athist or Sunni channel, especially by Shiite politicians and observers. According to Kadhim Al-Rikabi, Program Manager for IREX's Supporting Independent Media in Iraq programme, Al-Sharqiya's manager once stated: 'whoever pays, has his say in my station' (Wikileaks 2009b). Its owner, Sa'ad Al-Bazaz, who worked as the director of Iraqi National TV during Saddam Hussein's rule before opposing the Ba'ath regime, was described in one of the US Cables as a 'media tycoon' who is also a 'flexible/opportunist' (Wikileaks 2005a). More recently, Azzaman Institute established a new channel called Al-Sharqiya

News to devote more attention to the events in Iraq and giving more space for Al-Sharqiya TV to air other programmes. www.alsharqiya.com/

28. **Al-Taakhi TV:** This is a Kurdish channel supported by the Kurdistan Democratic Party (KDP) and led by Masud Barazani. It started broadcasting on the same frequency as Zagros TV on Hotbird on August 1, 2005, and some of its programmes were in Arabic. It stopped transmission after a couple of years. The KDP has a famous Arabic newspaper of the same name.

29. **Al-Ra'i TV:** This channel is based in Syria and is directed by the Sunni Misha'an Al-Jubouri, who previously owned the controversial Al-Zawraa channel. Al-Ra'i tries to imitate Al-Zawraa but to a lesser extent by showing subtitles that document most of the activities of the Iraqi insurgent groups. Al-Jubouri claims that the new channel is not his own because it is owned by his Syrian wife and he is only managing it. The channel has generated a great deal of controversy because of its anti-government stance and its support for armed struggle against the US-led forces in Iraq. In a confidential US cable leaked by Wikileaks, the US government pressured Syria to 'stop broadcasts from Damascus of Ba'thist-backed satellite channels glorifying terrorism and violence, but had not seen any action' (Wikileaks 2009i). This is a clear reference to Al-Ra'i. More recently, the channel became the only media outlet for the former Libyan leader Mu'amar Gadhafi, who has previously sent monetary aid to it (Kennedy 2011).

30. **Ashur TV:** This channel is supported by the Christian Assyrian Democratic Party and airs its programmes in Syriac and Arabic. It broadcasts from California, USA, and focuses on themes related to Iraqi Christians. Its website is not functioning at the moment. http://www.ashurtv.org/.

31. **Al-Zawraa TV:** This controversial channel is supported by Misha'an Al-Jubouri. It first aired from Iraq and then moved to Egypt. It was closed due to pressure from the US and Iraqi governments on the Egyptian authorities because the channel encouraged insurgency and continued broadcasting footage of insurgent groups. See Chapter 4 for more information on this channel.

32. **Baghdad TV:** This channel first aired from Baghdad then moved its main office to Jordan. It is run by Sa'd Al-Tikriti and is supported by the Sunni Iraqi Islamic Party, which is part of political group the Iraqi Accord Front. Its programmes are mostly devoted to covering the plight of Sunnis in the new government; Al-Tikriti once mentioned that the channel aims at representing the 'ambitions of the Sunnis in Baghdad' (Wikileaks 2008c). One of the popular programmes which the channel produces is 'Patron of the Oppressed', which is shown every Saturday and lasts an hour. The show airs the testimonies of Iraqis whose relatives were either detained, kidnapped, or just disappeared (Healy 2010). Also, Baghdad TV was probably the only Iraqi channel that aired the controversial Qatari TV series 'Al-Hasan and Al-Hussein' during the whole month of Ramadhan in 2011. The series chronicles the events that followed the death of the fourth Muslim Caliphate, Imam Ali. The Iraqi parliament, and consequently the CMC, decided to prohibit all Iraqi channels from airing this series because of the Shiite–Sunni conflicting interpretation of these historical events. See Chapter 4 for more information on this channel. http://www.baghdadch.tv/.

33. **Al-Baghdadia TV:** Its motto is 'The eye of Iraq on the world, and the world's eye on Iraq'. It is owned by the Iraqi businessman Uon Hussein Al-Khashluq, and it started broadcasting on September 12, 2005, from Cairo, Egypt. On its website the channel claims to be against sectarianism and favouritism, and calls for unity, freedom, and democracy. It became very famous after one of its correspondents, Muntadar Al-Zaidi, threw his shoes at US President George Bush during a press conference held in Baghdad in 2009. The channel faces tremendous pressures from official bodies because they do not give it the chance to air their advertisements, hoping to change its national policy. In one US report, Baghdadia TV was assigned to the category of channels opposing the US presence in Iraq, and its staff were regarded as 'one of the biggest sources of erroneous stories. But when presented with clarifying information, they would typically choose not to provide a retraction or this alternative point of view' (Cioppa 2009, p. 37). The channel produced several interesting and famous series and reality shows, like Minas Suheil's one-hour live show 'Baghdadia and the People', which aired the complaints of Iraqis in the streets (Fadel 2010), and 'Put Him in Bucca',[1] which created a great deal of controversy locally and internationally (Ghazi 2010). This show made the CMC revoke the channel's licence and order it to close its offices in Iraq on September 7, 2010, because it allegedly breached the media laws; though many observers believe that Maliki's press office was behind the closure. After restoring its licence, the channel was then permanently closed during the attack on Our Lady of Salvation Church in Baghdad on October 31, 2010. Maliki's government was infuriated by the channel's decision to air the demands of a number of kidnappers from Al-Qaeda, who took civilian hostages inside the church (Lelan and Ali 2010). http://www.albaghdadia.com/.

34. **Biladi TV:** This is a Shiite TV channel. According to its website, it 'reflects the pulse of the Iraqi street without siding with any group or sect in the society'. It further states that it 'speaks on behalf of the Iraqi people, and it is the voice of all Iraqis from various origins'. The channel describes itself as a 'national, political, and news channel that airs up-to-date news'. However, the channel usually focuses on issues relevant to the Shiites of Iraq. The channel airs Iranian-produced series that tackle Islamic history, dubbed into Arabic. It is run by the Shiite leader of the National Reformation Movement, Ibrahim Al-Ja'afari, who is also a former prime minister and leader of the Da'awa Party. http://www.beladitv.net/.

35. **Dijla TV:** The channel was established in 2008 and was supported by Diyala Governorate Council. The channel was secular and used to air cultural programmes and shows and had a moderate rhetoric. However, it stopped transmission in January 2010 due to financial difficulties, as its funding from the Council ceased in mid-2009. A new channel, entitled Diyala TV, has appeared on Nilesat. It is not yet airing programmes, but it appears to be supported by the Diyala Province Council, so it will replace Dijla TV.

36. **Iraqyia TV or Iraqia TV:** This is the official TV channel in Iraq, which aims to be a public broadcasting station; it is part of IMN. It broadcasts in three languages: Arabic, Kurdish, and English. There are other channels linked

to IMN: Iraqia Sport TV, Alforqan TV (religious programmes), Iraqia Education TV (programmes targeting students), and Iraqia Antikhabia (elections). The latter started broadcasting advertisements for political parties in 2009 in preparation for the 2010 elections, but it stopped transmission after the end of the elections. There was also Ittyaf Iraqia TV, which broadcast programmes in Kurdish, Turkomen, and other languages spoken in Iraq, but the channel stopped due to an IMN decision to reduce its budget in 2009. See Chapter 4 for detailed information on this channel. www.imn.iq

37. **Ishtar Broadcasting Corporation TV**: This channel airs from Erbil city in Iraqi Kurdistan in three languages: Arabic, Syriac, and Kurdish. It started broadcasting in 2005. The channel emphasises the legal, cultural, political, and historical rights of Iraqi Christians. According to its website, it 'gives sufficient importance to our Chaldean Syriac Assyrian people whose civilization and national identity were marginalised and obliterated for long decades'. The current head of the channel is Canadian Iraqi George Mansour, who first worked for the official channel Iraqia TV. http://www.ishtartv.com/.

38. **ITV (Iraq Television)**: This was another channel whose logo appeared without any aired programmes, and it was not clear who funded it. Its manager was the pro-government Kurdish media figure Ismael Zayer, who is also the editor-in-chief of *Al-Sabah Al-Jadeed* newspaper. According to its website, ITV 'aims to inform the Arab sphere and in particular Iraqis as citizen, consumers, employees and entrepreneurs. It provides a varied package of programs for all age groups, men and women, with a special focus on culture'. The channel was available on Nilesat, for a short time, but its website is no longer available. http://www.itv-iraq.com/.

39. **Karbala TV**: This is a Shiite channel devoted to airing the Shiite sermons and festivities of Karbala city. It was established on October 1, 2008, and started experimental transmission on August 22, 2009. It is supported by the Shiite Religious Endowment and is based in Karbala. http://www.karbala-tv.net/.

40. **Kirkuk TV**: This is a new channel that has not started broadcasting yet. The channel appears to be supported by Kirkuk City Council, which is largely run by Kurdish figures. Its logo uses the Kurdish language first, then Turkoman (Latin letters), then Arabic, and finally Syriac.

41. **Salah El-Din TV**: This airs from the Sunni Salahdeen governorate and focuses on the events of this governorate. It was originally established with funding from US forces (Wikileaks 2008e) and was affiliated with Salahdeen City Council. It was temporarily closed down for airing footage of Iraqis mourning the death of Saddam Hussein, whose hometown, Tikrit, is located in the same governorate. The channel's website is no longer functional. http://www.salahdintv.net/.

42. **Al-Sumeria TV**: This is a well-respected and famous channel broadcasting from Beirut, Lebanon, which was established in September 2004. Owned by Iraqi businessmen, it employs about 700 people, and it tries to show an objective account of the events taking place in Iraq. It has become famous after airing the popular 2005 show 'Iraq Star', which shows talented Iraqi singers competing to win (Hammond 2005). It has also produced several famous Iraqi TV series that were aired during the Muslim holy month of Ramadhan. According to its website, the channel follows a moderate policy that involves all the sects and groups of Iraqi society as the only way

for peaceful co-existence. Its slogan, 'We Promote life', reflects its editorial policy. http://www.alsumaria.tv/.

43. **Al-Afaq TV**: This is run by the Shiite Daawa Party, which is led by Prime Minister Nouri Maliki and airs programmes and news in favour of the Iraqi government's efforts to establish national unity and fight terrorism. Its slogan is 'the distinguished media message'. http://www.afaqtv.com/.

44. **Suroyo TV**: This is a Christian channel that is based in Sweden. It first started broadcasting in 2004 and its programmes are aired in six languages: Syriac, Arabic, English, Turkish, and Swedish. The channel is aimed at Christians living in the Middle East, especially in Iraq, Syria, and Turkey, though its transmission reaches other Christians from this region who have emigrated to Europe and the USA.

45. **Turkmen TV**: This is a Turkomen TV channel that airs in both Turkomen and Arabic, and is obviously supported by Turkey. The channel uses Latin words instead of Arabic, just like the modern Turkish language. Most of the programmes focus on the issue of Kirkuk and it favours the Turkomen and their culture by emphasising their rights and concerns. Its slogan is 'Irak'in Aydinlik Yüzü' (The bright side of Iraq). http://www.turkmenelitv.com/tv/.

Finally, there are a few Iraqi music channels that appeared on Nilesat, such as BMusic – Iraq TV; Al-Hanin – MH TV (Listen to it well); and MCP. Yet, most of these channels are only advertising for their programmes and have not started airing songs yet.

Notes

1 Iraqi Media: The Beginnings

1. The Iraqi National Library and Archives have scanned some of the monthly magazines that flourished at that time and posted them online, such as *Al-Uloom* (1910), *Al-'Alim* (1910), *Tanwir Al-afkar* (1910), and *Lughat Al-Arab* (1911), which was the most successful Arabic journal in Iraq, having readers from around the Arab world, and *Al-Risafa* (1913) (Iraqi National Library and Archives 2011a, 2011b, 2011c, 2011d).
2. One of the few exceptions to this rule was the newspaper *Al-Istiqlal*, which was published by political party Al-Ahad. It first appeared on September 28, 1920, and its editor was Abdul Ghafur Al-Badri.
3. Taisi was an open-minded writer and one of Iraq's pioneer thinkers. The book he wrote was entitled *Mahyat Al-Ruh* ('The Query about the Soul'), in which he advocated the philosophy of materialism and negated the existence of the soul.
4. This radio channel had a famous commentator, Ahmed Said, who once got a message after the 1958 Iraqi Revolution that contained one of Nouri Said's fingers, with a thank-you note for his contribution towards agitating the Iraqi public against the monarchy (Boyd 1982, p. 402).
5. This was a religious campaign which started in the 1990s during the economic sanctions. Saddam Hussein encouraged but did not force Iraqi women to wear the veil.

2 US Propaganda Efforts to Wage a War on Iraq: The Case of *Nassiriah* and *Babil* Newspapers

1. The US news site *Mother Jones* counted the false statement in a similar fashion under the title 'Lie by Lie' (see Mother Jones 2008). Also, the *Iraq on the Record* (IR) database collected the false statements made by the Bush Administration's key figures. IR mentioned that there were 237 'misleading' statements made by Bush, Cheney, Rumsfeld, Powell, and Rice. They were communicated on 125 separate occasions in press briefings, speeches, press conferences, congressional testimonies, and written statements (*Iraq on the Record* 2004, p. 2).
2. The newspaper's website was http://www.iraq2000.com/nasyriah/.
3. The newspaper's website was http://www.iraq2000.com/babil/.
4. The repetition of the word 'men' is used to add emphasis, denoting that the list comprises the names of brave men whose national actions and stances annoyed their enemies on the opposition.
5. Since the back issues of this newspaper are not available online, some issues can be viewed via *Waybackmachine* at www.archive.org. Also, the complete

list of names as they appeared in *Babil* is still available on the Shiite forum *Al-Hajar Cultural Network*, which was founded in 1998. The list was posted on August 26, 2002 (see http://hajr04.homeip.net/hajrvb/forum.php).

3 The US Role in Shaping Iraq's Post-2003 Media

This chapter is partly published as an article which appeared in the International Communication Gazett.

1. Contrary to prevalent views that Shiites were a repressed majority in pre-2003 Iraq, Hana Batatu mentions that Saddam Hussein 'associated the Shi'is more meaningfully with his regime and extended economic benefits to their areas' (2004, pp. 221–222). The head of the De-Ba'athification Committee, Ahmed Chalabi, privately admitted to the US Ambassador in Baghdad that 65 per cent of the Ba'ath members were Shiite (Wikileaks 2005d). Furthermore, during the 1991 Shiite revolt, Saddam Hussein depended on Muhammad Hamza Al-Zubaidi, a Shiite, to suppress the revolt. Al-Zubaidi, who was 'responsible for the bloodbath in the south...died in US custody in 2005' (Hiltermann 2007, p. 800). Even the list of 55 Iraqi officials whose names were shown in the US deck of cards contained Shiite figures more than Sunni ones.
2. INC's old website (http://209.50.252.70/p_en/inc_newspaper/index.shtml) is not functioning anymore, but it can be accessed through *archive.org*.
3. It is a well-known fact that the US government has a long history of interfering in the Republic of Nicaragua's media (see, for example, Norsworthy 1994).
4. The fortified Green Zone is the area in which the US administration and Iraqi officials are located. It is important to note that the US definition of the Green Zone (safe area) must be contrasted with the other term, the Red Zone (dangerous area), which refers to the rest of the country. Indeed, these terms clearly indicate the self-imposed isolation of the US and Iraqi authorities from the Iraqi people.
5. For more information, see the website of the US Army in Iraq on YouTube: http://www.youtube.com/MNFIRAQ.
6. It is important to note that USAID, which is mostly funded by the US Department of State, became one of the tools of the US military after 9/11 in terms of public relations or diplomacy, being a mild term for propaganda. The aim of public diplomacy is to 'seek international support for US policies'. Andrew Natsios, USAID director, revealed in 2003 that his organisation is 'an arm of the U.S. government', and it is very crucial to point out this link lest they should 'lose their funding' (*The Media Missionaries* 2004, p. 26).
7. The Dean of the College of Communication at Baghdad University, Abdul Salam Al-Samr, mentioned that IREX donated 400,000 dollars to a group of Iraqi media experts to form NINA. This news agency does not only disseminate news but also provides subscribed wireless Internet connections to some areas in Baghdad (Al-Samr 2011). It seems that IREX's main source of funding was USAID.

4   The Iraqi Media after the US-Led Invasion

1. Until January 2006, the Iraqi National Communications and Media Commission licensed 108 media channels: '28 terrestrial TV; 25 satellite TV; 41 FM radio; and 14 AM radio stations' (Wikileaks 2006b).
2. See, for example, the cases of Suadad Al-Salhy and Kilshan Al-Bayati, who both worked for the Saudi-owned *Al-Hayat* newspaper (Al-Rawi 2010, p. 230).
3. Majed Al-Brekan, an Iraqi journalist, observed that the majority of journalists in Basrah must have a 'benefactor' who would provide money and connections for the journalist. Al-Brekan mentioned that during a 'provincial press conference, a Governor's spokesman was openly handing out envelopes to journalists with 50,000 Iraqi dinar, or around $42, in each' (Wikileaks 2009g).
4. This statement is taken from a senior Iraqi female journalist whom I met in 2006 in Amman, Jordan.
5. Simon Haselock was later appointed as a leading member in the British Media Development and Advisory Team (MDAT) that worked with the CMC (Wikileaks 2005c).
6. Interview with one of Ayad Allawi's media officers in Baghdad in 2005.
7. Habib Al-Sadr himself told US Embassy officials in 2007 that 'his sister is Islamic Supreme Council of Iraq (ISCI) leader Abdulaziz Al-Hakim's wife and the mother of Amar al-Hakim. He noted he is a distant relative of Moqtada al-Sadr, too' (Wikileaks 2007d).
8. Shiite music here refers to the chants and rhythms that accompany the customary flagellation ceremonies held by devout Shiites.
9. For more information on the Iraqi government's media efforts, see the following websites: http://www.youtube.com/user/Iraqigov, www.nmc.gov. iq (Maliki's National Media Center), and http://www.pmo.iq/default.aspx. (Maliki's official website).
10. For example, Al-Arabiya channel covered Hakim and Maliki's slates in a negative manner during the 2010 general election, whereas Allawi's block was presented in a positive way with special programmes repeated 10 times that amount to 436 seconds (Al-Mir'at 2010, p. 8).

5   TV and Iraqi Elections

1. I have depended on the English version of the CMC's 'Code for Media during Election'.
2. Funding for the website of Bent Arafidain and Al-Mir'at organisations came from NDI, which paid 8985 dollars for their construction (United States Internal Revenue Service 2006, p. 20).

6   Iraqi TV Coverage of the 2010 General Election

1. For the detailed study of these TV channels, please see my unpublished PhD thesis, *TV Coverage of the 2010 Elections in Iraq: A Study of the Evening Newscasts of Four Iraqi Satellite Channels*, 2011. Department of Media and Communication, University of Leicester.

Appendix II

1. The name of the show is derived from Camp Bucca, which was the largest US detention facility in Iraq and was located in Basrah. The camp was named after Ronald Bucca, one of the firefighters who died in the 9/11 attack. Al-Baghdadia TV used a pun in the title of the show since it can also mean 'Let's (steal) kidnap him!', which is an indirect hint that some armed forces affiliated with the government are involved in kidnapping Iraqis near checkpoints.

References

AAG (Arab Advisors Group). 2011. 'Governments Continue to Dominate Terrestrial TV Channels in the Arab World'. January 11. Retrieved on January 12, 2011. http://www.arabadvisors.com/Pressers/presser-110111.htm

Abdel Majid, Ahmed. 2007. 'The Crisis of Professional Responsibility in Iraqi Journalism: Avoiding Incitement to Violence and Armed Conflict'. *International Review of the Red Cross*, 89, 868 (December): 893–913.

Abedin, Mahan. 2006. 'The Iraqi Media's Response to Recent Sectarian Tension in Iraq'. *Terrorism Focus: Middle East*, 3, 10 (March 14).

'Afas, Bahnam Fadheel. 1985. *Tarikh Al-Tiba'ah wa Al-Matbu'at Al-Iraqia (The History of the Iraqi Printing Press and Publications)*. Baghdad: Mattba'at al-Adib al-Baghdadiah.

Agence France Presse. 2008. 'Five Suspects Arrested after Iraq TV Crew Murder'. September 14.

Agence France Presse. 2009. 'Iraq "Best" in Mideast for Press Freedom: Maliki'. May 23.

Agence France Presse. 2011. 'Iraqi Kurd Journalist Attacked outside Office'. August 30.

Ahmed, N M. 2005. *The War on Truth: 9/11, Disinformation, and the Anatomy of Terrorism*. Northampton, MA: Olive Branch Press.

Al-'Adhami, Mudhafar Hashim. 1972. 'Jaridat al-Hukumah al-Iraqia' (The Newspaper of the Iraqi Government). In *Dirasat fi Al-Sahafah Al-Iraqia (Studies in the Iraqi Press)*. Baghdad: Mudiriat al-'Illam al-Amah, 41–52.

Al-Bayyna Al-Jadidah (Newspaper). 2007. 'Mahmood al-Mashhadani Warns Habib al-Sadr about a Near Harsh Questioning'. December 11, Issue 488.

Albin, Michael W. 1981. 'Iraq's First Printed Book'. *Libri*, 31, 1: 167–174.

Al-Daqouqi, Ibrahim. 1986. *Communication Law: A New Theory in the Modern Media Studies* (in Arabic). Baghdad: Ministry of Endowment and Religious Affairs Printing House.

Alexander, Anne. 2004. 'Iraq: The Battle for the Media'. *Middle East International*, Online (February 6). Retrieved on March 20, 2005. http://meionline.com/features/189.shtml

Al-Hassani, Abdul Razaq. 1957. *Tariskh Al-Sahafah Al-Iraqia (The History of the Iraqi Press)*. Baghdad: Mattba'at al-Zahraa.

Al-Hassani, Abdul Razaq. 1969. *Al-Sahafah Al-Iraqia fi Rubu' Qarn, 1908–1933 (The Iraqi Press in a Quarter of a Century, 1908–1933)*. Baghdad: Matb'aat Al-Jamhurriah.

Al-Hayat. 2009. 'Iraqi Official Censorship on Imported Books'. July 22. Retrieved on December 31, 2009. http://ksa.daralhayat.com/ksaarticle/40272

Al-Jezairy, Zuhair. 2006. *The Iraqi Press: The Heritage of the Past and the Challenges of the Future*. Lotte Dahlmann ed. International Media Support. October.

Al-Jezairy, Zuhair. 2010a. 'The Iraqi Media between the 2005 and 2009 Elections'. *Tawasol* Magazine. CMC. February. Fifth year, No. 9.

Al-Jezairy, Zuhair. 2010b. 'The Journalist and the State: A History of Marginal-ization'. In *Iraqi Media: Freedom of Expression and Access to Information, Book 1* (in Arabic). Baghdad: *Communication and Media Commission*, 92–108.

Al-Jubouri, Jamil. 1986. *Habazbuz fi Tarikh al-Hazall wa al-Karikatir fi Al-Iraq (Habazbuz Newspaper: The History of Comedy and Caricatures in Iraq)*. Baghdad: Dar al-Hurriah lil Tiba'ah.

Al-Khafaji, Isam. 2003. 'I Did Not Want to Be a Collaborator'. *The Guardian*. Mon-day, July 28. Retrieved on June 20, 2009. http://www.guardian.co.uk/world/2003/jul/28/iraq.comment

Allen, Jeffrey. 2006. 'World Press Freedom Day: Iraq's Fledgling Media Already Shaping Opinions'. *Oneworld.net*. May 3. Retrieved on August 27, 2010. http://oneworldus.civiblog.org/blog/_archives/2006/5/3/1935080.html

Al-Marashi, Ibrahim. 2007. 'The Dynamics of Iraq's Media: Ethno-Sectarian Vio-lence, Political Islam, Public Advocacy, and Globalisation'. *Cardozo Arts and Entertainment Law Journal*, 25, 95: 96–140.

Al-Mir'at Center for Media Monitoring. 2005. 'The First Monitoring Accessory: The Iraqi Election by Al-Mirat Network: The Final Statement' in 'Towards Impartial and Free Media'. December 30.

Al-Mir'at Center for Media Monitoring. 2010. 'Balanced Media Coverage for Fair Voting: Media Monitoring during the Iraqi Parliamentary Elections in 2010, from 15/11/2009 until 6/3/2010'. March.

Al-Mukhtar, Uthman. 2009. 'Baghdad Struggles to Stop Banned Books Trade'. *Institute for War and Peace Reporting*. ICR No. 314, December 3.

Al-Mu'tamar (Newspaper). 2001a. 'List of Dishonour'. No. 269, August 31.

Al-Mu'tamar (Newspaper). 2001b. 'List of Dishonour'. No. 270, September 7.

Al-Qaisi, Faris & Jabbar, Ali. 2010. 'Sunni and Shiite Iraqi Journalists Talk about War'. *The Associated Press*. September 4.

Al-Qattan, Khalid & Juma'a, Athra'a. 2006. 'First Policy: Iraqi Media Outlets are Invited to Abstain from the Sectarian Spirit'. *Al-Sabah* Newspaper. July 25.

Al-Qazwini, Iqbal Hassoon. 2004. 'On the Role of Media in the Current Transition Phase in Iraq'. *Transnational Broadcasting Studies*, Fall 13.

Al-Quds Al-Arabi. 2009. 'MP: Calling for Christians to Leave Iraq is Rejected and the Baghdad of Government's Promise to Protect them is only an Illusion'. July 16.

Al-Rawi, Ahmed K. 2011. 'Iraqi Women Journalists' Challenges and Predica-ments'. *Journal of Arab & Muslim Media Research*, 3, 3: 223–236.

Al-Rawi, Ahmed K. 2012. ' "The Campaign of Truth" Program': US Propaganda in Iraq During the early 1950s'. In *Race, Religion, and Ethnicity in the Cold War: A Global Perspective*. Muehlenbeck Philip (ed.). Tennessee: Vanderbilt University Press.

Al-Rawi, Khalid Habib. 1978. *Facets from the History of the Iraqi Press* (In Arabic). Baghdad: Ministry of Culture and Arts.

Al-Rawi, Khalid Habib. 1992. *Tarikh Al-Idha'ah wa al-Talfiziun fi Al-Iraq (The History of Radio and Television in Iraq)*. Baghdad: Dar Al-Hikma lil Tiba'ah wa Al-Nashir.

Al-Rawi, Khalid Habib. 2010. *Tarikh Al-Sahafah wa Al-'Illam fi Al-Iraq munthu Al-'Ahad Al-Othmani wa Hatta Harb Al-Khalij Al-Thaniah, 1816–1991 (The His-tory of the Press and Media in Iraq from the Ottoman Period until the Second Gulf War, 1816–1991)*. Damascus: Dar Safahat lil Dirasat wa Al-Nashir.

Al-Sabah Al-Jadeed. 2010. 'An Interview with Burhan Shawi, the CEO of NCMC'. Issue 1804. September 2.

Al-Samr, Abdul Salam. 2011. 'The American Propaganda Activity in Iraq' (In Arabic). *Center of Iraq for Studies.* June 21. Retrieved on September 30, 2011. http://www.markazaliraq.net/?state=news&viewId=7243

Althaus, Scott & Largio, Devon. 2004. 'When Osama Became Saddam: Origins and Consequences of the Change in America's Public Enemy #1'. *PS: Political Science and Politics,* October, 37: 795–799.

Altheide, David L. 1976. *Creating Reality: How TV News Distorts Events.* Beverly Hills, CA: Sage.

Al-Tikriti, Munir Bakr. 1969. *Al-Sahafah Al-Iraqia wa Ittijahatuha Al-Syasyah wa al-Ijtima'iah wa al-Thaqafiah min 1869–1921 (The Iraqi Press and its Political, Social, and Cultural Trends from 1869–1921).* Baghdad: Mattba'at al-Irshad.

American University of Iraq. 2010. 'Report Card: How the Press is Covering the Iraqi Elections'. March 3. Retrieved on June 27, 2010. http://www.auis.biz/?q=node/230

Amnesty International. 2010. 'New Order, Same Abuses: Unlawfaul Detentions and Torture in Iraq'. Retrieved on September 13, 2010. http://www.amnesty.org/en/library/asset/MDE14/006/2010/en/c7df062b-5d4c-4820-9f14-a4977f863666/mde140062010en.pdf

Amos, Deborah. 2010. 'Confusion, Contradiction and Irony: The Iraqi Media in 2010'. Joan Shorenstien Center on the Press, Politics and Public Policy Discussion Paper Series D-58, John F. Kennedy School of Government, Harvard University. Retrieved on August 12, 2011 3:46:15 AM EDT. http://www.hks.harvard.edu/presspol/publications/papers/discussion_papers/d58_amos.pdf

APFW (Arab Press Freedom Watch). 2003. 'Final Report of It's Fact Finding Mission to Iraq', June 10–17, 2003 and 'Working with Iraqi Journalists: Towards a Free and Independent Media', London, July 2, 2003. Retrieved on June 25, 2004. http://apfw.org/data/report/english/spe1100.pdf

Arango, Tim. 2011. 'Optimism of Intellectuals Ebbs in Iraq'. *The New York Times.* September 30.

Article 19. 2004. 'Freedom of Expression Essential to Iraq's Future'. Iraq Media Law Analysis: Global Campaign for Free Expression, London, February.

The Associated Press. 2005. 'Powell Calls Pre-Iraq U.N. Speech a "blot" on his Record'. *USA Today.* September 8. Retrieved on September 17, 2011. http://www.usatoday.com/news/washington/2005-09-08-powell-iraq_x.htm

The Associated Press. 2006. 'Iraqi Leader Warns Biased Media Outlets', July 12.

The Associated Press. 2010a. 'Iraq's New Parliament Seat Distribution', March 26.

The Associated Press. 2010b. 'More than a Thousand Protesters Rally in Northern Iraq against Killing of Kurdish Reporter', May 12.

Aumente, Jerome, Gross, Peter, Hiebert, Ray, Johnson, Owen & Mills, Dean. 1999. *Eastern European Journalism before, during and after Communism.* New York: The Hampton Press.

The Australian. 2006. 'Bush adviser casts doubt on Maliki'. November 30. Retrieved on November 2, 2011. http://www.theaustralian.com.au/news/world/bush-adviser-casts-doubt-on-maliki/story-e6frg6so-1111112605927

AWGMM (Arab Working Group for Media Monitoring). 2007. 'The Media in the 2006 Bahraini Elections.' Retrieved on June 22, 2010. http://www.awgmm.net/fr/node/180

AWGMM (Arab Working Group for Media Monitoring). 2009a. 'The Programme of Monitoring Media Performance During the Election Campaign of April 9, 2009'. Retrieved on June 25, 2010. http://www.awgmm.net/sites/default/files/Présentat.._0.ppt

AWGMM (Arab Working Group for Media Monitoring). 2009b. 'Monitoring the Parliamentary Election by Governmental and Private Media Channels in the Hashemite Kingdom of Jordan'. Retrieved on June 25, 2010. http://www.awgmm.net/node/211

AWGMM (Arab Working Group for Media Monitoring). 2009c. 'Tunisia October 2009: Media Monitoring of the Presidential and Legislative Elections'. December. Retrieved on July 14, 2011. http://awgmm.net/eng/wp-content/uploads/2011/03/Media-Monitoring-TN09-EN.pdf

AWGMM (Arab Working Group for Media Monitoring). 2010a. 'Media Coverage of the 2010 Parliamentary Elections in Jordan'. Retrieved on July 14, 2011. http://www.awgmm.net/eng/wp-content/uploads/2011/04/Elect-jordan-EN.pdf

AWGMM (Arab Working Group for Media Monitoring). 2010b. 'Media and Elections in Sudan: Monitoring the Coverage of Sudan 2010 Elections'. July 29. Retrieved on July 15, 2011. http://awgmm.net/eng/wpcontent/uploads/2010/11/MM_report_FINAL_english_29_July.pdf

AWGMM (Arab Working Group for Media Monitoring). 2010c. 'The Arabic Network Announces the Preliminary Indicators of Arabic Electronic News Sites Performance During The Egyptian Parliamentary Elections 2010: Youm7 Most Covering, Akhbar Misr and AlMasry AlYoum Most Impartial'. December 8. Retrieved on July 14, 2011. http://www.awgmm.net/eng/?p=27

AWGMM (Arab Working Group for Media Monitoring). 2011. 'The Results of Monitoring the Media in Bahrain's Elections – October 2010'. January. Retrieved on July 14, 2011. http://awgmm.net/eng/wp-content/uploads/2011/01/final-english.pdf

Axe, David. 2006. 'Propagandistan: Iraqi Kurdistan Is Free — but Its Media Sure Isn't'. *Worldpress.org*. April 5. Retrieved on July 1, 2009. http://www.worldpress.org/print_article.cfm?article_id=2428&dont=yes

Ayish, Muhammad I. 2002. 'Political Communication on Arab World Television: Evolving Patterns'. *Political Communication*, 19, 2: 137–154.

Azzildin, Yousif. 1976. *Fahmi Al-Mudaris min Rwad Al-Fikr Al-Hadith (Fahmi al-Mudaris: One of the Pioneers of [Iraq's] Modern Thought)*. Baghdad: Baghdad University Press.

Babil (Newspaper). 2002. 'List of Honour'. Issue 12, No. 3504, Thursday, November 14.

Badrakhan, Abdul Wahab. 2006. 'The Impact of Occupation on Media Freedom'. In *Arab Media in the Information Age*. Abu Dhabi: Emirates Center for Strategic Studies and Research.

Baker, James A, Hamilton, Lee H, Eagleburger, Lawrence S, Jordan, Vernon E, Meese, Edwin, O'Connor, Sandra Day, Panetta, Leon E, Perry, William J, Robb, Charles S, & Simpson, Alan K. 2006. 'The Iraq Study Group Report'. United States Institute of Peace. December. Retrieved on July 10, 2009. http://media.usip.org/reports/iraq_study_group_report.pdf

Baker, Pauline H. 2003/2007. 'A Way Out: The Union of Iraqi States'. *The Fund for Peace*. Report No. 7. March 2003 to June 2007.

Baker, Raymond W, Ismael, Shereen T, & Ismael, Tareq Y. 2010. *Cultural Cleansing in Iraq: Why Museums Were Looted, Libraries Burned and Academics Murdered.* London: Pluto Press.

Barakat, Rijab. 1977. *Min Sahaft al-Khalij al-Arabi: al-Sahafah Al-Basriah Bayn 'Amai 1889–1973 (From the Arab Gulf's Press: Basrah's Press between 1889–1973).* Baghdad: Mattba'at al-Irshad.

Barker, Michael J. 2008. 'Democracy or Polyarchy? US-funded Media developments in Afghanistan and Iraq Post 9/11'. *Media Culture Society*, 30: 109–130.

Barry, Ellen. 2003. 'US Restrictions on Iraqi Media Spark Criticism'. *The Boston Globe.* June 19.

Barzanji, Yahya. 2011. 'Gunmen in Iraq Attack Kurdish TV Station that Showed Protest'. *The Associated Press.* February 20.

Batatu, Hanna. 2004. *The Old Social Classes and the Revolutionary Movements of Iraq: A Study of Iraq's Old Landed and Commercial Classes and of its Communists, Ba'thists and Free Officers.* London: Saqi Books.

Battle, Joyce. 2007. 'Pentagon "Rapid Reaction Media Team" for Iraq'. *The National Security Archive.* May 8. Retrieved on June 16, 2009. http://www.gwu.edu/~ nsarchiv/NSAEBB/NSAEBB219/index.htm#20050600

BBC Arabic. 2010. 'Allawi and Maliki Resume Talks to Form a Government'. August 20. Retrieved on September 26, 2011. http://www.bbc.co.uk/arabic/middleeast/2010/08/100820_maliki_allawi.shtml

BBC News. 2003a. 'Radio Tikrit Changes Tune in Iraq'. February 23. Retrieved on July 10, 2009. http://news.bbc.co.uk/2/hi/middle_east/2791865.stm

BBC News. 2003b. 'Iraqi Leaders Expected Mid-May'. May 5. Retrieved on June 22, 2009. http://news.bbc.co.uk/2/hi/middle_east/3000845.stm

BBC News. 2006. 'Iraq Torture "Worse after Saddam"'. September 21. Retrieved on July 8, 2009. http://news.bbc.co.uk/2/hi/middle_east/5368360.stm

BBC Two. 2010. 'Secret Iraq: Awakening', part 2, TV Series. October 6.

BBC Two. 2010. 'Secret Iraq: Insurgency', part 1, TV Series. September 29.

BBC World Service Trust. 2003. 'The Current State of the Broadcast Media in Iraq'. *Iraqi Media Audit: Eight-City Report.* April and June. Retrieved on July 2, 2009. http://www.mict-international.org/pdf/BBC.pdf

BBC World Service Trust. 2006. 'Mirbad: Choice of Southern Iraq'. July 5. Retrieved on August 27, 2010. http://www.bbc.co.uk/worldservice/trust/mediadevelopment/story/2006/07/060620_almirbad_june_update.shtml

Beehner, Lionel. 2006. 'Maliki and Sadr: An Alliance of Convenience'. *Council on Foreign Relations.* October 24. Retrieved on September 16, 2010. http://www.cfr.org/publication/11787/maliki_and_sadr.html#p6

Bengio, Ofra. 1985. 'Shi'is and Politics in Ba'thi Iraq'. *Middle Eastern Studies*, 21, 1 (January): 1–14.

Bengio, Ofra. 1998. *Saddam's Word: Political Discourse in Iraq.* New York: Oxford University Press.

Bengio, Ofra. 2000. 'How Does Saddam Hold on?' *Foreign Affairs*, 79, 4 (July–August): 90–103.

Biles, Peter. 2010. 'Iraq Inquiry: Ex MI5 Chief Pulls no Punches'. *BBC.* July 23. Retrieved on September 16, 2011. http://www.bbc.co.uk/news/uk-politics-10740001

Blum, William. 2003. *Killing Hope: US Military and CIA Interventions Since World War II.* London: Zed Books Ltd.

Borger, Julian. 2003. 'The Spies Who Pushed for War'. *The Guardian*. Thursday, July 17. Retrieved on September 2, 2011. http://www.guardian.co.uk/world/2003/jul/17/iraq.usa

Boyd, Douglas A. 1982. 'Radio and Television in Iraq: The Electronic Media in a Transitionary Arab World Country'. *Middle Eastern Studies*, 18, 4 (October): 400–410.

Brahimi, Rym. 2003. 'Iraq's Media Wrestles with New Freedoms'. *CNN.com*. August 4. Retrieved on July 6, 2009. http://articles.cnn.com/2003-08-04/world/sprj.irq.media_1_iraqi-media-network-freedom-democracy?_s=PM:WORLD

Bryant, Jennings & Zillmann, Dolf (eds). 2002. *Media Effects: Advances in Theory and Research*. Hillsdale, NJ: Lawrence Erlbaum Associates.

Buckingham, James Silk. 1827. *Travels in Mesopotamia including a Journey from Ilepo to Bagdad, by the route of Beer, Orfah, Diarbeker, Mardan, and Mosul, with Researches on the Ruins of Nineveh, Babylon, and Other Ancient Cities*. vls. i and ii. London: Henry Colburn.

Bush, George W. 2005. 'Iraq Strategy'. November. Retrieved on June 12, 2009. http://georgewbushwhitehouse.archives.gov/infocus/iraq/text/iraq_strategy_nov2005.html

Butler, Jeremy G. 2002. *Television: Critical Methods and Applications*. Hillsdale, NJ: Lawrence Erlbaum Associates.

Butti, Fai'q. 1968. *Sahafat al-Iraq: Tarikhuha wa Kifah Ajialuha (Iraq's Press: Its History and the Struggle of its Generations)*. Baghdad: Mattba'at al-Adib Al-Baghdadiah.

Butti, Fai'q. 1972a. 'Mujaz li-Tarikh al-Sahafah fi Al-Iraq' (A Brief History of the Iraqi Press). Paper Presented During the Third Conference of Arab Journalists Union. Baghdad: Iraqi Journalists Syndicate.

Butti, Fai'q. 1972b. 'Tattawr Al-Maqal fi Al-Sahafah Al-Iraqia' (The Development of the Editorial in the Iraqi Press). In *Dirasat fi Al-Sahafah Al-Iraqia (Studies in the Iraqi Press)*. Baghdad: Mudiriat al-'Illam al-Amah: 28–40.

Butti, Fai'q. 1976. *Al-Musu'ah Al-Suhufiah Al-Iraqia (The Encyclopedia of the Iraqi Press)*. Baghdad: Mattba'at Al-Adib Al-Baghdadiah.

Butti, Rufa'il. 1926. 'Tarikh Al-Tiba'ah Al-Iraqia' (The History of the Iraqi Printing Press). *Lughat Al-Arab Journal*, year 4, 3, September: 147–152.

Butti, Rufa'il. 1955. *Al-Sahafa fi Al-Iraq (The Press in Iraq)*. Cairo: Dar al-Hanaa.

Byrne, Ciar. 2003. 'Iraqi TV was Coalition's "Stuff of Dreams"'. *The Guardian*. July 9. Retrieved on July 3, 2009. http://www.guardian.co.uk/media/2003/jul/09/Iraqandthemedia.broadcasting

Cabinet Minutes of Discussion. 2002. 'Iraq: Prime Minister's Meeting, 23 July'. Matthew Rycroft, Private Secretary to the Prime Minister, S 195/02, July 23, United Kingdom. Retrieved on September 18, 2011. http://www.gwu.edu/~nsarchiv/NSAEBB/NSAEBB328/II-Doc14.pdf

Cambridge Arab Media Project (CAMP) and the Prince al Waleed Bin Talal Centre of Islamic Studies. 2010. 'Sunni/Shiite Broadcasting Divide in Iraq' in 'Religious Broadcasting in the Middle East Islamic, Christian and Jewish Channels: Programmes and Discourses'. University of Cambridge (CIS), April 29–33.

Caterinicchia, Dan. 2003. 'DOD Confirms Iraq E-Mail Campaign'. *Federal Computer Week*. January 16.

Channel 4. 2007. 'Dispatches: Iraq's Death Squads'. TV documentary. January 19.

Chatterjee, Pratap. 2004 'Information Warfare or Yesterday's News? Pentagon Media Contractor Loses Battle for Iraqi Audiences'. *CorpWatch*. January 6. Retrieved on January 15, 2005. http://www.corpwatch.org/article. php?id=9508

Chulov, Martin. 2010. 'Tariq Aziz: "Britain and the US killed Iraq. I Wish I was Martyred"'. *The Guardian*. August 5. Retrieved on September 18, 2011. http:// www.guardian.co.uk/world/2010/aug/05/iraq-us-tariq-aziz-iran

Chulov, Martin & Borger, Julian. 2009. 'Iraqi Court Rules Guardian Defamed Nouri al-Maliki'. *The Guardian*. November 10. Retrieved on September 23, 2011. http://www.guardian.co.uk/world/2009/nov/10/guardian-nour-al-maliki-iraq

Cioppa, Thomas M. 2009. 'Operation Iraqi Freedom Strategic Communication Analysis and Assessment'. *Media, War & Conflict*, 2: 25–45.

Clark, Andrew M & Christie, Thomas B. 2005. 'Ready...Ready...Drop!: A Content Analysis of Coalition Leaflets Used in the Iraq War'. *Gazette: The International Journal for Communication Studies*, 67: 141–154.

Clark, William R. 2005. *Petrodollar Warfare: Oil, Iraq, and the Future of the Dollar*. Gabriola Island: New Society Publishers.

Claypole, Stephen. 2003. 'Beams over Baghdad'. *Liebreich.com*. September 9. Retrieved on July 3, 2009. http://www.liebreich.com/LDC/HTML/Opinion/ Iraq/IraqTV.html

CMC (Communications and Media Commission). 2005. 'Mass Media and the Election Campaign: National, Regional and Local Elections January 30, 2005'. Retrieved on June 29, 2010. http://www.nmc.gov.iq/doc/electionarabic.pdf

CMC (Communications and Media Commission). 2007. 'Policy Recommendations Concerning Broadcasting in Iraq'. Stanhope Centre for Communications Policy Research. January.

CMC (Communications and Media Commission). 2009. 'Broadcasting Programme Code and Practice'. Retrieved on May 24, 2010. http://www.icmc.iq/ pdfcmc/22.pdf

CMC (Communications and Media Commission). 2010a. 'The Periodical Report of Evaluating the Media Performance of Iraqi Satellite Channels from 22/07/2010 to 09/08/2010'. Media Monitoring Department. Retrieved on September 6, 2010. http://www.icmc.iq/pdfcmc/22-7—9-8-2010.pdf

CMC (Communications and Media Commission). 2010b. 'The Periodical Report of Evaluating the Media Performance of Iraqi Satellite Channels from 10/08/2010 to 09/09/2010'. Media Monitoring Department. Retrieved on October 7, 2010. http://www.icmc.iq/pdfcmc/Media%20Report.doc

CMC (Communications and Media Commission). 2010c. 'The Periodical Report of Evaluating the Media Performance of Iraqi Satellite Channels from 1/10/2010 to 15/10/2010'. Media Monitoring Department. Retrieved on October 29, 2010. http://www.icmc.iq/pdfcmc/1—15-10-2010.pdf

CMC (Communications and Media Commission). 2010d. 'Rassed'. Year one, vol. 1. Retrieved on September 24, 2011. http://www.cmc.iq/ar/pdfcmc/ rased.pdf

CMC (Communications and Media Commission). 2010e. 'Rassed'. Year one, vol. 2. Retrieved on September 24, 2011. http://www.cmc.iq/ar/pdfcmc/ rasad2.pdf

CMC (Communications and Media Commission). 2010f. 'The 2010 Annual Report of the Media Monitoring Department'. Retrieved on September 24, 2011. http://www.cmc.iq/ar/pdfcmc/mreport2010.docx

CNN Broadcast. 2006. International Correspondents. November 17, 14:00 EST. http://www.cnn.com/2003/WORLD/meast/08/04/sprj.irq.media/index.html? iref=newssearch

Coalition Provisional Authority. 2003. 'Annex: Coalition Provisional Authority Order Number 2: Dissolution of Entities'.CPA/ORD/23 May 003/02.

Coalition Provisional Authority. 2003. 'Order Number Seven: Penal Code'. CPA/ORD/9 June.

Coalition Provisional Authority. 2003. 'Prohibited Media Activity'. CPA/ORD/10 June 2003/14.

Coalition Provisional Authority. 2003. 'TV Is a Crucial Information Source for Iraqis'. M-146-03. October 16. Retrieved on November 19, 2003. www.cpa-iraq.org/audio/20031117_Nov-16-INR-media_habits_survey.html

Coalition Provisional Authority. 2003. 'Closure of Al Mustaqila Newspaper'. PR NO. 22. July 21. Retrieved on July 6, 2009. http://www.nahrain.com/d/cpa/pressreleases/PR22mustaqila21July03.html

Coalition Provisional Authority. 2004a. 'Iraqi Communications and Media Commission'. CPA/ORD/20 March 2004/65.

Coalition Provisional Authority. 2004b. 'Bremer Appoints Iraqis to the National Communications and Media Commission'. *Press Release*. April 20. Retrieved on June 10, 2009. http://www.iraqcoalition.org/pressreleases/20040420_media_commission.html

Coalition Provisional Authority. 2004. 'Transition of Laws, Regulations, Orders, and Directives Issued by the Coalition Provisional Authority'. CPA/ORD/28 June 2004/100.

Cochrane, Paul. 2006. 'The "Lebanonization" of the Iraqi Media: An Overview of Iraq's Television Landscape'. *Transnational Broadcasting Studies*, 16.

Collyns, Sam. 2010. 'Iraq's Militia Leaders Reveal Why They Turned on al-Qaeda'. *BBC News*. September 29. Retrieved on September 29, 2010. http://www.bbc.co.uk/news/world-middle-east-11417211

Coughlin, Con. 2003. 'Terrorist behind September 11 Strike was Trained by Saddam'. *The Telegraph*. December 14. Retrieved on September 2, 2001. http://www.telegraph.co.uk/news/worldnews/middleeast/iraq/1449442/Terrorist-behind-September-11-strike-was-trained-by-Saddam.html

The 9/11 Commission Report. 2004. 'The National Commission on Terrorist Attacks upon the United States'. Retrieved on September 14, 2011. www.9-11commission.gov/report/911Report.pdf

CPJ (Committee to Protect Journalists). 2008. 'Special Reports: For Sixth Straight Year, Iraq Deadliest Nation for Press'. December 18. Retrieved on June 25, 2009. http://cpj.org/reports/2008/12/for-sixth-straight-year-iraq-deadliest-nation-for.php

CPJ (Committee to Protect Journalists). 2011. 'Special Reports: Getting Away with Murder: CPJ's 2011 Impunity Index Spotlights Countries where Journalists are Slain and Killers Go Free'. June 1. Retrieved on August 5, 2011. http://cpj.org/reports/2011/06/2011-impunity-index-getting-away-murder.php#index

CPJ (Committee to Protect Journalists). 2012. '151 Journalists Killed in Iraq since 1992/Motive Confirmed'. Retrieved on April 7, 2012. http://cpj.org/killed/mideast/iraq/

Curtius, Mary. 2004. 'Some Find Ties to CIA, Baath Party Worrisome'. *Los Angeles Times*. May 29. Retrieved on July 6, 2009. http://articles.latimes.com/2004/may/29/world/fg-allawi29

Damon, Arwa. 2007. 'Shadowy Iraq Office Accused of Sectarian Agenda'. *CNN.com*. May 1. Retrieved on July 9, 2009. http://www.cnn.com/2007/WORLD/meast/05/01/iraq.office/

Daragahi, Borzou. 2003. 'Occupiers Propose Iraqi Media "Code of Conduct"'. *The Associated Press*. June 4.

Dauenhauer, K. & Lobe, J. 2003. 'Iraq: Media Venture by Major Military Contractor under Fire'. *Inter Press Service*. August 13.

Davis, Eric. 2005. *Memories of State: Politics, History, and Collective Identity in Modern Iraq*. Berkeley: University of California Press.

Dawisha, Adeed. 2005. 'Democratic Attitudes and Practices in Iraq, 1921–1958'. *Middle East Journal*, 59, 1 (Winter): 11–30.

De Beer, Arnold & Merrill, John. 2004. *Global Journalism: Topical Issues and Media Systems*. Boston: Pearson Education.

DeCarvalho, Frank B, Kivett, Spring, & Lindsey, Matthew. 2008. 'Reaching Out: Partnering with Iraqi Media'. *Military Review* (July–August): 87–95.

Democracy Now 2004. 'U.S. Journalist Quits Pentagon Iraqi Media Project Calling it U.S. Propaganda'. Radio Interview with Don North. January 14. Retrieved on July 5, 2009. http://www.democracynow.org/2004/1/14/u_s_journalist_quits_pentagon_iraqi

Detenber, B H, Simons, R F, & Bennett, G G, Jr. 1998. 'Roll 'em!: The Effects of Picture Motion on Emotional Responses'. *Journal of Broadcasting & Electronic Media*, 4: 113–128.

Donsbach, W Olfgang. 1997. 'Media Thrust in the German Bundestag Election, 1994: News Values and Professional Norms in Political Communication'. *Political Communication*, 14, 2: 149–170.

Dreyfuss, Robert & Vest, Jason. 2004. 'The Inside Story of how the Bush Administration Pushed Disinformation and Bogus Intelligence and Led the Nation to War'. *Mother Jones*. January/February.

Drogin, Bob. 2004. 'Spy Work in Iraq Riddled by Failures'. *Los Angeles Times*. June 17. Retrieved on July 6, 2009. http://articles.latimes.com/2004/jun/17/world/fg-intel17

D'Souza, Frances & Boyle, Kevin. (eds). 1992. *Striking a Balance: Hate Speech, Freedom of Expression, and Non-Discrimination*. London: Article 1.

Edwardson, M, Kent, Kurt, Engstrom, Erika, & Hofmann, Richard. 1992. 'Audio Recall Immediately Following Video in Television News'. *Journal of Broadcasting and Electronic Media*, 36: 395–410.

Eissa, Razuq. 1926. 'Istidrak'. *Lughat al-Arab*, year 4, 4 (October): 206.

Eissa, Razuq. 1934. 'Tarikh Al-Sahafah fi Al-Iraq' (The History of the Press in Iraq). *Al-Najim* magazine, issue 7, volume 6 (September 30).

Ellis, J. 2000. *Seeing Things: Television in the Age of Uncertainty*. London: I. B. Taurus.

Encyclopedia Judaica. 2007. V.s. 'Press'. vl. 16. Detroit: Thompson Gale.

Entman, R M. 1989. 'How the Media Affect What People Think: An Information Processing Approach'. *Journal of Politics*, 51, 2: 347–370.

Entman, R M. 1993. 'Framing: Toward Clarification of a Fractured Paradigm'. *Journal of Communication*, 43, 4: 51–58.

Erni, John Nguyet. 2005. 'War, Incendiary Media, and International Law (Part I)'. *Flow TV*. September 23. Retrieved on September 20, 2010. http://flowtv.org/2005/09/war-incendiary-media-and-international-law-part-i/

Erni, John Nguyet. 2006. 'War, "Incendiary Media," and International Law' (Part III). *Flow TV*. Volume 3. January 26. Retrieved on July 7, 2009. http:// flowtv.org/?p=211

European Commission. 1996–99. *Eurobarometer 46–50*. Brussels: Directorate-General X.

Everette, D E & Merrill, J C. 1996. *Media Debates: Issues in Mass Communication*. New York: Longman.

Everts, Philip & Isernia, Pierangelo. 2005. 'The Polls–Trends: The War in Iraq'. *Public Opinion Quarterly*, 69, 2: 264–323.

Fadel, Leila. 2010. 'Iraqi TV Personality Takes on a Perilous Job: Giving a Microphone to the Masses'. *The New York Times*. October 28.

Fadhil, Ali. 2006. 'The Night the Americans Came'. *The Guardian*. January 11. Retrieved on November 3, 2011. http://www.guardian.co.uk/media/2006/jan/11/channel4.Iraqandthemedia

Farouk-Sluglett, Marion & Sluglett, Peter. 1990. 'Iraq since 1986: The Strengthening of Saddam'. *Middle East Report*, 167 (November–December): 19–24.

Fawzi, Ahmed. 1986. *Al-Jaridah wa Sira'iha ma'a al-Sultah (The Newspaper and its Struggle Against the Authority)*. Baghdad: Mattba'at al-Diwani.

Fedarko, Kevin. 2001. 'Saddam's CIA Coup'. *Time*. June 24. Retrieved on July 3, 2009. http://www.time.com/time/magazine/article/0,9171,136540,00.html

Feith, Douglas. 2009. *War and Decision: Inside the Pentagon at the Dawn of the War on Terrorism*. New York: HarperCollins.

Finer, Jonathan. 2005. 'Press in Iraq Gains Rights but No Refuge: 85 Workers Killed in 2 Years'. *The Washington Post*. June 6.

Fisk, Robert. 2003. 'Iraq: News, but Not as We Know It'. *The Independent*. October 7. Retrieved on July 1, 2009. http://www.independent.co.uk/opinion/commentators/fisk/news-but-not-as-we-know-it-582542.html

Foreign and Commonwealth Office. 2002. 'Iraq: Advice for the Prime Minister'. Letter from Peter Ricketts, Political Director, to Foreign Secretary Jack Straw, March 22. Retrieved on September 18, 2011. http://www.gwu.edu/~nsarchiv/NSAEBB/NSAEBB330/III-Doc02.pdf

Fraser, Baillie J. 1840. *Travels in Koordistan, Mesopotamia, Including an Account of Parts of those Countries Hitherto Unvisited by Europeans, with Sketches of the Character and Manners of the Koordish and Arab Tribes*. London: Richard Bentley.

Fraser, Baillie J. 1841. *Mesopotamia and Assyria, from the Earliest Ages to the Present Time*. Edinburgh: Oliver & Boyd, Tweeddale Court.

Freedom House. 2004. 'Liberated and Occupied Iraq – New Beginnings and Challenges for Press Freedom'. August. Retrieved on July 4, 2009. http://www.unhcr.org/refworld/docid/473b1fb72.html

Freedom House. 2009. 'Freedom of the Press 2009'. Retrieved on July 19, 2009. http://www.freedomhouse.org/uploads/fop/2009/FreedomofthePress2009_tables.pdf

Gambill, Gary. 2009. 'The Iraqi Media'. *Global Journalist*. May 14.

Garyantes, Dianne M & Murphy, Priscilla J. 2010. 'National Elections: Success or Chaos?: Framing and Ideology in News Coverage of the Iraqi'. *International Communication Gazette*, 72, 2: 151–170.

Georgiadis, Basil D. 2004. 'The Romanian Media in Transition'. Unpublished Ph.D. thesis, The Florida State University, College of Arts and Sciences.

Ghafur, Abdul & Ghani, Abdul. 1974. *al-'Illam wa Al-Thaqafah wa Al-Tanimiah Al-Qawmiah (Media, Culture and National Development)*. Baghdad: Dar al-Hurriah lil Tiba'ha.

Ghazi, Mazen. 2006. 'Mixed Reaction Over Iraqi Satellite Channels'. January 31. IslamOnline.net. Retrieved on June 29, 2009. http://www.islamonline.net/ English/News/2006-01/31/article05.shtml

Ghazi, Yasir. 2010. 'Punk'd, Iraqi-Style, at a Checkpoint'. *The New York Times*. September 3.

Gerth, Jeff. 2005. 'Military's Information War Is Vast and Often Secretive'. *The New York Times*. December 11. Retrieved on July 2, 2009. http://www.nytimes. com/2005/12/11/politics/11propaganda.html?hp&ex=1134363600&en=

Gosh, Bobby. 2006. 'Doubts Grow Over Iraq's Prime Minister'. *Time*. October 25. Retrieved on July 9, 2009. http://www.time.com/time/world/article/0,8599, 1550694,00.html

Gowen, Annie & Alwan, Aziz. 2011. 'Hadi al-Mahdi, Slain Iraqi Journalist, had Warned of Threats'. *The Washington Post*. September 9. Retrieved on September 23, 2011. http://www.washingtonpost.com/world/middle-east/hadi-al-mahdi-slain-iraqi-journalist-had-warned-of-threats/2011/09/09/ gIQAsy52DK_story.html

Grabe, Maria & Bucy, Erik. 2009. *Image Bite Politics: News and Visual Framing of Elections*. New York: Oxford University Press, Inc.

Graber, Doris A. 2001. *Processing Politics: Learning from Television in the Internet Age*. Chicago: University of Chicago Press. Studies in Communication, Media, and Public Opinion.

Gray, Matthew. 2010. 'Revisiting Saddam Hussein's Political Language: The Sources and Roles of Conspiracy Theories'. *Arab Studies Quarterly*, 15, 20: 28–46.

Groves, Anthony N. 1832. *Journal of a Residence at Bagdad during the Years 1830 and 1831*. London: James Nisbet.

The Guardian. 2006. 'US Troops Seize Award-Winning Iraqi Journalist'. January 9. Retrieved on July 9, 2009. http://www.guardian.co.uk/media/2006/jan/ 09/pressandpublishing.iraq

Gunter, Barrie. 1979. 'Recall of Television News Items: Effects of Presentation Mode, Picture Content and Serial Position'. *Journal of Education Television*, 5: 57–61.

Gunter, Barrie. 1997. *Measuring Bias on Television*. Bedfordshire: University of Luton Press.

Hachten, William A. & Scotton, James Francis. 2007. *The World News Prism: Global Information in a Satellite Age*. New Jersey: Wiley-Blackwell.

Hakak, Lev., 2009. *The Emergence of Modern Hebrew Literature in Babylon from 1735–1950*. Purdue: Purdue University Press.

Hall, S. 1985. 'Signification, Representation, Ideology: Althusser and the Post-Structuralist Debates'. *Critical Studies in Mass Communication*, 2, 2: 91–114.

Hammond, Andrew. 2005. 'Iraq "Pop Idol" Offers Escape from Daily Grind'. *Reuters*. 21 August.

Haner, Noelle C. 2004. 'How Harris Corp. Became a Media Player – in Iraq'. *Orlando Business Journal*. December 10. Retrieved on July 3, 2009. http:// orlando.bizjournals.com/orlando/stories/2004/12/13/story1.html

Hanieh, Adam. 2006. ' "Democracy Promotion" and Neo-Liberalism in the Middle East'. *State of Nature (online journal)*, Spring.

Harris, Paul. 2010. 'CIA's Secret Iraq Weapon Revealed: A Saddam Gay Sex Tape'. Wednesday, May 26. Retrieved on September 5, 2011. http://www.guardian.co. uk/world/2010/may/26/cia-saddam-hussein-gay-sex-smear-plot

Harrison, Jackie. 2006. *News*. London: Routledge.

Hartley, John. 1988. *Understanding News*. New York: Routledge.

Hartley, John. 1995. *Understanding News*. New York: Routledge.

Hasoon, Faissal. 2007. *Sahafat Al-Iraq ma Bayn 1945–1970 (Iraq's Press Between 1945–1970)*. Damascus: Dar al-Mada.

Hassen, Farah. 2006. 'New State Department Releases on the "Future of Iraq" Project'. *The National Security Archive*. September 1. Retrieved on September 20, 2011. http://www.gwu.edu/~ nsarchiv/NSAEBB/NSAEBB198/index.htm

Hayes, Stephen F. 2003a. 'The Al Qaeda Connection: Saddam's Links to Osama were no Secret'. *The Weekly Standard*. May 12. Retrieved on September 18, 2011. http://www.weeklystandard.com/Content/Public/Articles/000/000/002/628wqxma.asp?nopager=1

Hayes, Stephen F. 2003b. 'The Al Qaeda Connection, cont.: More Reason to Suspect that bin Laden and Saddam may have been in League'. *The Weekly Standard*. July 11. Retrieved on September 18, 2011. http://www.weeklystandard.com/Content/Public/Articles/000/000/002/889jldct.asp

Healy, Jack. 2010. 'On Iraqi Television, Crying Out for the Missing'. *The New York Times*. November 29.

Hersh, Seymour M. 2003. 'Selective Intelligence'. *New Yorker*. May 12.

Heude, William. 1819. *A Voyage up the Persian Gulf, and a Journey Overland from India to England in 1817*. London: Longman, Hurst, Rees, Orme, and Brown.

Hilmi, Ibrahim. 1913. 'Al-Tiba'ah fi Dar al-Salam wa Al-Najaf wa Karbala'. *Lughat al-Arab*. January. 7: 303–309.

Hiltermann, Joost. 2007. 'A New Sectarian Threat in the Middle East?' *International Review of the Red Cross*, 89, 868: 795–808.

Hollings, Ernest F. 2003. 'Commentary'. *The State*. Sunday, November 9.

Human Rights Watch. 2011. 'At a Crossroads: Human Rights in Iraq Eight Years after the US-Led Invasion'. February.

Hussein, Jenan & Ashton, Adam. 2009. 'Baghdad Makes a Comeback – on Iraqi TV'. *McClatchy* Newspapers. September 1. Retrieved on September 23, 2011. http://www.mcclatchydc.com/2009/09/01/74694/baghdad-makes-a-comeback-on-iraqi.html

Huston, Aletha C, Donnerstein, Edward, Fairchild, Halford, Feshbach, Norma D, Katz, Phyllis A, Murray, John P, Rubinstien, Eli A, Wilcox, Brian L, & Zuckerman, Diana M. 1992. *Big World, Small Screen: The Role of Television in American Society*. Nebraska: University of Nebraska Press.

Ibrahim, Zahda. 1976. *Kashaf Al-Jaraid wa Al-Majalt Al-Iraqia (The Prospectus of Iraqi Newspapers and Magazines)*. Baghdad: Dar al-Hurriah lil Tiba'ah.

Independent High Electoral Commission. n.d. 'Factsheet: Electoral System and Seat Allocation'. Retrieved on September 9, 2010. http://www.ihec-iq.com/en/files/95.pdf

Institute for Economics and Peace. 2010. 'Global Peace Index'. Retrieved on August 28, 2010. http://www.visionofhumanity.org/wp-content/uploads/PDF/2010/2010%20GPI%20Results%20Report.pdf

International Crisis Group. 2006. 'In Their Own Words: Reading the Iraqi Insurgency' Middle East Report No. 50, February 15. Retrieved on April 7, 2012. http://www.crisisgroup.org/~/media/Files/Middle%20East

%20North%20Africa/Iraq%20Syria%20Lebanon/Iraq/In%20Their%20Own %20Words%20Reading%20the%20Iraqi%20Insurgency.pdf
International Federation of Journalists. 2004. 'IFJ Says Iraq Elections "Pipe Dream of Deluded Politicians" As Media Face New Pressure'. November 18. Retrieved on November 3, 2011. http://www.ifj.org/en/articles/ifj-says-iraq-elections-pipe-dream-of-deluded-politicians-as-media-face-new-pressure
International Media Support. 2003. 'Media Development in Post-war Iraq Report'. April 24. Retrieved on June 16, 2009. http://www.i-m-s.dk/files/ publications/Iraq%20post%20war%20media%20development%202003.pdf
International Media Support. 2009. 'Iraqi Media Conference Breaks Isolation'. April 6. Accessed on September 2, 2011. http://www.i-m-s.dk/article/iraqi-media-conference-breaks-isolation
International Media Support. 2010. 'Democracy Stutters in Iraq'. March 12. Retrieved on June 28, 2010. http://www.i-m-s.dk/article/democracy-iraq-stutters
Internet World Stats. 2011. 'Internet Usage in the Middle East: Middle East Internet Usage & Population Statistics'. Retrieved on September 26, 2011. http:// www.internetworldstats.com/middle.htm#iq
Internews. 2003. 'Designing Democratic Media for Iraq'. Internews Newsletter. Winter 2003/2004.
Iraq Centre for Research and Strategic Studies. 2005. 'Public Opinion Survey in Iraq: Media Survey Media "Nationwide"'. November. Retrieved on November 4, 2011. http://www.irqcrss.org/pdf/16.pdf
Iraq on the Record: The Bush Administration Public Statements on Iraq. 2004. 'United States House of Representatives Committee on Government Reform – Minority Staff Investigations Division'. March 16. Prepared for Rep. Henry A Waxman. Retrieved on June 9, 2008. http://oversight.house.gov/ IraqOnTheRecord/pdf_admin_iraq_on_the_record_rep.pdf
Iraqi National Accord. n.d. 'Iraqi National Accord: The Establishment and the Struggle'. Retrieved on July 6, 2009. http://www.wifaq.com/abouta.htm
Iraqi National Congress. 2001. 'List of Dishonour'. September 6.
Iraqi National Library and Archives. 2011a. *Al-Uloom* Magazine. November 1910. Retrieved on August 25, 2011. http://www.nmc.gov.iq/public-html/library/ uloom/index.htm
Iraqi National Library and Archives. 2011b. *Al-'Alim* Magazine (1910). Retrieved on August 25, 2011. http://www.nmc.gov.iq/public-html/library/ 3alam/index.htm
Iraqi National Library and Archives. 2011c. *Tanweer al-Afkar* Magazine (1910). Retrieved on August 25, 2011. http://www.nmc.gov.iq/public-html/library/ tanweerafkar/index.htm
Iraqi National Library and Archives. 2011d. *Al-Risafa* Magazine (1913). Retrieved on August 25, 2011. http://www.nmc.gov.iq/public-html/library/rasafa/index. htm
Iraqi National Library and Archives. 2011e. *Al-Nadi al-'Almi* Magazine (1919). Retrieved on August 25, 2011. http://www.nmc.gov.iq/public-html/library/ nadi3lmi/index.htm
Iraqi National Library and Archives. 2011f. *Mir'at al-Iraq* Magazine (1919). Retrieved on August 25, 2011. http://www.nmc.gov.iq/public-html/library/ mraat/index.htm
Iraqi Publication Law. 1933. 'Iraqi Legal Database'. Retrieved on September 10, 2011. http://www.iraq-ild.org/LoadLawBook.aspx?SP= ALL&SC= 210920059058435

Iraqia TV. 2009. 'Maliki's Visit to IMN'. September 28. Monday 9:30–10:00 pm.

IREX. 2010. 'Iraq Media Study: National Audience Analysis'. April 21. Retrieved on May 22, 2010. http://www.irex.org/newsroom/news/2010/0428_iraq_media_survey_national.pdf

Isakhan, Benjamin. 2008. 'Mediated Hegemony: Interference in the Post-Saddam Iraqi Media Sector'. A Paper Presented at Australian Political Studies Association Conference. Brisbane, Australia. July 6–9.

Ismael, Tareq & Fuller Max. 2009. 'The Disintegration of Iraq: The Manufacturing and Politicization of Sectarianism'. *International Journal of Contemporary Iraqi Studies*, 2, 3: 443–473.

IWPR (Institute for War and Peace Reporting). 2003. 'Media Development in Post-war Iraq Report'. April 24. Retrieved on December 31, 2009. http://iwpr.net/docs/iraq_Media_in_Iraq_Meeting.html

IWPR (Institute for War and Peace Reporting). 2009. 'Small Bribes Keep Iraqi Press Sweet'. August 25. Retrieved on December 30, 2009. http://www.unhcr.org/refworld/docid/4a97840e1bc57.html

IWPR (Institute for War and Peace Reporting). 2010. 'Iraq Event Charts Course for Information Age'. September 26. Retrieved on October 5, 2010. http://iwpr.net/report-news/iraq-event-charts-course-information-age

Iyengar, Shanto & Kinder, Donald R. 1987. *News That Matters: Television and American Opinion*. Chicago: The University of Chicago Press.

Jakubowicz, Karol. 2001. 'Rude Awakening: Social and Media Change in Central and Eastern Europe'. *The Public*, 8, 4: 59–80.

Jakubowicz, Karol & Sukosd, Miklos (eds). 2008. *Finding the Right Place on the Map: Central and Eastern European Media Change in a Global Perspective*. Bristol: Intellect Books.

Jamail, Dhar. 2007. 'Iraqi Media Under Growing Siege'. *Antiwar.com*. January 12. Retrieved on July 5, 2009. http://www.antiwar.com/jamail/?articleid=10312

Jassim, Lattif Nussaif. 1990. *Al-Tariq ala Al-Ghad: Ahadith fi Al-Thaqafah wa Al-Syasah wa al-'Illam (The Path to the Future: Discussions on Culture, Politics, and Media)*. Baghdad: Dar al-Shu'n Al-Thaqafiah al-'Amah.

Jayasekera, Rohan. 2003a. 'Free Media in a Free-for-All'. *Indexonline*. May 23. Retrieved on June 5, 2003. www.indexonline.org/news/20030523_iraq.shtml

Jayasekera, Rohan. 2003b. 'Gives with One Hand, Takes Away with the Other'. *Indexonline*. June 11. Retrieved on June 13, 2003. http://www.indexonline.org/news/20030611_iraq.shtml

Jayasekera, Rohan. 2004. 'Options for Media Development in Iraq'. Index on Censorship. SPO/CI/FED/2004/PI/1. December. Retrieved on July 5, 2009. http://www.i-m-s.dk/files/publications/Iraq%20Media%20Development%202003-05%20pdf.pdf

Jebnoun, Noureddine. 2009. 'Iraqi Media Landscape, Six Years after the Invasion'. *Middle East Times*. April 9.

Jennings, Ray Salvatore. 2003. 'After Saddam Hussein: Winning a Peace If It Comes to War'. United States Institute of Peace. Special Report 102, February. Retrieved on July 8, 2004. http://www.usip.org/pubs/specialreports/sr102.pdf

JFO (Journalistic Freedoms Observatory). 2008. 'Foreign Interference in the Iraqi Media Channels'. June 28. Retrieved on July 9, 2009. http://www.jfoiraq.org/newsdetails.aspx?back=1&id=415&page=32=EF=BB=BF

JFO (Journalistic Freedoms Observatory). 2009. 'A Satellite Channel Must Pay a Fine for a Defamation Case'. April 19. Retrieved on July 8, 2009. http://www.jfoiraq.org/newsdetails.aspx?back=1&id=557&page=5=EF=BB=BF

JFO (Journalistic Freedoms Observatory). 2010. 'Ruling Party Demands One BillionDollars in Defamation Lawsuit'. August 2. Retrieved on August 27, 2010. http://www.jfoiraq.org/newsdetails.aspx?back=1&id=719&page=

Jones, Tony. 2006. 'Lateline: Robert Fisk Shares his Middle East Knowledge'. Interview on the Australian Broadcasting Corporation. March 2. Interview transcript retrieved on September 19, 2011. http://www.abc.net.au/lateline/content/2006/s1582067.htm

Joseph, Edward P & O'Hanlon, Michael E. 2007. 'The Case for Soft Partition in Iraq'. No. 12, June. The Saban Center for Middle East Policy at the Brookings Institution. Retrieved on September 8, 2010. http://www.brookings.edu/~/media/Files/rc/papers/2007/06iraq_joseph/06iraq_joseph.pdf

Kedourie, Elie. 1988. 'Anti-Shiism in Iraq under the Monarchy'. *Middle Eastern Studies*, 24, 2 (April): 249–253.

Kennedy, Elizabeth A. 2011. 'An Iraqi Exile Gives Outlet to Gadhafi's Voice'. *Associated Press*. September 9.

Kepplinger, H. 1982. 'Visual Biases in Television Coverage'. *Communication Research*, 9: 432–446.

Kepplinger, H. 1983. 'Visual Biases in Television Campaign Coverage'. In *Mass Communication Review Yearbook*. vl. 4, E Wartella, C Whitney, & S Windahl (eds). Beverly Hills, CA: Sage: 391–405.

Kerr, Malcolm H. 1971. *The Arab Cold War: Gamal 'Abd al-Nasir and His Rivals, 1958–1970*. London: Oxford University Press.

Keyes, Charley. 2011. 'It's "Good Night, Baghdad" for U.S. Army Radio'. *CNN*. September 23. Retrieved on September 24, 2011. http://edition.cnn.com/2011/09/23/world/meast/iraq-us-army-radio/index.html

Khadduri, Majid. 1951. *Independent Iraq: A Study in Iraqi Politics since 1932*. London: Oxford University Press.

Khadduri, Walid. 1979. 'The Jews of Iraq in the Nineteenth Century: A Case Study of Social Harmony'. In *Zionism, Imperialism, and Racism*. 'Abd al-Wahhab Kayyali (ed.). London: Croom Helm.

Khalil, Ibrahim. 1982. *Nash'at al-Sahafah al-Arabiah fi Al-Mosul (The Formation of the Arab Press in Mosul)*. Mosul: Mudiriat Dar al-Kutub lil Tibahah wa al-Nashir.

Khalil, Ibrahim. 1985a. 'Al-Tiba'ah' (The Printing Press). In *Hadharat Al-Iraq (The Civilization of Iraq)*. vl. 11. Baghdad: Dar al-Hurria lil Tiba'ah.

Khalil, Ibrahim 1985b. 'Al-Sahafah' (The Press). In *Hadharat Al-Iraq, (The Civilization of Iraq)*. vl. 11. Baghdad: Dar al-Hurria lil Tiba'ah.

Kim, Hun Shik. 2007. 'Emerging Press Under Fire: Iraqi Media System in the Post-Saddam Hussein Era'. Communication and New Media Programme. University of Colorado at Boulder. Retrieved on July 2, 2009. http://www.fas.nus.edu.sg/cnm/news/071109%20talk%202.pdf

Kim, Hun Shik & Hama-Saeed, Mariwan. 2008. 'Emerging Media in Peril: Iraqi Journalism in the Post-Saddam Hussein Era'. *Journalism Studies*, 9, 4: 578–594.

Kimmage, Daniel & Ridolfo, Kathleen. 2007. 'Iraqi Insurgent Media: The War of Ideas and Images: How Sunni Insurgents in Iraq and their Supporters Worldwide are using the Media'. *Radio Free Europe: Radio Liberty*. Retrieved on September 21, 2011. http://realaudio.rferl.org/online/OLPDFfiles/insurgent.pdf

King, David C & Morehouse, David. 2004. 'Moving Voters in the 2000 Presidential Campaign: Local Visits, Local Media'. In *Lights, Camera, Campaign: Media, Politics, and Political Advertising*. David A Shultz (ed.). New York: Peter Lang Publishing: 301–318.

Knights, Michael. 2003. 'The Role of Broadcast Media in Influence Operations in Iraq'. *Policy Watch*, No. 758. May 19. Retrieved on June 25, 2009. http://www.washingtoninstitute.org/templateC05.php?CID=1636

Kowalski, Tadeusz. 1988. 'Evolution after Revolution: The Polish Press System in Transition'. *Media Culture Society*, 10: 183–196.

Krosnick, J & Kinder, D. 1990. 'Altering the Foundations of Support for the President through Priming'. *American Political Science Review*, 84, 2: 497–512.

Kubey, Robert & Csíkszentmihályi, Mihály. 1990. *Television and the Quality of Life: How Viewing Shapes Everyday Experience*. Hillsdale, NJ: Lawrence Erlbaum Associates.

Kukis, Mark. 2006. 'Ethnic Cleansing in a Baghdad Neighborhood?' *Time*. October 25. Retrieved on July 9, 2009. http://www.time.com/time/world/article/0,8599,1550441,00.html

Kurdnet. 2011. 'Iraqi Kurdistan Magazine Chief Jailed on Libel Charges'. June 6. Retrieved on January 23, 2012. http://www.ekurd.net/mismas/articles/misc2011/6/state5165.htm

Kuusi, Antti, Jayasekera, Rohan, Borden, Anthony, Flint, Julie, & Furey, Duncan. 2003. 'A New Voice in the Middle East: A Provisional Needs Assessment for the Iraqi Media'. Index on Censorship. May–June.

Kwiatkowski, Karen. 2004. 'The new Pentagon Papers'. March 10. Retrieved on September 10, 2011. http://www.salon.com/news/opinion/feature/2004/03/10/osp/print.html

Lawson, Chappell & McCann, James. 2005. 'Television News, Mexico's 2000 Elections and Media Effects in Emerging Democracies'. *British Journal of Political Science*, 35: 1–30.

Leland, John & Ali, Khalid D. 2010. 'Baghdad Studio of Feisty TV Station Shut Down in Dispute with Iraqi Government'. *The New York Times*. November 4.

Levinson, Charles. 2006. 'Iraq's "PBS" Accused of Sectarian Slant'. *The Christian Science Monitor*. January 10. http://www.csmonitor.com/2006/0110/p06s01-woiq.html

Levinson, Charles. 2010. 'An Architect of U.S. Strategy Waits to Pop Cork'. *The Wall Street Journal*. August 27. Retrieved on September 16, 2010. http://online.wsj.com/article/SB10001424052748704125604575449171253677444.html

Lewis, Charles & Reading-Smith, Mark. 2008. 'False Pretenses'. The Center for Public Integrity. January 23. Retrieved on September 16, 2011. http://projects.publicintegrity.org/WarCard/

Lobe, Jim. 2007. 'Pentagon Moved to Fix Iraqi Media Before Invasion'. *Inter Press Service*. May 9.

Mahajan, Rahul. 2003. 'Gunpoint Democracy in Iraq'. *The Progressive*. September 3. Retrieved on July 4, 2009. http://www.progressive.org/node/1093

Mahmood, Essam Mohammed. 1971. *Matubatat al-Mosul munthu Sanat 1861–1970 (Mosul's Publications Since 1861–1970)*. Mosul: Matba'at al-Jamhur.

Margasak, L. 2005. 'Former Journalism Adviser in Iraq Says U.S. Officials Steered Coverage to Themselves'. *The Associated Press*. February 14.

Marra, Andrew. 2009. 'Boca Man Recalls how his Army Unit Spread Messages through Music in Iraq on a Makeshift Radio Station'. *Palm Beach Post.* September 19. Retrieved on September 19, 2011. http://www.palmbeachpost. com/localnews/content/local_news/epaper/2009/09/19/a1a_iraq_radio_0920. html

Marrs, Jim. 2006. *The Terror Conspiracy: Deception, 9/11, and the Loss of Liberty.* New York: The Disinformation Company Ltd.

Mazzetti, Mark & Daragahi, Borzou. 2005. 'U.S. Military Covertly Pays to Run Stories in Iraqi Press'. *Los Angeles Times.* November 30.

Mazzoleni, Gianpietro. 1987. 'Logic and Party Logic in Campaign Coverage: The Italian General Election of 1983'. *European Journal of Communication*, 2, 1 (March): 81–103.

McCaul, Kathleen. 2003. 'The Iraqi Media Network'. *Baghdad Bulletin.* July 21. Retrieved on July 2, 2009. http://www.baghdadbulletin.com/pageArticle.php? article_id=77&cat_id=

McCombs, Maxwell E. 2004. *Setting the Agenda: The Mass Media and Public Opinion.* Cambridge: Polity Press.

McCombs, Maxwell E & Shaw, D L. 1972. 'The Agenda-Setting Function of Mass Media'. *Public Opinion Quarterly*, 36: 176–187.

McDonough, Challiss. 2007. 'US Pressures Egypt to Stop Iraqi Insurgent TV Broadcasts'. *Voice of America.* January 18. Retrieved on July 9, 2009. http://www. globalsecurity.org/wmd/library/news/iraq/2007/01/iraq-070118-voa07.htm

McEvers, Kelly. 2010. 'In Iraq, Getting The Story Gets Tougher For Reporters'. *NPR.* October 1. Retrieved on October 4, 2010. http://www.npr.org/templates/ story/story.php?storyId=130241509

The Media Missionaries. 2004. 'Bush Policy: Independent Media or Pro-U.S. Media?' Report for the John S. and James L. Knight Foundation, February.

Merritt, Gilbert S. 2003. 'Document Links Saddam, Bin Laden'. *The Tennessean.* Wednesday, June 25.

Messing, Michael. 2004. *Now They Tell us: The American Press and Iraq.* New York: The New York Review of Books.

Metcalf, Steve. 2006. 'Analysis: Iraq's Media Three Years on'. *BBC.* April 6. Retrieved on July 7, 2009. http://news.bbc.co.uk/2/hi/middle_east/ 4884246.stm

Middle East Online. 2009a. 'Iraqi journalists Cry Foul Over War of Words'. August 9. Retrieved on December 31, 2009. http://www.middle-east-online. com/english/iraq/?id=33631

Middle East Online. 2009b. 'Iraqi Journalists Protest 'Intimidation', Censorship'. August 14. Retrieved on December 31, 2009. http://www.middle-east-online. com/english/?id=33720

Miller, D. 2004. *Tell Me Lies: Propaganda and Media Distortion in the Attack on Iraq.* London: Pluto.

Mink, A C. 2004. 'Local Iraqi Starts Independent Newspaper'. *Marine Link.* May 14.

Mohammed, Abeer. 2010. 'Journalists Decry Iraq's Biased Media'. Institute for War and Peace Reporting. ICR Issue 361, December 6. Retrieved on December 10, 2010. http://iwpr.net/report-news/journalists-decry-iraq%E2% 80%99s-biased-media

Morris, Jonathan S. 2007. 'Slanted Objectivity? Perceived Media Bias, Cable News Exposure, and Political Attitudes'. *Social Science Quarterly*, 88, 3 (September): 707–728.

Mother Jones. 2008. 'Lie by Lie: The Mother Jones Iraq War Timeline (8/1/90–2/14/08)'. Retrieved on September 9, 2011. http://motherjones.com/bush_war_timeline

Muhalhal, Naeem 'Abd. 2001. 'America: A Fear Called Osama Bin Laden'. *Nassiriah* Newspaper, issue 64. July 21.

Muhalhal, Naeem'Abd. 2006. 'Bin Laden, the Prophecy of the Article, and the Iraqi War Dairies'. *Azzaman* Newspaper, No. 2357. March 22.

Muhalhal, Naeem'Abd 2009. Email correspondence with the author. Monday, June 15.

Murphy, Caryle & Saffar, Khalid. 2005. 'Terror Suspects Grilled, Mocked on Hit Iraqi Show'. *The Washington Post*. April 5.

Murphy, Janet. 1998. 'An Analysis of Political Bias in Evening Network News during the 1996 Presidential Campaigns' Unpublished Ph.D. thesis, University of Oklahoma.

Murrell, Colleen 2010. 'Baghdad Bureaux: An Exploration of the Interconnected World of Fixers and Correspondents at the BBC and CNN'. *Media, War & Conflict*, 3, 2 (August): 125–137.

Myers, Steven Lee. 1999. 'Toppling Dictators; Guns Don't Scare Them? Try Campaign Spending'. *The New York Times*. November 7.

Najjar, Orayb A. 2009. '"The Pathology of Media Intervention" in Iraq 2003–2008: The US Attempt to Restructure Iraqi Media Law and Content'. *International Journal of Contemporary Iraqi Studies*, 3, 1: 27–52.

National Endowment for Democracy. 2004. 'Democracy Projects Database: Iraq'. Retrieved on July 1, 2010. http://geniehost25.inmagic.com/dbtw-wpd/projects-search.htm

National Intelligence Estimate. 2007. 'Prospects for Iraq's Stability: A Challenging Road Ahead'. January. Retrieved on September 18, 2010. http://www.dni.gov/press_releases/20070202_release.pdf

National Media Center, Monitoring and Research Department. n.d. 'Government Media Rules'. Retrieved on May 24, 2010. http://www.nmc.gov.iq/eelamgov.htm

The National Security Archive. 1998. 'Statement by the President'. Retrieved on September 10, 2011. http://www.gwu.edu/~nsarchiv/NSAEBB/NSAEBB326/doc02.pdf

The National Security Archive. 2001a. 'Origins of the Iraq Regime Change Policy'. From Edward S. Walker. January 23. Retrieved on September 10, 2011. http://www.gwu.edu/~nsarchiv/NSAEBB/NSAEBB326/doc03.pdf

The National Security Archive. 2001b. 'Rumsfeld's Handwritten Notes'. Retrieved on September 10, 2011. http://www.gwu.edu/~nsarchiv/NSAEBB/NSAEBB326/doc07.pdf

The National Security Archive. 2002a. 'Factsheet on Iraq Liberation Act (ILA), Drawdown, and Economic Support Funds (ESF)'. August 22. Retrieved on September 20, 2011. http://www.gwu.edu/~nsarchiv/NSAEBB/NSAEBB328/IIDoc09.pdf

The National Security Archive. 2002b. 'Future of Iraq Project: Free Media Working Group'. December. Date/Case Released June 17 2005, 200304121. Retrieved on June 16, 2009. http://www.gwu.edu/~nsarchiv/NSAEBB/NSAEBB198/FOI%20Free%20Media.pdf

The National Security Archive. 2003. 'The Future of Iraq Project: Local Government Working Group'. January 28. Retrieved on September 20, 2011. http://www.gwu.edu/~nsarchiv/NSAEBB/NSAEBB198/FOI%20Local%20Govt.pdf

NAVY mil. 2005. 'Iraqi TV Tells Coalition Story from Firsthand Experience'. Story No. NNS050330-09. March 30. Retrieved on July 6, 2009. http://www.navy.mil/search/display.asp?story_id=17698

NDI. n.d. 'Iraq'. Retrieved on October 4, 2011. http://www.ndi.org/iraq

The New York Times. 2010. 'Iraq Elections'. July 20. Retrieved on September 9, 2010. http://topics.nytimes.com/top/news/international/countriesandterritories/iraq/elections/index.html

Nicols, John. 2003. 'Electoral Raid on Baghdad'. The Nation. November 30. Retrieved on July 5, 2009. http://www.thenation.com/blogs/thebeat/1097

Norsworthy, Kent W. 1994. 'Television Broadcasting and Media Reform in Nicaragua (1956–1994): U.S. intervention in Nicaragua's 1990 Elections: The Case of the Media'. Unpublished M.A. thesis, University of Texas at Austin.

North, Don. 2003. 'Project Frustration: One Newsman's Take on How Things Went Wrong'. *Television Week.* December 15. Retrieved on June 3, 2004. http://www.tvweek.com/topstorys/121503iraqproject.html

Oates, Sarah. 2006. *Television, Democracy, and Elections in Russia.* London: Routledge.

Opel, Richard A. 2003. 'Iraqis Get the News but Often Don't Believe It'. *The New York Times.* August 5. Retrieved on July 2, 2009. http://www.nytimes.com/2003/08/05/international/worldspecial/05MEDI.html?pagewanted=1

OpenNet Initiative. 2007. 'Iraq'. May 10. Retrieved on August 3, 2009. http://opennet.net/sites/opennet.net/files/iraq.pdf

ORHA (Office of Reconstruction and Humanitarian Assistance). 2003. 'Inter-Agency Rehearsal and Planning Conference'. February 21–22. The National Security Archive. Retrieved on September 20, 2011. http://www.gwu.edu/~nsarchiv/NSAEBB/NSAEBB328/II-Doc09.pdf

Otterman, Michael, Hil, Richard, & Wilson, Paul. 2010. *Erasing Iraq: The Human Costs of Carnage.* London: Pluto Press.

Oweis, Khaled Yacoub. 2003. 'Iraqi TV Head Quits, Says US Losing Propaganda War'. *Reuters.* August 6.

Oxford Research International. 2004. 'National Survey of Iraq'. February. Retrieved on July 3, 2009. http://news.bbc.co.uk/nol/shared/bsp/hi/pdfs/15_03_04_iraqsurvey.pdf

Pallister, David. 2005. 'Media Mogul Accused of Running Saudi-funded Propaganda Campaign'. *The Guardian.* January 26. Retrieved on September 26, 2011. http://www.guardian.co.uk/world/2005/jan/26/pressandpublishing. media

Palmer, Jerry & Fontan, Victoria. 2007. ' "Our Ears and Our Eyes": Journalists and Fixers in Iraq?' *Journalism*, 8, 1: 5–24.

Parker, Ned & Salman, Raheem. 2010. 'Iraqi Reporter Risks it all for the Story'. Los Angeles Times. July 15. Retrieved on 25 August 2010. http://articles.latimes.com/2010/jul/15/world/la-fg-iraq-press-20100715

Patterson, T E & McClure, R D. 1976. *The Unseeing Eye: The Myth of Television Powers in the National Politics.* New York: G. P. Putnam's Sons.

Pelham, Nicolas. 2004. 'Iraq Sets up Committee to Impose Restrictions on News Reporting'. *The Financial Times*. July 27.

Pincus, Walter. 2003. 'U.S. General May Censor Iraqi TV Station's Programs'. *Washington Post*. A24, May 9.

Piper, Ian. 2004. 'Rebuilding Iraq's Media One Year on'. *BBC Monitoring*. April 11. Retrieved on July 5, 2009. http://news.bbc.co.uk/2/hi/middle_east/3610671.stm

Pipes, Daniel. 2006. 'Civil War in Iraq?' *The Jerusalem Post*. March 1.

Porter, Robert Ker. 1822. *Travels in Georgia, Persia, Armenia, Ancient Baylonia During the Years 1817, 1818, 1819, and 1820*. vl. ii. London: Longman, Hurst, Rees, Orme, and Brown.

Prados, John. 2004. *Hoodwinked: The Documents that Reveal How Bush Sold Us a War*. New York: The New Press.

Presidency Council. 2009. 'National Media Center Law'. Retrieved on May 24, 2010. http://www.nmc.gov.iq/slaws/markzlaw.pdf

Price, Monroe E. 2007. 'Foreword: Iraq and the Making of State Media Policy'. *Cardozo Arts & Entertainment*, 25, 5: 5–21.

Prusher, Ilene. 2003a. 'Free Media Blossom in Iraq City'. *The Christian Science Monitor*. April 29.

Prusher, Ilene. 2003b. 'In Volatile Iraq, US Curbs Press: US Issues an Order against Inciting Attacks on Minorities or US Troops'. *The Christian Science Monitor*. June 19.

Radio Netherlands – RNW Arabic Service. 2011. 'Al-Dujail Massacre...Did it Really Happen?' July. Retrieved on September 23, 2011. http://www.rnw.nl/arabic/article/444333

Redorbit.com. 2003. 'Pentagon Funds Pro-U.S. Network in Iraq'. November 29. Retrieved on July 3, 2009. http://www.redorbit.com/news/general/34224/pentagon_funds_prous_network_in_iraq/index.html

Reuters. 2006. 'Bush Warns Iraqis that American Patience has Limits'. October 26.

Rich, James Claudius. 1836. *Narrative of a Residence in Koordistan and on the Site of Ancient Nineveh: With a Journal of a Voyage down the Tigris to Bagdad and an Account of a Visit to Shirauz and Persepolis*. vl. ii. London: James Duncan, Paternoster Row.

Rieff, David. 2003. 'Blueprint for a Mess'. *The New York Times*. November 2.

Robison, Gordon. 2003. *Rebuilding Iraqi Television: A Personal Account*. USC Centre on Public Diplomacy. Middle East Media Project October 27.

Rohde, David. 2003. 'Iraqis were Set to Vote, but U.S. Wielded a Veto'. *The New York Times*. June 19.

Rosen, Nir. 2004a. 'US Newspaper Ban Plays into Cleric's Hands'. *Asia Times Online*. March 31. Retrieved on July 1, 2009. http://www.atimes.com/atimes/Middle_East/FC31Ak01.html

Rosen, Nir. 2004b. 'The Shi'ite Voice that Will be Heard'. *Asia Times Online*. April 8. Retrieved on July 1, 2009. http://www.atimes.com/atimes/Middle_East/FD08Ak06.html

Rosen, Nir. 2006a. 'Anatomy of a Civil War: Iraq's Descent into Chaos'. *Boston Review*. November/December. Retrieved on September 7, 2010. http://www.bostonreview.net/BR31.6/rosen.php

Rosen, Nir. 2006b. 'Iraq's Jordanian Jihadis'. *The New York Times*. February 19. Retrieved on September 20, 2011. http://www.nytimes.com/2006/02/19/magazine/iraq.html?pagewanted=all

Roug, Louise. 2006. 'Unfair, Unbalanced Channels'. *Los Angeles Times*. March 28. Retrieved on July 5, 2009. http://articles.latimes.com/2006/mar/28/world/fg-media28

RSF (Reporters Sans Frontières). 2002a. 'Iraq 2002 Annual Report'. April 24. Retrieved on July 3, 2009. http://www.rsf.org/Iraq-annual-Report-2002.html

RSF (Reporters Sans Frontières). 2002b. 'Press Freedom Index'. October. Retrieved on June 19, 2009. http://www.rsf.org/Reporters-Without-Borders,4116.html

RSF (Reporters Sans Frontières). 2003a. 'The Iraqi Media: 25 Years of Relentless Repression'. February. Retrieved on July 4, 2009. http://www.rsf.org/IMG/pdf/doc-1919.pdf

RSF (Reporters Sans Frontières). 2003b. 'The Iraqi Media Three Months after the War: A New but Fragile Freedom'. July 22. Retrieved on July 3, 2009. http://www.rsf.org/The-Iraqi-media-three-months-after,7583.html

RSF (Reporters Sans Frontières). 2009a. 'Trade Minister Drops Lawsuits against Two Newspapers'. May 15. Retrieved on July 10, 2009. http://www.rsf.org/Trade-minister-drops-lawsuits.html

RSF (Reporters Sans Frontières). 2009b. 'News Website Latest Target in Government's Legal Offensive against Independent Media'. May 20. Retrieved on July 10, 2009. http://www.rsf.org/News-website-latest-target-in.html

RSF (Reporters Sans Frontières). 2010. 'The Iraq War: A Heavy Death Toll for the Media, 2003–2010'. August. Retrieved on September 7, 2010. http://en.rsf.org/IMG/pdf/rapport_irak_2003-2010_gb.pdf

Rugh, William A. 1975. 'Arab Media and Politics during the October War'. *Middle East Journal*, 29, 3 (Summer, 1975): 310–328.

Rugh, William A. 2004a. *Arab Mass Media: Newspapers, Radio, and Television in Arab Politics*. Westport, CT: Praeger Publishers.

Rugh, William A. 2004b. 'How Washington Confronts Arab Media'. *Global Media Journal*, 5.

Ryan, Buck & O'Donnell, Michael J. 2001. *The Editor's Toolbox: A Reference Guide for Beginners and Professionals*. Iowa: Iowa State University Press.

Saadi, Salam & Ahmed, Hevidar. 2011. 'Head of KDP's Baghdad Branch: The Number of Kurds in Baghdad is Wrongly Inflated'. *Rudaw*. June 2.

The Saban Center for Middle East Policy. 2007. 'Crisis in the Middle East Task Force: The Sunni-Shi'i Divide: How Important has it Become?' July 30. Retrieved on September 7, 2010. http://www.brookings.edu/events/2007/0730middle-east.aspx

Said, Sinan. 1970–1971. 'Al-Sahafah fi 'Ahad Abdul Hamid (The Press during Abdul Hamid's Rule)'. *Journal of the College of Arts*, Baghdad University, 14: 335–346.

Sakr, Naomi. 2006. 'Foreign Support for Media Freedom Advocacy in the Arab Mediterranean: Globalization from Above or Below?' *Mediterranean Politics*, 11, 1: 1–20.

Salaheddin, Sinan. 2009. 'Iraq to Impose Controls on Internet Content, Sparking Freedom of Speech Debate'. *AP*. August 4.

Schlesinger, Philip. 1987. *Putting 'Reality' Together: BBC News*. London: Methuen & Co. Ltd.

Semetko, H, Blumler, J, Gurevitch, M, & Weaver, D. 1991. *The Formation of Campaign Agendas: A Comparative Analysis of Party and Media Roles in Recent American and British Elections*. Hillsdale, NJ: Lawrence Erlbaum.

Semetko, Holli & Canel, Maria J. 1997. 'Agenda-Senders Versus Agenda-Setter: Television in Spain's 1996 Election Campaign'. *Political Communication*, 14: 459–479.

Shadid, Anthony. 2009. 'In the City of Cement'. *The Washington Post*. July 12.

Shadid, Anthony. 2010. 'The Long, Long Shadow of Early Missteps in Iraq'. *The New York Times*, WK4. February 21.

Shadid, Anthony. 2011. 'Iraq's Last Patriot'. *The New York Times*. February 6.

Shukur, Malih Salih. 2010. *Tarikh Al-Sahafa Al-Iraqia fi Al-'Ahdin Al-Malaki wa Al-Jamhuri 1932–1967 (The History of the Iraqi Press in the Monarchy and Republican Eras, 1932–1967)*. Beirut: al-Dar al-Arabia lil Musu'at.

Sinjari, Hussein. 2006. 'The Iraqi Press after Liberation: Problems and Prospects for Developing a Free Press'. In *Arab Media in the Information Age*. Abu Dhabi: Emirates Center for Strategic Studies and Research.

Sipress, Alan. 2004. 'For Many Iraqis, U.S.-Backed TV Echoes the Voice of its Sponsor: Station Staffers Acknowledge their Reluctance to Criticize'. *The Washington Post*. January 8, 2004.

Sloan, William David & Mackay, Jenn Burleson. (eds). 2007. *Media Bias: Finding It, Fixing It*. North Carolina: McFarland & Company.

Sly, Liz. 2009. 'Iraq's Maliki Declines U.S. Offer on National Reconciliation'. *Los Angeles Times*. July 4.

Solomon, Norman & Erlich, Reese. 2003. *Target Iraq: What the News Media Didn't Tell You*. New York: Context Books.

Stalinsky, Steven. 2005. 'Reality TV, Iraq-Style'. *FrontPageMagazine.com*. March 31. Retrieved on July 6, 2009. http://www.frontpagemag.com/readArticle.aspx? ARTID= 9083

Straw, Jack. 2010. 'Memorandum of Evidence to the Iraq Inquiry'. January 21. Iraq Inquiry. Retrieved on September 18, 2011. http://www.iraqinquiry.org.uk/ media/43119/jackstraw-memorandum.pdf

Suskind, Ron. 2009. *The Way of the World: A Story of Truth and Hope in an Age of Extremism*. New York: Harper Perennial.

Tammuz Organization for Social Development. 2010. 'The Complete Report on Monitoring the Media Campaign for the 2010 Iraqi Parliament Elections'. March 6. Retrieved on October 4, 2011. http://www.tammuz.net/news/arabic/ 06-03-010a4.pdf

Tawfeeq, Mohammed. 2011. 'Two Students Killed in Sunni Neighborhood of Baghdad'. *CNN.com*. March 7. Retrieved on March 26, 2011. http://articles. cnn.com/2011-03-07/world/iraq.violence_1_baghdad-s-zafaraniya-civilians-falluja?_s=PM:WORLD

Telegraph.co.uk. 2005. 'The Buds of Democracy are Showing in Iraq'. April 13. Retrieved on July 1, 2009. http://www.telegraph.co.uk/comment/telegraph-view/3616191/The-buds-of-democracy-are-showing-in-Iraq.html

Telephone Interview with Sabah Nahi. 2011. September 18. 11:30 am.

Therese, Marie. 2005. 'Torture TV: Hottest Show in Iraq is Run by Americans'. *News Hounds*. May 22. Retrieved on July 4, 2009. http://www.newshounds.us/ 2005/05/22/torture_tv_hottest_show_in_iraq_is_run_by_americans.php

Thompson, John B. 1990. *Ideology and Modern Culture. Stanford.* California: Stanford University Press.

Thompson, Paul. 2004. *The Terror Timeline: Year by Year, Day by Day, Minute by Minute: A Comprehensive Chronicle of the Road to 9/11–and America's Response.* New York: Regan Books.

Transparency International. 2009. 'Global Corruption Barometer.' Retrieved on April 20, 2010. http://www.transparency.org/content/download/43788/701097/

Transparency International. 2010. 'Corruption Perception Index 2010 Results'. Retrieved on March 21, 2011. http://www.transparency.org/policy_research/surveys_indices/cpi/2010/results

UK Cabinet Office. 2002. 'Iraq: Options Paper'. Overseas and Defense Secretariat, United Kingdom, March 8. Downing Street Documents. Retrieved on September 18, 2011. http://downingstreetmemo.com/docs/iraqoptions.pdf

UNDP (United Nations Development Programme), and Arab Fund for Economic and Social Development. 2003. 'Arab Human Development Report: Building a Knowledge Society'. Retrieved on December 12, 2009. http://www.arab-hdr.org/publications/other/ahdr/ahdr2003e.pdf

UNESCO. 2008. 'Launch of Professional Code of Conduct for Iraqi Media'. *UNESCOPRESS.* March 25. Retrieved on July 9, 2009. http://portal.unesco.org/en/ev.php-URL_ID=42110&URL_DO=DO_TOPIC&URL_SECTION=201.html

UNESCO. 2010. 'Literacy in Iraq; Fact Sheet'. September. Retrieved on October 5, 2010. http://www.iauiraq.org/documents/1050/Literacy%20Day%20Factsheet_Sep8.pdf

UNESCO Conference. 2007. 'Towards a Free, Pluralistic and Vibrant Media in Iraq: An International Conference on Freedom of Expression and Media Development in Iraq'. Paris, France. January 8–10. Retrieved on July 1, 2009. http://portal.unesco.org/ci/en/files/23849/11691287391declaration_engl.pdf/declaration+engl.pdf

UNESCO; International News Safety Institute; Index on Censorship; Reuters Foundation; Article 19. 2008. *A Reporter's Guide to Election Coverage.* Retrieved on July 15, 2010. http://www.reuterslink.org/docs/electionhandbook.pdf

United States Department of Defense. 2003. 'White Paper: "Rapid Reaction Team" Concept'. The National Security Archive. Retrieved on June 18, 2009. http://www.gwu.edu/~ nsarchiv/NSAEBB/NSAEBB219/iraq_media_01.pdf

United States Department of Defense, Inspector General. 2007. 'Review of the Pre-Iraqi War Activities of the Office of the Under Secretary of Defense for Policy'. Report No. 07-INTEL-04, February 9. Retrieved on June 13, 2009. http://www.gwu.edu/~ nsarchiv/NSAEBB/NSAEBB219/iraq_media_03.pdf

United States Department of Defense, Office of the Inspector General. 2004. 'Quality Integrity Accountability Contracts Awarded for the Coalition Provisional Authority by the Defense Contracting Command-Washington (D-2004-057)'. March 18. Retrieved on June 22, 2009. http://www.dodig.mil/audit/reports/fy04/04-057.pdf

United States Internal Revenue Service. 2006. 'Return of Organization Exempt from Income Tax'. Retrieved on October 3, 2011. http://apps.sos.wv.gov/business/charities/readpdf.aspx?DocID=76292

USAID. 2004. 'USAID Iraq Reconstruction Financial Summary'. Retrieved on July 2, 2009. http://www.reliefweb.int/library/documents/2004/usaid-irq-27apr.pdf

USAID. 2007. 'America's Development Foundation (ICSP)'. Retrieved on July 1, 2009. http://www.usaid.gov/iraq/contracts/

US Army Field Manual. 1994. 'Psychological Operations Techniques and Procedures'. Headquarters, Department of the Army, FM 33-1-1. May 5.

US Army Field Manual. 2003. 'Information Operations: Doctrine, Tactics, Techniques, and Procedures'. Headquarters, Department of the Army, FM 3-13 (FM 100-6), November.

US Army Field Manual. 2006. 'Counterinsurgency'. FM3-24, MCWP 3-33.5, December.

USATODAY. 2005. 'Key Findings: Nationwide Survey of 3,500 Iraqis'. The USA TODAY/CNN/Gallup Poll. May 20. Retrieved on July 10, 2009. http://www.usatoday.com/news/world/iraq/2004-04-28-gallup-iraq-findings.htm#data

US Congress. 1998. 'An Act to Establish a Program to Support a Transition to Democracy in Iraq'. H.R. 4655. January 27. National Security Archive. Retrieved on September 10, 2011. http://www.gwu.edu/~nsarchiv/NSAEBB/NSAEBB326/doc02.pdf

US Department of Justice. 2004. No title. Federal Bureau of Investigation, Baghdad Operations Center, June 28. The National Security Archive. Retrieved on September 18, 2011. http://www.gwu.edu/~nsarchiv/NSAEBB/NSAEBB279/26.pdf

Usher, Sebastian. 2005a. 'Iraqi Media Urges High Turnout'. *BBC News*. January 28. http://news.bbc.co.uk/2/hi/middle_east/4216997.stm

Usher, Sebastian 2005b. 'Hard TV Sell for Iraqi Electorate'. *BBC News*. December 14. http://news.bbc.co.uk/2/hi/middle_east/4526174.stm

Van Dijk, T A. 1998. 'Opinion and Ideologies in the Press'. In *Approaches to Media Discourse*. A Bell & P Garrett (eds). Oxford: Blackwell: 22–63.

Vannatta, Don. 2006. 'Bush Was Set on Path to War, British Memo Says'. *The New York Times*. March 27. Retrieved on September 10, 2011. http://www.nytimes.com/2006/03/27/international/europe/27memo.html

Vaughan, James. 2002. 'Propaganda by Proxy?: Britain, America, and Arab Radio Broadcasting, 1953–1957'. *Historical Journal of Film, Radio and Television*, 22, 2: 157–172.

Visser, Reider. 2007/2008. 'The Western Imposition of Sectarianism on Iraqi Politics'. *Arab Studies Journal*, Fall/Spring: 83–99.

Voltmer, K. 2000. 'Constructing Political Reality in Russia Izvestiya: Between Old and New Journalistic Practices'. *European Journal of Communication*, 15, 4: 469–500.

Vultee, Fred. 2009. 'The Second Casualty: Effects of Interstate Conflict and Civil War on Press Freedom'. *Media, War & Conflict*, 2, 2: 111–127.

Waisbord, Silvio. 2000. *Watchdog Journalism in South America: News, Accountability, and Democracy*. New York: Columbia University Press.

The Washington Times. 2004. 'For Iraqi, the End Justifies Means'. February 19. Retrieved on September 10, 2011. http://www.washingtontimes.com/news/2004/feb/19/20040219-115614-3297r/

Wellsted, J R. 1840. *Travels of the City of the Calliphs along the Shores of the Persian Gulf and the Mediterranean*. vl. i. London: Henry Colburn, Publisher.

Westerståhl, J. 1983. 'Objective News Reporting: General Premises'. *Communication Research* (July), 10: 403–424.

White, Josh & Graham, Bradley. 2003. 'Military Says It Paid Iraq Papers for News: Possible "Improprieties" to Be Investigated'. *The Washington Post.* December 3.

Wikileaks. 2003. 'Media Training Workshop combines Iraqi, Palestinian, and Jordanian journalists'. 03AMMAN6912. Embassy Amman. October 27. Retrieved on September 30, 2011. http://wikileaks.org/cable/2003/10/03AMMAN6912.html

Wikileaks. 2004a. 'Iraq: Italy Trains Iraq TV Journalists'. 04ROME1806. Embassy Rome. May 8. Retrieved on September 30, 2011. http://wikileaks.org/cable/2004/05/04ROME1806.html

Wikileaks. 2004b. 'Embassies Abu Dhabi and Baghdad Join Forces to Train Iraqi Journalists on Effective Use of the Internet, September 25th to 30th, 2004'. 04ABUDHABI3583. Embassy ABU DHABI. October 12. Retrieved on September 24, 2011. http://wikileaks.org/cable/2004/10/04ABUDHABI3583.html

Wikileaks. 2005a. 'Iraqis in Jordan: Well-Integrated, Economically'. 05AMMAN3963. Embassy Amman. May 20. Retrieved on October 4, 2011. http://wikileaks.org/cable/2005/05/05AMMAN3963.html

Wikileaks. 2005b. 'The Remaking of "Al-Iraqiyya" – Primitive but Effective Programming'. 05BAGHDAD2616. Embassy Baghdad. June 20. Retrieved on September 23, 2011. http://wikileaks.org/cable/2005/06/05BAGHDAD2616.html

Wikileaks. 2005c. 'NCMC Board Under Quorum'. 05BAGHDAD2807. Embassy Baghdad. July 3. Retrieved on September 28, 2011. http://wikileaks.org/cable/2005/07/05BAGHDAD2807.html

Wikileaks. 2005d. 'Iraqi DPM Chalabi Supports Outreach To Sunnis, Moderation In De-baathification'. 05BAGHDAD3111. Baghdad Embassy. July 27. Retrieved on September 19, 2011. http://wikileaks.org/cable/2005/07/05BAGHDAD3111.html

Wikileaks. 2005e. 'Al-Baghdadiya TV: Is The Former Iraqi Regime'. 05BAGHDAD4411. Embassy Baghdad. October 27. Retrieved on October 6, 2011. http://wikileaks.org/cable/2005/10/05BAGHDAD4411.html

Wikileaks. 2005f. 'Iraqi Media Developments in November: Kurdish Independent Satellite Radio Starts up, New Polling and Media Monitoring Activity London for Arabic Media Unit'. Embassy Baghdad. 05BAGHDAD4849. December 5. Retrieved on October 5, 2011. http://wikileaks.org/cable/2005/12/05BAGHDAD4849.html

Wikileaks. 2005g. 'What Campaigning in IRAQ Looks Like'. 05BAGHDAD4912. Embassy Baghdad. December 8. Retrieved on October 3, 2011. http://wikileaks.org/cable/2005/12/05BAGHDAD4912.html

Wikileaks. 2005h. 'Newspaper Editors Look To Play A Role In Building Democracy After The December 15 Elections'. 05BAGHDAD5001. Embassy Baghdad. December 14. Retrieved on September 27, 2011. http://wikileaks.org/cable/2005/12/05BAGHDAD5001.html

Wikileaks. 2005i. 'Electoral War Heats Up – Jazeera And Furat Channel Feuds Spark Demonstrations In Baghdad'. 05BAGHDAD5012. Embassy Baghdad. December 15. Retrieved on October 3, 2011. http://wikileaks.org/cable/2005/12/05BAGHDAD5012.html

Wikileaks. 2006a. 'Muqtada Sadr Debuts on Al-Jazeera with Iraqi Nationalist Message, Rejecting "Sectarian" or "Occupation" Federalism'. 06BAGHDAD549.

Embassy Baghdad. February 21. Retrieved on November 2, 2011. http://wikileaks.org/cable/2006/02/06BAGHDAD549.html

Wikileaks. 2006b. 'Freedom Of Speech In Iraq 2006, Part I: Media Gold Rush In A "virtual" Marketplace'. 06BAGHDAD554. Embassy Baghdad. February 22. Retrieved on September 30, 2011. http://wikileaks.org/cable/2006/02/06BAGHDAD554.html

Wikileaks. 2006c. 'Sectarian Concerns At Imn'. 06BAGHDAD1560. Embassy Baghdad. May 10. Retrieved on September 30, 2011. http://wikileaks.org/cable/2006/05/06BAGHDAD1560.html

Wikileaks. 2006d. 'Baghdad Threatens Regional Newspapers'. 06HILLAH101. REO Hillah. June 11. Retrieved on September 30, 2011. http://wikileaks.org/cable/2006/06/06HILLAH101.html

Wikileaks. 2006e. 'Media in Basrah'. 06BASRAH167. REO Basrah. October 26. Retrieved on September 29, 2011. http://wikileaks.org/cable/2006/10/06BASRAH167.html

Wikileaks. 2006f. 'Public Diplomacy in Closed Societies: Lessons Learned From Czech Experience'. 06PRAGUE1349. Embassy Prague. October 30. Retrieved on September 30, 2011. http://wikileaks.org/cable/2006/10/06PRAGUE1349.html

Wikileaks. 2007a. 'UNESCO Conference on Freedom of Expression and Media Development in IRAQ'. 07PARIS168. Embassy Paris. January 18. Retrieved on September 24, 2011. http://wikileaks.org/cable/2007/01/07PARIS168.html

Wikileaks. 2007b. 'PM Media Advisor Talks about TV Station Shutdowns, Al Jazeera English, and Baghdad Security Plan'. 07BAGHDAD350. Embassy Baghdad. February 2. Retrieved on October 1, 2011. http://wikileaks.org/cable/2007/02/07BAGHDAD350.html

Wikileaks. 2007c. 'Iraqi Public Broadcasting Board Member Comments on New Board Appointed by PM Without Parliamentary Approval'. 07BAGHDAD1082. Embassy Baghdad. March 28. Retrieved on September 30, 2011. http://wikileaks.org/cable/2007/03/07BAGHDAD1082.html

Wikileaks. 2007d. 'Journalists on the State of Press Freedom'. 07BAGHDAD4065. Embassy Baghdad. December 14. Retrieved on September 30, 2011. http://wikileaks.org/cable/2007/12/07BAGHDAD4065.html

Wikileaks. 2008a. 'Request to Close Down Al-Rafidayn Satellite TV'. 08BAGHDAD984. Embassy Baghdad. March 31. Retrieved on October 6, 2011. http://wikileaks.org/cable/2008/03/08BAGHDAD984.html

Wikileaks. 2008b. 'State of Freedom of Press'. 08BAGHDAD3585. Embassy Baghdad. November 12. Retrieved on September 23, 2011. http://wikileaks.org/cable/2008/11/08BAGHDAD3585.html

Wikileaks. 2008c. 'IRAQI Media Outlets Based in Jordan: Profiles'. 08BAGHDAD984. Embassy Amman. November 17. Retrieved on October 5, 2011. http://wikileaks.org/cable/2008/11/08AMMAN3125.html#help_1

Wikileaks. 2008d. 'Erbil and Kirkuk: Murder and Intimidation Threaten the Survival of Independent Media in Northern Iraq. 08BAGHDAD2815'. RRT Erbil – PRT Kirkuk Reporting Cable. Embassy Baghdad. September 2. Retrieved September 15, 2011. http://wikileaks.org/cable/2008/09/08BAGHDAD2815.html

Wikileaks. 2008e. 'Prt Salah Ad Din: Independent Media Face Intimidation'. 08BAGHDAD3771. Embassy Baghdad. December 1. Retrieved on September 29, 2011. http://wikileaks.org/cable/2008/12/08BAGHDAD3771.html

Wikileaks. 2008f. 'Centcom Commander Petraeus' Meeting With Sultan Qaboos (November 30)'. 08MUSCAT853. Embassy Muscat. December 17. Retrieved September 10, 2011. http://wikileaks.org/cable/2008/12/08MUSCAT853.html

Wikileaks. 2009a. 'Journalists Assess Iraq's Provincial Elections'. 09BAGHDAD721. Embassy Baghdad. March 17. Retrieved on October 3, 2011. http://wikileaks.org/cable/2009/03/09BAGHDAD721.html

Wikileaks. 2009b. 'Journalists' Rights Defenders Worry Goi Clamping Down on Media'. 09BAGHDAD1077. Embassy Baghdad. April 21. Retrieved on October 1, 2011. http://wikileaks.org/cable/2009/04/09BAGHDAD1077.html

Wikileaks. 2009c. 'Iraqi Journalists Continue the Elusive Search for Freedom of the Press'. 09BAGHDAD1433. Embassy Baghdad. June 1. Retrieved on October 2, 2011. http://wikileaks.org/cable/2009/06/09BAGHDAD1433.html

Wikileaks. 2009d. 'Iraqi Journalists Express Concern Over Draft Legislation'. 09BAGHDAD2151. Embassy Baghdad. August 10. Retrieved on October 2, 2011. http://wikileaks.org/cable/2009/08/09BAGHDAD2151.html

Wikileaks. 2009e. 'Iraqi Telecommunications: At The Frontline of the Battle For Iraq's Economic Ideology'. 09BAGHDAD2677. Embassy Baghdad. October 5. Retrieved on September 30, 2011. http://wikileaks.org/cable/2009/10/09BAGHDAD2677.html

Wikileaks. 2009f. 'Iraq's Telecom Regulator: Pushing for Independence and Concerned about Foreign Media Influences on Election'. 09BAGHDAD2677. Embassy Baghdad. November 16. Retrieved on September 28, 2011. http://wikileaks.org/cable/2009/11/09BAGHDAD3007.html

Wikileaks. 2009g. 'Basra Journalist Discusses Maliki Visit, Journalistic Challenges, U.S. Iraq Legacy'. 09BASRAH53. REO Basrah. September 24. Retrieved on October 2, 2011. http://wikileaks.org/cable/2009/09/09BASRAH53.html

Wikileaks. 2009h. 'Four Iraqi Journalists Given Awards for Courageous Reporting in Face of Threats'. 09BAGHDAD3192. Embassy Baghdad. December 13. Retrieved on September 30, 2011. http://wikileaks.org/cable/2009/12/09BAGHDAD3192.html

Wikileaks. 2009i. 'Nea A/S Feltman's Meeting with President Talabani'. 09BAGHDAD3316. Embassy Baghdad. December 23. Retrieved on November 2, 2011. http://wikileaks.org/cable/2009/12/09BAGHDAD3316.html

Wikileaks. 2009j. 'Prt Ninewa: Mosuliyya in a Muddle: Pressure on U.S.-Backed Station Intensifies'. 09BAGHDAD3371. Embassy Baghdad. December 30. Retrieved on November 2, 2011. http://wikileaks.org/cable/2009/12/09BAGHDAD3371.html

Wikileaks. 2010a. 'Basrah's Press: A Work in Progress'. 10BASRAH3. REO Basrah. February 6. Retrieved on October 2, 2011. http://wikileaks.org/cable/2010/02/10BASRAH3.html

Wikileaks. 2010b. 'Iraqi Election Campaign Update: February 22, 2010'. 10BAGHDAD475. Embassy Baghdad. February 22. Retrieved on October 3, 2011. http://wikileaks.org/cable/2010/02/10BAGHDAD475.html

Wikileaks. 2010bb. 'Corrected Copy: Iraq's Pre-election Trends: The North'. 10BAGHDAD473. Embassy Baghdad. February 22. Retrieved on October 1, 2011. http://wikileaks.org/cable/2010/02/10BAGHDAD473.html

Wikileaks. 2010c. 'Coalition Profile: PM Maliki's State of Law'. 10BAGHDAD499. Embassy Baghdad. February 24. Retrieved on October 2, 2011. http://wikileaks.org/cable/2010/02/10BAGHDAD499.html

Wikileaks. 2010d. 'Iraqi Election Campaign Week Two: Political Roundup'. 10BAGHDAD509. Embassy Baghdad. February 25. Retrieved on October 3, 2011. http://wikileaks.org/cable/2010/02/10BAGHDAD509.html

Wikileaks. 2010e. 'PRT Kirkuk: Kurdish Campaign Behavior – Unheeded'. 10BAGHDAD514. Embassy Baghdad. February 26. Retrieved on October 3, 2011. http://wikileaks.org/cable/2010/02/10BAGHDAD514.html

Wikileaks. 2010f. 'Coalition Profile: Tawafuq Confronts Diminished'. 10BAGHDAD517. Embassy Baghdad. February 27. Retrieved on October 3, 2011. http://wikileaks.org/cable/2010/02/10BAGHDAD517.html

Wikileaks. 2010g. 'Coalition Profile: The IRAQI National Alliance'. 10BAGHDAD537. Embassy Baghdad. February 28. Retrieved on October 1, 2011. http://wikileaks.org/cable/2010/02/10BAGHDAD537.html

Williams, Daniel. 2003. 'U.S. Taps Media Chief for Iraq; Regulation Attempted Without Appearing Heavy-Handed'. *The Washington Post*. August 18.

Wong, Edward. 2005a. 'Iraqi Constitution May Curb Women's Rights'. *The New York Times*. July 20. Retrieved on October 4, 2009.

Wong, Edward. 2005b. 'On the Air, on Their Own: Iraqi Women Find a Forum'. *The New York Times*. September 4. Retrieved on September 23, 2011. http://www.nytimes.com/2005/09/04/international/middleeast/04broadcast.html; http://www.nytimes.com/2005/07/20/international/middleeast/20women.html

World Free Press. 2003. 'Framework for Change: Transforming Iraq's Media Landscape'. June 1–3. Athens. Retrieved on June 30, 2009. http://www.worldfreepress.org/Documents/IraqMediaFramework.pdf

Yahya, Mazin. 2011. 'Iraqi Reporter who Criticized Government Shot Dead'. *Associated Press*. September 8.

Ya'qbub Sarkis. 1955. *Mabahith Iraqia (Iraqi Papers)*. vol. ii. Baghdad: Sharikat Al-Tiba'ah wa Al-Tijarah al-Mahdudah.

Young, Karen De & Pincus, Walter. 2008. 'U.S. to Fund Pro-American Publicity in Iraqi Media'. *The Washington Post*. October 3.

YouTube. 2009a. November 24. Retrieved on August 27, 2010. http://www.youtube.com/user/Iraqigov#p/u/251/6N6Bi_Gid2A

YouTube. 2009b. October 4. Retrieved on January 24, 2012. http://www.youtube.com/watch?v=Of-KXqEnnAU

YouTube. 2009c. December 21. Retrieved on August 27, 2010. http://www.youtube.com/user/Iraqigov#p/u/197/gsOHa7ZzT1w

Zunes, Stephen. 2006. 'The U.S. Role in Iraq's Sectarian Violence'. *Foreign Policy in Focus*. March 6. Retrieved on June 15, 2009. http://www.fpif.org/fpiftxt/3139

Index